the gods of diyala

TEXAS A&M UNIVERSITY
118
MILITARY HISTORY SERIES

the gods of diyala
TRANSFER OF COMMAND IN IRAQ

CALEB S. CAGE AND GREGORY M. TOMLIN

Texas A&M University Press
College Station

This paper meets the requirements of ANSI/NISO Z39.48-1992 (Permanence of Paper).
Binding materials have been chosen for durability.

Library Of Congress Cataloging-in-Publication Data

Cage, Caleb S., 1979–
    The gods of Diyala : transfer of command in Iraq / Caleb S. Cage and Gregory M.
Tomlin. — 1st ed.
        p. cm. — (Texas A & M University military history series ; 118)
    Includes index.
    ISBN-13: 978-1-60344-038-7 (cloth : alk. paper)
    ISBN-10: 1-60344-038-0 (cloth : alk. paper)
    1. Cage, Caleb S., 1979– 2. Tomlin, Gregory M., 1979– 3. Iraq War, 2003—Personal
narratives, American. 4. Iraq War, 2003—Campaigns—Iraq—Diyalá. I. Tomlin,
Gregory M., 1979– II. Title.
DS79.76.C34 2008
956.7044'3092273—dc22

                                                                    2007052619

This book is dedicated to the soldiers of 1st and 3rd Platoons, C Company, Task Force 1-6 Field Artillery, and is in memory of Pvt. First Class Jason Nathaniel Lynch, killed in action in Buhriz, Iraq, on June 18, 2004. You inspired us with your courage, and it was our honor to serve with each of you.

contents

Acknowledgments   ix

Map of Baquba and Buhriz   1

PART 1: EVOLUTION

    CHAPTER 1. Genesis   3

    CHAPTER 2. Insurgency: A Prelude   19

PART 2: THE EASTER OFFENSIVE

    CHAPTER 3. Insurgency: A Primer   39

    CHAPTER 4. All Things Conventional   48

PART 3: JUNE

    CHAPTER 5. Insurgency: A Practicum   69

    CHAPTER 6. IEDs: The Menace Beneath   79

    CHAPTER 7. A City Upon a Hill: The Urban Morass   87

    CHAPTER 8. A City Upon a Hill: The High Ground   97

PART 4: GOOD THINGS, BAD PEOPLE, AND THE PICTURES TO PROVE IT

    CHAPTER 9. The Moral Fight: Photogs   119

    CHAPTER 10. Regime Change   134

    CHAPTER 11. Revisionistas: An Interlude   147

PART 5: HOLIDAYS: ORIENT AND OCCIDENT

    CHAPTER 12. Ramadan in America   173

    CHAPTER 13. Christmas in Iraq   195

    CHAPTER 14. The Eve of a Nation   213

PART 6:   REFORMATION

        CHAPTER 15. Hope and Salvation   227

        CHAPTER 16. To Be or Not to Be   248

PART 7:   UP TO THE TASK

        CHAPTER 17. Security   277

        CHAPTER 18. Democracy   286

        Index   299

acknowledgments

So many people were tangentially or directly involved in the success of this publication that, rightfully, little credit remains for its authors. Primarily, we would like to express our deepest gratitude to the subjects of the dedication of this volume: the soldiers and sergeants of 1st and 3rd Platoons, C Company, 1-6 Field Artillery, and specifically, Pvt. First Class Jason Lynch, without whom we would have surely failed as leaders, let alone as writers. Our peers and their platoons deserve ample credit as well, because they endured the same successes and frustrations during the deployment, yet unfairly eluded serious mention in this book of our personal experiences.

Capt. Douglas Chadwick and 1st Sgt. James Ford, our rocks through bad times and worse, deserve many sincere thanks for their every effort in leading our company. Col. Steven Bullimore not only transformed his field artillery battalion into a capable counterinsurgency task force, but he personally selected both of us for the positions we held. Without his confidence in our leadership potential or his extraordinary patience with us, we would not have experienced many of the life-altering missions shared in this book.

Our parents, Harry and Donna Tomlin and Gary and Charlotte Cage, and siblings, Michael, Cheryl, Zach, and Charlie, experienced the same excruciating pangs of fear and frustration that every family of a deployed soldier experiences, yet their support and prayers were unwavering. For four months, Donna endured the tremendous burden of having both her husband and son deployed to the same combat zone. Her poise and support proved as unflappable as they did throughout her thirty years as a military spouse. Caleb's extended family, Rob and Christine McDonald, shared their customary love and support throughout this period as well. Our families' enthusiasm for this work was unconditional and wise, and many of their comments shaped it for the better. We could not ask for better from those we love.

T. J. Grider, Travis Cox, Peter Guellnitz, Jim Gifford, Chris Boggiano, and John Bushman proved to be irreplaceable friends and colleagues during our time in Germany and in Iraq, and since. Their support for our common mission and for this publication went far beyond the friendships we fostered on and off the battlefields of Iraq. It is true that combat makes friends into comrades for life, and we are grateful.

Three authors were instrumental in taking this work from a manuscript draft to its final form. Steve Mumford, author and painter of *Baghdad Journal,* read an early draft of several chapters in Caleb's dirty room in Baquba, and offered a crucial early critique of the work. Bill Murphy Jr., while writing a work about Caleb's graduating class from West Point, was instrumental in taking this from an absurdly disorganized and uncoordinated set of paragraphs to a logical and chronological memoir. Col. Edward Metzner (U.S. Army, Retired), the American most decorated by the Republic of Vietnam, moved us from oblivion to the Texas A&M University Press where his two books were also published.

Col. Ty Seidule, Head of Military History at the United States Military Academy, West Point, and Dr. Dennis Showalter, Professor of History at Colorado College, offered positive and motivating reviews of a draft of this volume for Texas A&M. The staff and editorial board at TAMU Press proved gracious, patient, diligent, and incredibly professional throughout the entire publication process, especially Dr. Mary Lenn Dixon, Marina Trninic, Diana Vance, Jennifer Gardner, Thom Lemmons, and Andrea Brennan. We are extremely proud and eternally grateful for the opportunity to publish this small work at such a wonderful press.

Of course, the glory goes to the friends, mentors, colleagues and family mentioned and not mentioned above, while the responsibility for errors and shortcomings of this book belongs to the authors alone.

PART 1
evolution

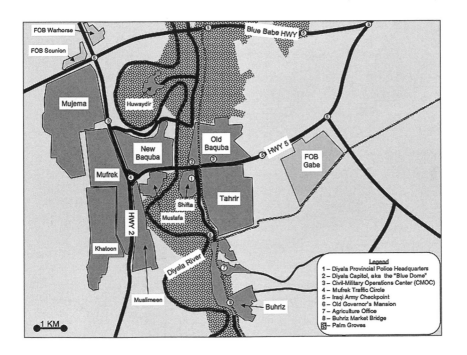

Legend
1 – Diyala Provincial Police Headquarters
2 – Diyala Capitol, aka the "Blue Dome"
3 – Civil-Military Operations Center (CMOC)
4 – Mufrek Traffic Circle
5 – Iraqi Army Checkpoint
6 – Old Governor's Mansion
7 – Agriculture Office
8 – Buhriz Market Bridge
    – Palm Groves

chapter 1
GENESIS

he village sheikh sauntered up the small hill towards the waiting lieutenant and interpreter. At just after 10:00 in the morning, he already reeked of alcohol and was fifteen minutes late. His traditional robe was askew and his headdress was sitting nearly sideways on top of his head, the result of a mild spill he took on the way up the hill a few minutes prior. He looked like he was in his late fifties, but was probably in his early forties. The interpreter was notably sober at the early hour and wearing black jeans, a brown leather jacket, and other symbols of western fashion. The young U.S. Army lieutenant stood, feigning patience as best he could. Both he and the sheikh managed smiles and even less sincere salutations before moving into their scheduled conversation.

The conversation slowly progressed, moving through the security threat and the vast infrastructural needs of the tiny village. After a brief time, it became annoyingly clear that neither required the use of the interpreter, each grasping enough of the other's foreign language to pass the details of their questions and concerns. But, if for no other reason than to appreciate the full absurdity of their charade, they paused after each of their sentences to allow time for the interpreter to translate.

The conversation ended with no real change in the preconceptions with which each had entered. In the lieutenant's mind, the sheikh would not take ownership of his village and its problems. Instead, he wanted promises of supplies and improvements that would increase his stature as the provider within his community of followers. Similarly, in the sheikh's mind, the lieutenant seemed to merely want to gather information that would lead him to the insurgents in the village who had been challenging his ability to be seen as a protector.

When the little standoff on the hilltop was over, and having time to kill before talking over the high and low points, the three stood on top of the hill discussing the politics of the war in Iraq that had kicked off a few months before. The sheikh admitted, in near perfect English, that his parents had told him what life was like in Germany before the Allied invasion of his homeland, and that he saw the war as probably necessary given the present state of the world.

The interpreter, like most German kids his age, sputtered something about the war being for oil, the possibility that the World Trade Center attacks were planned by the U.S. government, and that war was clearly no way to achieve peace. Although there were obviously clashing worldviews and cultural perspectives, the actual war in Iraq provided a cushion for the amiable conversation.

The three men were actors, and were taking part in a pre-deployment training exercise designed to prepare the soldiers of the 3rd Brigade Combat Team, 1st Infantry Division at the Combined Maneuver Training Center in Hohenfels, Germany. The so-called sheikh was, in all likelihood, a seasonally-employed resident of a nearby Bavarian town, who had been hired by the U.S. Army to play the part of the Middle Eastern tribal leader for a few weeks that fall. The interpreter was probably a high school student from the area who spoke enough English to secure the job. The lieutenant was actually a commissioned Army officer, and his role was so ill-defined that his authenticity was simply irrelevant. All were taking part in a month-long affair designed to prepare the brigade's 3,000 soldiers for their upcoming deployment to Iraq.

The environment at the training center was overtly staged and had been for decades. Hohenfels had long been used to duplicate the areas of possible future conflict. In the 1930s the German Army confiscated thousands of acres of farmland to prepare a mock military landscape that might resemble western Poland or Czechoslovakia. In the name of the Fuehrer, the peasant residents of entire villages regrettably located among the rolling hills of the new training area were relocated to rapidly fabricated communities kilometers away. Ruins of their truly ancient homes and churches could still be seen in the training area. At the conclusion of the Second World War, with the United States deliberating the likelihood of a Soviet invasion of Western Europe, the American Army assumed control of the former *Wehrmacht* facility in order to practice hypothetical tank battles against an encroaching Red Army. It was used in this manner for the remainder of the Cold War.

In the years following the Cold War, the sweeping changes in warfare resulted in an appropriate scramble by defense leaders to update the training center as well. In the mid-1990s, after the 1st Armored Division deployed to Bosnia for the Army's maiden deployment to the Balkans, Hohenfels gained a new dimension. Mock villages that included police departments, schools and minaret-complemented mosques began to dot the post–Cold War battlefield. During scenarios intended to better prepare soldiers to interact with Bosnians and Kosovars during peacekeeping missions, hundreds of German nationals gained employment with the U.S. Army by playing beleaguered residents of the fake towns. Conveniently, as the U.S. prepared for operations in the Middle East, the same villages meant to house fictitious Muslim Bosniaks and Orthodox Serbs could easily serve as the homes of fictitious Iraqis.

The makeshift villages that peppered the once-open Bavarian countryside assumed names like Khan Bani Sa'ad, Mualimeen, and Salman Pak, all towns that the 3rd Brigade would grow intimately acquainted with in the Iraqi province of Diyala. Three times a day, the makeshift minarets played a crucial role in converting an obviously European pastoral scene into a more foreign Muslim community. Starting at first light, the rhythmic whir of a distant call to prayer crept across the coniferous valleys, encouraging the local Christians in the surrounding communities to celebrate their devotion to Allah above. The unanimous response was consistently secular.

The tent city, serving as the operating base for the brigade, made an interesting contrast to the haphazardly arranged, makeshift villages. Countless rows of perfectly aligned vehicles balanced countless rows of perfectly aligned tents. The mud roads, thick and sappy from rainfall during the day and frozen by nightfall, formed symmetrical grids across the camp. The huge white fest tent was the centerpiece for the operating base. Although normally used for summer beer festivals in southern Germany, the tent housed the field mess facility established to modestly handle the nutritional needs of the brigade.

The climate was anything but that of an austere desert. The few November days that yielded sunlight in Hohenfels were quickly forgotten in the fog and the wind. It was seldom when a person could not see the heavy signature of his breath, or curse himself for inadvertently leaving a patch of skin exposed to the unforgiving elements. A month of training for the Middle East passed for the brigade without a single soul having to deal with dehydration, heat exhaustion, or any other real health issues that they would be forced to endure in the hotter climate to come. Northern Bavaria stuck out in contrast to the desert to such an extent that the brigade engineers were forced to bring in truckloads of sand to fill the requisite number of sandbags for camp position improvements against imaginary mortar attacks.

If the weather prohibited the soldiers from preparing for the aridity of the "Cradle of Civilization," the minds of the U.S. Army attempted to counteract the perceivable flaw with other measures. They hired beleaguered villagers, all eager to participate in what they must have seen as a spectacular absurdity for the most powerful army in the world, who filled out the hierarchy of the mock villages, and put a human face on sustainment operations. Military observer-controllers instructed the actors to only speak their native German, and they were briefed on a daily script that dictated their persona, their actions and reactions, and their level of distrust in the American regime. Some of the actors were scripted to be informants, working on the sly for the American cause or for monetary compensation. Others acted as hostiles, out to dismantle whatever good deeds might be proffered by the occupiers.

The female actors presented a peculiar situation for the soldiers operating in their communities. They, too, originated from the same local communities as their mock patriarchal oppressors. They received instructions to pretend to be forced to wear the chador and burqa, to walk behind their leading men, to bring hot tea in during important meetings, and to sit quietly in the social setting. As would be expected from the long-liberated German women, they were not going to take such demands sitting down. They appeared to be shrewdly revolting against their oppressors by wearing western-style blue jeans, T-shirts with American band names, and clearly indulging in the ills of make-up, all of which nicely contrasted with their wearing of eastern veils.

Certainly, between the investment in infrastructure and the hiring of civilian actors, the Army's tremendous effort to simulate the Iraqi experience deserved credit. Although the absurdities were many, the training was necessary and offered a real opportunity for the platoons to operate as teams. Also, the pressing reality of the upcoming deployment often counteracted much of the training's surreal nature and encouraged the American forces to at least play along.

During the evenings, when the exercise was no longer in full swing, the companies were given opportunities to continue to develop their procedures based on the lessons learned from the day's activities. Clearly the soldiers were beginning to grasp the gist of their violent role in defeating an insurgency, but their leaders needed further training in the nuances of dealing with the indigenous people of a war-torn country. On at least one occasion, the junior and senior leaders of the entire 3rd Brigade were assembled for a culture briefing that aimed to assist in exactly that. The main speaker of the event was a Harvard-educated civilian who was currently teaching Middle Eastern culture at the Naval Postgraduate School in Monterey, California.

He spoke mostly of the delicate interaction between a company of military personnel and a local Iraqi population. He gave pointers on the differences in social structure, provided explanations on cultural taboos, and demonstrated cultural greeting procedures that would assist the young leaders in developing the community's security, infrastructure, and quality of life. He cautioned the assembled group to be attentive to their own words and gestures in front of an Iraqi people who, it appeared, generally appreciated the work of their liberators in freeing them from a self-serving despot.

One point in his lecture proved to be highly poignant, and even inspired. Describing the perception of the locals regarding their saviors, he noted that the company commander responsible for the town was a "god" to that town; that the lieutenants who oversaw the workings of the local infrastructure under that commander were the "gods" of the hospitals, of the police stations, and other pieces of a city's infrastructure.

Sitting in the back of the mess tent, Greg Tomlin and Caleb Cage, both lieutenants in C Company, quietly laughed at the obvious overstatement the lecturer was using in such serious tones. More precisely, they laughed at how literally their company commander was taking this new information. After the lecture, Greg and Caleb walked back to their tents with their fellow C Company lieutenants, James Gifford and Christopher Lacour, joking about how their commander undoubtedly translated the lecturer's overstatement in his mind.

They were not surprised when the company commander called them into his private tent. He wanted to discuss his excitement about the forthcoming deployment, he said as they arrived. He was animated and candid because he believed that his officers worshipped him and enjoyed growing from his constant mentorship. Neither was the case.

As his three platoon leaders and executive officer settled in, the commander disclosed what he thought was important from the lecture from the "Harvard dude," as he called him. He talked quickly through their roles during the following year in Iraq, recapped a few of the customs and courtesies, and then excitedly delved into what he really wanted to discuss. He reminded the lieutenants that he, as the company commander, was to be a

god to the people of Iraq. And the lieutenants, he remarked in a concilia-
tory way, would be lesser gods. He was serious, much to the amazement
of his lieutenants. Departing the tent shortly after the commander's ego-
tistical rant, the lieutenants engaged in what had become a standard cop-
ing mechanism: mockery, followed by thorough preparation that would
mitigate their commander's ineptitude.

His comments evoked awestruck laughter, which could not be thoroughly enjoyed because of the thin canvas walls of their tent. It took several minutes for the sheer hilarity of the experience to wear off before the
four were able to talk. "What exactly does the god of a police station do,"
Greg quietly asked through his laughter to no one in particular. "I lami-
nated security badges," Jim sarcastically exclaimed, referring to his time
as the sole Army officer at the government building for the Kurdish city
of Kirkuk during the ground war.

Eventually, more theological questions evolved. Was the god of a
hospital granted powers to heal? Was the god of a police station empow-
ered with omniscience and omnipresence? Would the lieutenants have the
power to both give and take away? Would they have the power to smite
their enemies with relative ease? Perhaps most importantly, would they
be able to both comprehend and master reality? Exhausted by a day's
worth of training, the apprentice gods set off to prepare for the last few
weeks of theatrical missions.

The training at Hohenfels eventually came to an end with the platoons and companies learning a great deal about the war they would fight.
No matter what their commander tried to tell them that night, though,
the four lieutenants knew that they were not quite gods. There were
simply too many questions left unanswered and fears left to be dealt with
later. How exactly would they fight a primitive insurgency in Iraq with
the world's most modern forces and equipment? How would the real beleaguered local populace react to their presence? Could they accomplish
their mission and bring all of their soldiers home alive?

The post–Cold War world brought alien translations of old themes to
the world stage as well. The world was apparently unipolar, markets were
increasingly global, wars were asymmetric, and history was resurrected.
Balance had been broken and the fundamentals of the modern world had
been shaken. Although no less confused by the world into which they
graduated, and often unaware of what the changes would mean to them
personally, Greg and Caleb had been watching the shift for several years
before they met in Germany.

Over the second weekend of November 2000, several hundred young, optimistic college students from all over the United States gathered at the United States Military Academy, West Point. The purpose of the gathering was the 52nd Annual Student Conference on United States Affairs (SCUSA). Although unbeknownst to them at the time, both Caleb Cage and Greg Tomlin were sitting in the audience of students on the opening night of SCUSA.

Had the conference been held six months later, it would have been presented with more domestic consciousness. The very contentious presidential election pitting George W. Bush against Vice President Al Gore was not determined on election night, and it would not be for several weeks to come. The event's panel of speakers on its opening night included Enron executive Rick Waddell and Fox News political analyst John Ellis. Ellis was later exposed as a member of the Bush family; he had prematurely called the state of Florida in favor of his cousin earlier the same day of the conference's opening. Of course, during the conference, no one knew the complex nature of the domestic scandals that would unfold with respect to these panel participants.

Had the conference been ten months later, it would have been presented with a profoundly different focus on United States foreign policy. As it was, ten months before the Al Qaeda attacks on America's shores, the conference was noticeably steeped in the traditions of the optimism that accompanied the End of History. The theme of SCUSA in 2000 was, appropriately reflecting the pre-September 11 fixation on the mystery of the new millennium, "U.S. Leadership into the New Century: Defining the Puzzle." This theme intended to spark dialogue bent on determining America's role in the new, post–Cold War times that did not particularly fit any schemes or rubrics that our nation had grown to appreciate on its way to hegemony.

The optimism and benign ignorance of America's position in the world and the world's views of this position were clearly and, in hindsight, humorously detailed in the information packet distributed to the delegates of the conference. "We find ourselves at the dawn of a new millennium without a major threat to our security, but facing an abundance of minor threats requiring competing policy options," one particularly optimistic passage read. "Guided by vague and sometimes troubling clues and aided by half-completed ideas and overlapping, interconnected options," it was up to the conference participants to attempt to approximate an intellectually coherent policy stance for the United States in the coming century.

Luckily for the majority of the several hundred participants at that time, SCUSA was a world of theoretical conjecture that was heavy on the hypothetical and light on realistic application.

Breaking into twenty-person round tables, discussion leaders hailing from the academic, federal and private sectors led students through a three-day dialogue on specific themes. The timing and focus of the conference set the participants ablaze with fascination regarding domestic politics and international affairs. Youthful idealism clashed mightily with the realism of some of the best minds in the field of U.S. public and foreign policy.

For the most part, as the students would later find out, the basic assumptions of those in attendance were desperately immature. The Cold War was dead, and most at the conference could hardly even begin to understand the threat that their parents' generation saw from the Evil Empire. They had known peace, prosperity and ground wars that lasted all of a hundred hours. In those few days at West Point, students were trying to apply their perspectives, experiences, assumptions and beliefs to a United States and a world that would flip completely upside down in only a matter of months.

Caleb participated in the democratization roundtable, which focused on determining the guidelines that would keep U.S. policymakers in check when it came to spreading democracy throughout the rest of the world. Discussions of the likelihood of countries with McDonald's franchises going to war with each other, peaceful transitions of power, and regime change abounded. Most of the discussions at the democratization roundtable were focused on the quiet assumption that democracy was certainly a political "good," but that the United States and its allies would have to be increasingly careful with how they packaged and pushed for democratization elsewhere. If we were not careful as a country, the panel members argued around the table, the U.S. could come away looking incredibly arrogant, which would probably hurt our cause tremendously.

Greg participated in the roundtable focusing on global threats to national security. Here, students examined the 2000 National Security Strategy written by the White House and postulated what stood as the most serious external threats to the country's well-being. As the required readings for the panel all emphasized, the twenty-first century promised to be a challenging environment for defining and realizing American foreign policy. In the previous century, especially during the Cold War, friendly alliances stood unanimously in support of a common goal. Opponents to democracy and the free global market stood distinctively in the opposite corner of a bipolar world. However, as the final years of the twentieth century unfolded, identifying enemies grew more difficult.

The 1993 World Trade Center bombing and the releasing of a nerve gas in a Tokyo subway station in 1995 alarmed the world to terrorists who held little regard for innocent civilians. Some statesmen also began to question the continued validity of well-established international organizations. Political disagreements between its member states during the 1999 Kosovo air campaign, for example, nearly became the catalyst for disbanding the North Atlantic Treaty Organization.

Such ambiguities left the roundtable at West Point uncertain about what exactly the enemy of the future would look like in the next decade. Certainly there were concerns about a weapon of mass destruction (WMD) falling into the wrong hands, and the rise of ethnically-based wars as seen in the Balkans, Africa, and East Timor—conflicts that could destabilize entire regions of the globe. However, the students could not identify which threat deserved the greatest attention of the U.S. government.

If SCUSA had existed in 1935, students would have identified the rise of Japanese hegemony in East Asia as a threat to the United States, based on Imperial Japan's growing navy and territorial annexations on mainland Asia. With a few modifications, conference participants from the 1950s through the 1980s could have used a facsimile of the previous year's paper to tout the threat of a nuclear holocaust caused by the Soviets.

Following two days of fervent discussions, the students of the Global Threats to National Security Panel prioritized asymmetric threats, including the possession of a WMD by a rogue state, and state-supported terrorism, as the most serious threats to the future of the United States. Neither the words "asymmetric" nor "rogue," however, annotated the specific source or method of delivery for the next global threat to national security. The roundtable members left the Military Academy on November 11, 2000 just as unsure about the specifics of the next viable threat as they did about who would be their 43rd president. Regardless of whatever threats the future possessed, no one in the group anticipated the unconventionally brazen attacks that would shake the United States exactly ten months to the day after the conference concluded.

In the months that followed, world leaders and renowned thinkers continued to deal with the global situation in various vacuums, through various lenses, and relying on various constructs. George W. Bush would prevail as the President of the United States and appoint Donald Rumsfeld

to the post of Secretary of Defense. One of the secretary's most contentious initiatives was the Defense Department's proposal for transformation. Dedicated to radical change within his realm, the defense secretary
embarked on a campaign to reconfigure ground forces into smaller, more
mobile units able to rapidly respond to any contingency mission across
the globe.

Additionally, politicians, academics, and policymakers fiercely debated the second Bush Administration's high profile National Missile Defense Program. The Defense Department projected the development to
be the next generation of President Ronald Reagan's Star Wars program,
intended to shield the U.S. from rockets launched in the country's direction. Indeed, in early 2001, Americans seemed to have plenty of time to
ponder new security initiatives. Of course, this only lasted long enough
for Americans to get comfortable.

On September 11th, 2001, Cage and Tomlin sat on opposite ends of
the U.S. Army's education system. Caleb was in his senior year at West
Point, while Greg was serving as the faculty assistant for the Department
of Military Strategy, Planning and Operations at the United States Army
War College, Carlisle Barracks, Pennsylvania. Regardless of their seats, the
terrorist attacks changed the world as they understood it.

For Caleb, the change was quite palpable. With the exception of
those who lost loved ones, it would probably be difficult to find a concentrated group of Americans who felt the impact of the events of September
11th as much as the cadets at West Point. If any of the senior cadets had
believed for the previous three years that they would give the Army five
years of time, with possibly a cruise or two through the Balkans, and then
step right out onto Wall Street, they now understood that they were going
to war.

Changes at the military academy were quickly implemented. The
academic departments wisely took their cue from the terrorists and immediately started integrating important and relevant information into existing courses. Sometimes it meant bringing back previous graduates to
talk to the cadets about their deployments to Kosovo or Macedonia. There
was also the instructors' amazing talent for managing to work a *Blackhawk
Down* reading or reference into almost any situation. Many people outside
of the academic departments were starting to recognize the trivialities of
cadet life as well. The changes, either academic or tactical, were neither
robust nor sweeping, but in the few months separating graduation from

the terrorist attacks, people were thinking and adapting as well as they could.

Of course, much like the academy's administration and faculty, the cadets had very little idea of what they were stepping into. By Christmas of 2001, many thought, the battle against Afghanistan's Taliban seemed to be pretty well contained. Soldiers there would probably only need a few years of Bosnia-style peacekeeping deployments to complete the isolated country's democratization.

Such denial would be cured on June 1, 2002 during a forty-five minute speech by President George W. Bush, who told West Point's graduating class in fairly certain terms that the United States would be going to war against the dictatorship of Saddam Hussein. From their seats in the stadium, Caleb's parents sat stone-faced, listening to their son's commander-in-chief outline his next campaign in the war on terrorism.

Greg's experience at the U.S. Army War College offered another take on the events. Unlike Caleb, instead of being surrounded by his peers, a cohort of apprentice officers, he was at the Army's senior post-graduate school, where lieutenant colonels and colonels study the implementation of national military policy and campaign planning. As the only lieutenant working for a faculty comprised entirely of colonels and career professors, Greg benefited from mentors who were as generous with their time for entertaining questions as they were patient at handling the naiveté of a new lieutenant.

The full implications of the attack on American soil could not be completely appreciated by a newly minted second lieutenant. However, as Greg spoke to faculty members and students at the War College, two things became clear. First, the United States would go to war imminently with some state or entity. This meant that significant portions of the Army would deploy, potentially including the first tactical unit that he would join. Second, the Army's involvement in the upcoming war would affect his entire military career.

If the attacks impressed the graduating cadets at West Point with a realization of their fleeting innocence, they merely provoked measured and rational wisdom from some of the Army's most experienced leaders and sharpest thinkers. Although well seasoned in the art and science of warfare, the colonels in Carlisle seemed to recognize that the new mission requirements and enemy forces would be more ambiguous than any previously encountered by the Army.

As the instructors considered revamping their syllabi, the garrison of Carlisle Barracks feverishly worked to implement an assortment of new force protection measures. These requirements were directed by the Department of the Army, for improving security at installations across the country and around the world. With so many senior American and international military officers working on the small post, would the terrorists' next selection of targets include Carlisle?

One specific directive required each post to conduct a nightly roving patrol of its perimeter. Without the normal complement of Military Police (MP) shared by larger installations, Carlisle Barracks needed to improvise to meet the new force protection standard. The garrison headquarters established a roving guard, consisting of two members of the faculty or post headquarters driving around the post in a golf cart with a radio and flashlight from seven at night until seven the next morning.

Aside from the golf cart security force, the Army also tasked every garrison to create an installation operations center to function twenty-four hours a day as the hub for security management and for the development of situational awareness. Leaning on the faculty for a room design, the post gained an elaborate response center more akin to an Army division's tactical operations center than to a small town's police dispatch office. With desks for chemical officers and civilian police liaisons, every visitor knew that the designers of the Carlisle operations center had spent many years in senior-level headquarters. Until an Army Reserve element of soldiers and officers could be activated to operate the operations center, the garrison turned once again to the faculty for manning requisites.

Working in twelve-hour shifts, two colonels and an MP soldier monitored radios, remained current on world events, wrote mundane reports, and shared information with other Army posts in the continental United States. The commandant exempted students from the task of working in the operations center or the roving guard in order to allow them to remain focused on their studies. Greg spent more than a week working alongside a colonel in the Carlisle operations center, thinking how strange it was for a field artillery lieutenant to be involved with managing installation security. Little did he know that three years later he would be the officer in charge of an even more sophisticated operations center with responsibility for an entire province in Iraq.

As serious, and sometimes as amusing as the Army's reactions may have been to the terrorist attack, one specific event made it clear that the military was not the only sphere of American society unsure of how to respond to the unthinkable act. Maj. James Putnam had served as company commander for Greg's dad in 1993, and in the small world that is the Army, he was escorting the Saudi Defense Minister on an official visit to the War College on September 11. With all air traffic grounded indefinitely, Major Putnam had to entertain the Saudi delegation in Carlisle until suitable transportation could be arranged to take them home. On the evening of September 11, the Saudi exchange student to the War College, a Saudi Army brigadier, scheduled a dinner party at his home. Following the morning's attack, the host sagely scaled down the guest list for a somber supper to a handful of professors and the foreign visitors.

Sometime during the course of the dinner, two Carlisle police officers arrived at the door of the brigadier's suburban home. The police arrived at the house in response to a call made by a neighbor who reported that "the damn Arabs next door are celebrating the attacks." Major Putnam and a couple of the American colonels explained to the police, and later to the neighbor, that the complaint was entirely unsubstantiated. The officers identified the "damn Arabs" as a senior military delegation from one of America's allies whose visit was scheduled months in advance of the terrorist attack. The individual who notified the police may have accepted the Army officers' explanation. However, it was immediately clear that America's shock caused average citizens to make uninformed and irrational accusations.

Three years after the SCUSA conference, and four months following the March 2003 launch of Operation Iraqi Freedom, Greg and Caleb finally had a chance to meet. Both were assigned to the 1st Battalion, 6th Field Artillery Regiment, a battalion in the 1st Infantry Division, in Bamberg, Germany. Greg arrived after completing a nine-month deployment to Kosovo. Caleb came straight from the Field Artillery Officers Basic Course at Fort Sill, Oklahoma, where he had studied the fundamentals of conventional artillery. One week after their first meeting, the battalion received news that changed the lieutenants' duty positions as sharply as Al Qaeda redefined America's enemy threat.

It was just another Monday morning battalion formation in August 2003, but everyone had been expecting for several months to receive official word on the widely discussed deployment to Iraq. Standing in front of his battalion was the commander, Lt. Col. Steven Bullimore. The commander was a hulking figure who gained the admiration and respect of his troops for both his down-home style as well as his confident swagger. He ordered his nearly 700 soldiers to fall out of formation and huddle around him so that he could be heard more clearly as he read the newly published orders.

With the exception of a few small elements, the entire 1st Infantry Division had been left behind to watch their friends and fellow soldiers invade Mesopotamia that spring. It was one of the most controversial political decisions an American president had made in decades. There were plans assembled to use portions of the 1st Infantry Division in Northern Iraq, which dissolved due to failed diplomatic negotiations with Turkey. After the invasion, plausible rumors of the 1st Infantry Division becoming one of the two divisions to replace the 3rd and 4th Infantry Divisions ran rampant through Germany.

On that August morning, Lieutenant Colonel Bullimore substantiated the rumor as clearly and with as much detail as he could pass, as he had often promised. There was no other from whom the battalion would have preferred to receive the news, and it took him nearly half an hour to read and discuss the order. The moment had arrived, and most, if not all, realized its gravity with respect to their lives and the lives of their families. Yet, even as it provided concrete answers to the battalion, it also left thousands of open-ended questions in everyone's mind.

Traditionally, 1-6 Field Artillery provided artillery fires for the 3rd Brigade Combat Team of the 1st Infantry Division, but as the invasion rapidly ended, the need for traditional artillery quickly dissipated. As per the order, we learned that the brigade would be assigned to a portion of the Iraqi province of Diyala, situated directly north of Baghdad. 1-6 Field Artillery, as a part of 3rd Brigade, was tasked with a portion of the brigade footprint, the city called Baquba in the famed Sunni Triangle.

Two of the battalion's three cannon batteries, B and C Batteries, were to transition out of their traditional artillery role and reorganize as motorized rifle companies. In this role they would be responsible for providing security in the city of 280,000 inhabitants. B Battery would operate in the northern half, and C Battery would operate in the south. The third battery, A Battery, would remain true to its conventional mission of shooting artillery for the entire brigade.

Reorganizing the batteries into companies became an immediate concern, and it took a fair amount of creativity. A heavy artillery battery is composed of two firing platoons and a headquarters platoon, each consisting of thirty to forty soldiers. The final model developed for a motorized rifle company consisted of breaking the battery's two firing platoons

Third Platoon, C Company, Task Force 1-6 stands before the main entrance of the Diyala Provincial Capitol, the "Blue Dome," in May 2004. From left to right (front row): Staff Sgt. Wade Hunter, Sgt. William Joy, Sgt. Will Douglas, Sgt. Clayton Williams, Pvt. First Class Manuel Vargas, Pvt. Carlos Martinez, Pvt. Richard Roman, Spc. Middleton Wolf, Pvt. Wesley Waggoner. Left to right (second row): Pvt. Cory Hernandez, Sgt. Barry Poynter, Spc. Phillip Ramos, Spc. Frankie Cortes, Spc. Stewart Eubanks, Pvt. First Class Michael Lina, Sgt. Ray Villanueva. Left to right (third row): 1st Lt. Gregory Tomlin, Sgt. Winston Martinez, Spc. Charles Copp, Pvt. First Class Jason Lynch (KIA June 18, 2004), Sgt. Jarrod Matthews, Spc. Jesse Garcia, Staff Sgt. Bogdan Burduselu. (Gregory Tomlin Collection)

into three twenty-five-man platoons, and decreasing the size of the head-quarters platoon.

C Battery informally changed its name to C Company, thus distancing itself from its artillery heritage and mindset. Lts. James Gifford and Chris Lacour were assigned as the platoon leaders for the 1st and 2nd platoons, respectively, while Greg headed up the 3rd Platoon. Caleb assumed the role of executive officer, with oversight responsibilities for supply and maintenance.

Even with all of its frustrations, it turned out that determining the makeup of the two converted batteries was the easiest task. Learning how to operate as a rifle platoon in a motorized rifle company proved to be much harder. Transitioning into rifle platoons in the seven-month period between the delivery of the orders and the deployment date nearly over-whelmed the leadership within the newly formed companies.

Questions were plentiful at every level of the new platoons, and an-swers, of course, were often scarce and difficult to grasp. From the most senior leader to the most junior soldier in the battalion, this transition re-quired an entirely new set of material to be mastered. Infantry manuals helped in explaining small unit tactics, but often they contained large gaps with respect to urban combat operations. In late September, C Company trained through a circuit of basic individual infantryman skills, as well as those specific to the urban environment. A month later it was time to see how well soldiers utilized their newfound skills in collaborating on pla-toon and company-sized missions during the elaborate Mission Readiness Exercise at Hohenfels.

The field training at Hohenfels ended just in time to redeploy back to the battalion's home station in Bamberg, to clean and inventory equip-ment, and to take leave in December for the holidays. The deployment to Iraq was rapidly approaching, and after a long six months of field train-ing, the soldiers were eager to enjoy a few weeks of leave with their fami-lies and friends. The training had been rigorous, long, and frustrating, but when it was over, the soldiers had a better idea of what their mission would be.

Nothing was concrete, but at least they knew that much.

chapter 2
INSURGENCY: A PRELUDE

february 2004 arrived before anyone knew it. Our equipment, initially shipped across Germany, sailed on cargo ships from ports in Antwerp, Belgium, to ports outside of Kuwait City. The battalion's planners published rosters dating when soldiers were leaving, and all the various other minutiae seemed to fall into place to prepare men to depart from home for an entire year. The artillerymen of 1-6 Field Artillery were now soldiers of Task Force 1-6, awaiting the final call forward to say good-bye to their families and fly to Kuwait. Like his biblical namesake, Caleb, as the company executive officer, was sent ahead of the rest of the company with the advance party. Greg and the rest of the company arrived at Camp New York, Kuwait a few days later, where C Company prepared for a brief sojourn in the desert before "crossing the berm" into Iraq.

Kuwait was to be a transition area where the task force would gather its original equipment, receive more specialized equipment for the region, and conduct final training exercises before journeying north. Of course, the transition was mental as well. Perhaps it was the lack of distraction in the barren desert, or perhaps it was the rapidly approaching final trip into Iraq. Either way, the focus turned from the personal needs of pre-deployment to the communal need to train, prepare, and most importantly, to focus. For the first time, the task force was moving away from the notional world of the training centers to the real world of Diyala Province.

The seriousness, gained all the way down to the lowest level, was partly due to the focused information that started to flow in regarding the city of Baquba. When the unit left Germany, Baquba was a red star on a gray map of Iraq. It was a city that had several different pronunciations, varying from a Western bastardization by some and attempts to pronounce it with a higher degree of fidelity by others. Aside from the ground war, it had no history to speak of, with no practical reference points to help the task force understand it better. Baquba was Iraq, and Iraq was unknown.

In the tent that served as the battalion headquarters in Kuwait, the key leadership of the companies within the task force gathered nightly to coordinate logistics and receive intelligence updates on the city. The large maps of Iraq were replaced with satellite imagery of Baquba, revealing a complexity that seemed to be hiding behind the superimposed star on the former. The northern edge of the city was a highway that had been dubbed "RPG Alley" (Rocket-Propelled Grenade) during the ground war due to the high incidence of near ambushes from the heavy foliage on the flanks of the highway. In the west-central portion of the city was Mufrek Traffic Circle, which was actually triangular. Baquba's "green zone," consisting of the city's three main government buildings, was situated directly in the center of the city. Although the briefings had just exchanged one broad set of maps for a more narrow view, a skeleton of understanding was beginning to form, and perceptions of the city were beginning to refine into real understanding.

Little red explosions marked the maps in places where improvised explosive devices (IEDs), or roadside bombs, had exploded among convoys and civilians alike. For those who did not support the foreign military presence in Iraq, IEDs were favored and economical weapons. Wiring an artillery shell or a mortar round to a cell phone, hand-held transceiver or garage door opener, the insurgent could detonate the bomb from a safe distance. Often the triggerman clandestinely observed his enemy from a rooftop, a second story window, or a crowded storefront.

Baquba had one of the highest instances of IEDs in Iraq, especially around Mufrek Traffic Circle. Larger and more pronounced yellow explosions on the map indicated instances of direct fire engagements. Although the IED threat had increased within the city, direct fire engagements were relatively rare during Operation Iraqi Freedom (OIF) I. However, since Ramadan in the fall of 2003, RPG and rifle fire against U.S. forces began to rise.

The 588th Engineer Battalion, the 4th Infantry Division unit that Task Force 1-6 would replace, disseminated intelligence reports among 1-6's staff and commanders. Pictures of "High Value Targets," the locals suspected of masterminding the criminal and insurgent activity, were passed around. Lists of statistics detailed the threat and helped leaders to understand what they would face. Most of this data was taken as fact, merely numbers that heightened awareness; other pieces of information emphasized the gravity of the unit's training. The most sobering fact was learned through a *Stars and Stripes* newspaper and corroborated by the nightly updates: The 588th had suffered more American casualties than any other unit in the entire first year of the war. The names of the soldiers, names like Spc. Joseph C. Nordquist and Sgt. First Class Dan Henry Gabrielson, personalized the intelligence.

Aside from the intelligence, Kuwait itself increased awareness and focus as well. First was the strangeness of the environment to the Americans' eye, with its open ranges of sand dunes and Bedouins herding camels just outside the gates of Camp New York. The Army capitalized on the remote proximity of the desert to peacetime American garrisons to remind the soldiers of the closing proximity to the enemy. One poignant example was the relaxed training bureaucracy at the Udari Ranges in Kuwait, which allowed the platoons to train intensely without being smothered with regulations.

Back in Germany, contractors meticulously manicured the lawns of ranges in the European training centers. Range Control personnel virtually made a game out of faulting visiting officers who overlooked a small step outlined in one of the eleven annexes to the range safety manual. As a platoon leader conducting a familiarization range for the MK-19 automatic grenade launcher in Germany, Greg had to write a detailed plan to open, operate, and close the range. He had to maintain regular phone contact with Range Control from the MK-19 range tower, and he needed to coordinate for a military ambulance to be positioned by the firing line during hours of training.

When the C Company commander tasked him to run an M-16 qualification range at the Udari Ranges in Kuwait, Greg traveled with two buses packed with soldiers and ammunition on a barely distinguishable road to a location in the desert miles from Camp New York. Planted in the sand, a dozen simple wooden frames capable of holding six paper targets apiece served as the only indicator to soldiers that they had arrived at the range. Once the riflemen were dropped off, the buses began their hour-long return trip to Camp New York to pick up an additional set of soldiers to participate at the range.

Under the watchful eye of their non-commissioned officers, soldiers stapled targets to the frames, shot forty rounds apiece, and sat under the blazing sun until the buses returned to take them back to their tents. Should someone accidentally get shot, the platoon's medic would apply first aid and wait for an ambulance to arrive from Camp New York. Should a bus break down, the platoon would be stranded until they could fix it themselves or until help arrived. The safety net had been replaced by the sand of the Kuwaiti desert, which was as liberating as it was daunting.

Precious realistic training like this marked the majority of the days in Kuwait. At another range where soldiers practiced room clearing procedures, "shoot houses" constructed of plywood contained a series of rooms where soldiers were expected to shoot real bullets at paper targets. Each building included an overhead gangplank where the platoon leader could oversee his soldiers' performance. Greg found this particularly useful and spent hours watching his two squad leaders, Staff Sgt. Bogdan Burduselu and Staff Sgt. Wade Hunter, lead their soldiers through the buildings. He would never be afforded the omnipresence to watch their actions from above in a real combat environment. Instead, he would be expected to command his entire platoon from the street outside the building, anticipating developing threats to his forces and remaining in radio contact with headquarters.

Training events like the shoot houses were often overseen by civilian contractors who were all previous military special operators or police SWAT team members. Although the soldiers enjoyed working with the trainers and were willing to tweak their methods based on the expert advice of the contractors, their advice was seldom consistent. The gospel according to one contractor was that weapon slings were an unnecessary accoutrement, while another would stand by his conviction that the slings would mean the difference between wounding and killing the enemy. Another would insist that vehicle windows should be open in order to quickly return fire to an aggressive enemy, while others would assert that the bulletproof glass should be between the enemy and the passenger for the sake of safety.

The heightened sense of what was to come, and the opportunity to actually train with real ammunition in a real urban environment in a real Middle Eastern country, made the platoon leaders anxious to objectively nail down their tactics. The varying tactical advice given by the experts created a sense of relativity to their mission that was at first frustrating beyond words. Eventually, though, company leaders fostered a realization about the fight that was to come. The platoons would be autonomous elements, charged with engaging an amorphous enemy using methods that no military doctrine could prescribe, resulting in the disparate approaches taught in Kuwait. The reality of the moment of the fight would dictate the response. They could only hope to fall back on a few time-tested principles of combat, and otherwise react with the flow of events as they came. Although it was hardly an organized effort by the trainers to teach this lesson regarding the essential subjectivity of urban combat, the point was clear.

While Greg was leading his platoon through the training events, Caleb spent his time focusing on the support needs of the company. The three platoons needed the training, but the company needed to finalize plans to move north. Luckily, many of the preparations were completed in Germany, which left ample amounts of time for him to chase the commander's many ill-conceived whims.

Even at this late stage in the preparation for the deployment, major changes were taking place. Over the course of the first two weeks in Kuwait, C Company learned that it would be growing in numbers and capabilities. The 88 soldiers who made up C Company would be augmented by a platoon of infantry soldiers from another battalion in the brigade, 2-2 Infantry, under the leadership of platoon leader Lt. Kirby Jones and platoon sergeant Dwayne White. The company's fourth platoon, Punisher Platoon, consisted of approximately 40 soldiers, and came complete with four Bradley Fighting Vehicles. Their infantry expertise and their infantry equipment were welcomed to the company.

With the last-minute addition of Punisher Platoon, the evolution from peacetime artillery battery to a combat rifle company was nearly complete. The members of C Company were focused on beginning the mission, even if they had no idea how the future would unfold. The leaders had learned just as much as the soldiers did during the months of training, and still had plenty of questions left unanswered.

The complexity and absolute reality of the mission ahead greatly focused attention towards the questions that really mattered. The muddled new world of combat would present opportunities to create reality afresh for everyone. Collectively and individually, the company would face the incredible differences between the Islamic and Western worldviews. 24-year-old platoon leaders would be charged with adapting tactics and equipment designed for the previous war in order to simultaneously destroy the enemy and assist in the construction of a free and democratic Iraq. But they were also in the overwhelming position to create a reasonable truth that they could apply and understand in order to win. After just over three weeks of reorganizing and training in Kuwait, Task Force 1-6 repacked its gear and headed north. Once again, Caleb left with the advance party and flew into Iraq, while Greg traveled with the company's convoy of unarmored humvees through half of Iraq before arriving in Baquba.

A few days later, in early March, the two groups of soldiers met at Camp Gabe. The camp was named by the 588th Engineers after Sgt. Dan Henry Gabrielson; he was one of their comrades killed in Baquba. The members of C Company were happy to see each other and even more grateful that the long trip from Germany was over. First glimpses of the city did little to preserve the confidence that accompanied them in Kuwait. Not surprisingly, the landscape of the city as they drove to the camp consisted of unrecognizable left and right turns on an otherwise straight path. All attempts to associate key landmarks with those that had been displayed on the briefing maps in Kuwait were futile, even though the convoys had driven directly through the enormous traffic circle about which they had heard so much. Upon arrival at Camp Gabe, no one knew which direction was north.

The five-ton transport trucks Caleb and a few hundred other soldiers rode for the forty-five minute drive from the airfield quickly emptied when they reached their last stop. Forty-five minutes earlier, the trucks were loaded with anxious soldiers who realized for the first time that they were in Iraq. The uncertainty inspired bravado and a flippancy that often accompanies the unknown. Some made hopeful remarks about possible enemy attacks and others wrote their wives' names in black marker on the first round they intended to load into their weapon. Others sat quietly, looking outward at the mysterious terrain as it passed.

The Iraq that the group saw was not quite the terror zone most had expected. The country road wound through small farming villages where children ran to the street at the sound of the passing American convoy. Women, clad in black robes, held their scarves in place in front of their faces and ensured that the children did not run into the dangerous street. Traffic slowed and cleared for the heavily armed convoy as it sped through the bottlenecks. The obligatory combat hyperbole transformed into more authentic banter as the uneventful ride ended and the soldiers jumped down from the trucks onto the grounds of Camp Gabe. Discussions were curtailed out of necessity once the soldiers were off the trucks, though, as the wired, over-hydrated soldiers dismounted and unintentionally formed a massive circle, and then urinated on their new home in unchoreographed unison.

The ruins and overlaying military equipment on Camp Gabe approximately as it appeared upon our arrival in February 2004. (Provided with permission by Douglas Chadwick)

Although it was not intended in such a way, or intended at all, this first unified act of the new soldiers exemplified the initial opinions of the camp, which generally ranged from negative to extremely negative. Taking in the grounds for the first time, the soldiers noted the single-story, tan brick buildings that were poorly constructed on hard, tan dirt. They noticed the absence of life besides the few pathetic trees struggling to pull water out of the desert floor, and the kind of heat that makes you lethargic and sick to your stomach. The specter of the year to come seemed to mix in the air with the wavy, transparent exhaust fumes as the transport trucks drove away. Plenty of context was necessary to fully understand how anyone could live in such a drab environment, and the hosting engineers were eager to pass along what they knew.

Camp Gabe, formerly the headquarters of a 41st Armored Brigade of the Iraqi Republican Guard, sat in the southeast corner of Baquba and occupied approximately four square kilometers of land. The entire installation was divided into two parts, with Task Force 1-6 occupying the eastern half and the 82nd Engineer Battalion, another component of the 3rd Brigade, inhabiting the western half. The 82nd Engineers would be responsible for the vast, open farmlands that surrounded Baquba while Task Force 1-6 would be responsible for the city proper.

The former Republican Guard headquarters may have not been too impressive before the invasion, but what remained stood in shambles. Rubble surrounded the main camp in every direction and spread out for kilometers past the concertina wire and berm obstacles preventing access to the base. Enormous, rusted shards of metal were littered everywhere and seemed to criticize more than complement the ruins of the relatively modern structures in the camp. Carcasses of military vehicles seemed to only be connected to their rusted entrails by the miles of knee-high barbed wire that stretched across the camp. The soldiers remained vigilant so as not to insult the state of their hosts' home as they were shown around for the first time.

Such vigilance often resulted in theories that attempted to make some logical sense of the value of such a place when the soldiers were alone. A commonly expressed idea was that the Battle of Baquba fought by the 588th Engineers caused the destruction they had seen around them on their first day. The only inconsistency, of course, was that the Battle of Baquba never occurred during OIF I. The explanation was far more human.

By the time American troops entered Baquba for the first time, Baghdad had already fallen, and policymakers were already exchanging war plans for reconstruction policy. The occupation of the capital and the absence of occupying forces in cities like Baquba resulted in the dissolution of a legitimate military and police presence, and, in turn, a collapse of order. Policeman, former soldiers, imaginative townspeople, and shrewd entrepreneurs removed every fixture and object of conceivable value from the camp, first taking what was readily available, then gutting what still remained.

As the news had shown throughout the ground war, such looting occurred rampantly across the country. It happened in nearly all of the government buildings, and on occasion private homes and businesses were dismantled as well. While this meant acquiring exquisite antiques from Saddam's palaces in Baghdad, in Baquba it meant accumulating a plethora of construction material for locals methodical enough to chip cinder blocks from barracks walls.

Like the remainder of the camp, the ordnance depots of the former

Iraqi Army brigade had been looted by locals. However, unlike the floor tiles and bricks stripped from buildings, the ammunition could not be used to improve personal homes. Much of the stolen ammunition—from machine-gun ammunition to RPGs, and mortar rounds to larger artillery rounds—found their way into what would become enemy caches, reserved for future use. Intelligence indicated that 588th soldiers had been attacked by the enemy more than once with weapons that originated from the camp they presently occupied.

The weapons depot remaining at Camp Gabe, of which the engineers took control, still contained countless munitions that had been picked over and left. The massive 500-pound and two-ton bombs were too heavy for most donkey carts to pull away, but still posed a threat and needed to be destroyed. So the engineers embarked upon a mission to rid the camp of ordnance the best way they knew how: controlled detonation. Three to five times a day for several months on end, the ground shuddered beneath Baquba, causing the local Iraqis to refer to the camp as "Camp Boom." Referring to the state of the camp after most of the ordnance had been disposed of, Staff Sgt. Jason Bacon, the platoon sergeant for 2nd Platoon, C Company, piously referred to it as "Camp Doo Doo."

It was a hilariously appropriate title for the camp, but the new nickname did not reflect the efforts the engineers had taken to create a home for themselves. Although they hardly improved the camp aesthetically, giant cubical baskets were positioned around the buildings to protect against the numerous mortar attacks the engineers endured during their stay. Dirt roads had been lightly paved, bathrooms had been installed, and American military symbols and emblems marked doorways, signposts, and buildings. Once necessity allowed you to look through the rubble, dust and heat, Camp Gabe actually appeared habitable.

After the impact of the first impression was absorbed, these finer points of the camp became more easily discernable. There was a comfortable dining facility that served as the main social hub of the camp. A building had been rearranged to house an adequate but deceptively named Internet café, which had enough computers and phones to allow everyone to contact home. Generators had been trucked in to provide fairly reliable electricity for the countless air conditioners, televisions, and refrigerators that had likewise been shipped over. And although it was a relatively large installation, all of the real living went on in a fairly centralized location, meaning that one only had to be bothered by Gabe's lack of beauty when leaving his room with a purpose in mind.

The rampant disbelief that the soldiers of Task Force 1-6 initially expressed about the camp was short-lived and came out as forced and artificial. The sarcastic and incredulous expletives provoked by the loud generators and the barely functioning toilets quickly yielded to less self-conscious forms of humor. It was as if their generational irony was leaving them for awhile and being replaced by the realization that everything in the world was not the way they had grown to expect.

The generators were there because the city did not have electricity that functioned for more than a few hours at a time. The toilets had to be flushed with a bucket of often unavailable water because the locality lacked the infrastructure to provide such luxuries. Mostly, though, the soldiers knew how men were supposed to react to such conditions, and enjoyed a secret pride in what they were asked to endure. And after many conversations with the engineers about their experiences in Baquba, the pride the soldiers felt was replaced by a hint of shame in their expectations.

Baquba was generally overpopulated with few jobs or resources for its citizenry, leaving its dense and dirty footprint straddling the Diyala River. Because of its proximity to Baghdad, Baquba was often visited by members of Saddam's family during the previous regime. Uday and Qusay Hussein even owned several businesses and homes in the city, including a date processing plant and horse stables. Although it was a major city, it was not Tikrit, Saddam's hometown, or Baghdad, the capital of the Arab empire.

The city consisted of eleven smaller districts, all with varying personalities, people, and views of the American presence in their country. With the exception of Buhriz to the south and Huwaydir to the north, all of the districts were situated within the dense urban design of Baquba and were clearly planned in some way, as seen in the grid pattern of their roads and the placement of their scant utility provisions. Aside from the canal that split the greater city directly in half from east to west, and the major throughway (Highway 5) that split the city from north to south, there was little demarcation between any one district and another.

Many of the districts were quiet and some were even friendly. The neighborhoods of Shifta, Huwaydir, and Mustafa were almost inviting to the American presence. Other districts, like Khatoon, Mualimeen, Mufrek, New Baquba, and Mujema seemed relatively indifferent to the American presence most of the time. Residents had their rundown cars to fix, their classes to teach, their open-air market to attend, and often they just wished that their lives could return to normal. Tahrir and Old Baquba were often quiet and calm, but were classified on the bad side of "neutral" because of attack trends that appeared to originate in these districts. The town of Buhriz, the engineers offered, seemed to be as neutral as many of the other districts in the city, although it did seem to sparkle with activity from time to time.

Buhriz was not actually a part of Baquba. Rather, it was its own municipality, with land reaching as far as the northern outskirts of Baghdad. Because of this, the town was known as Baghdad's "gateway from the north," which should have been more ominous than it sounded. The heavily populated town of Buhriz sat centrally on the southern edge of Baquba, divided into two sections, east and west, by the canal. The rest of the district, stretching from Baquba to Baghdad, was comprised of many lesser populated and sparse farming communities, which made it difficult to patrol with any regularity. Task Force 1-6, and more precisely, C Company would assume responsibility for patrolling Buhriz.

Although believed to be a benign part of the area of operations, there were many indicators suggesting that Buhriz was a boiling pot of Jihadist sentiments. First, the vast majority of its citizens were Sunni Muslims, the minority in Iraq although they were protected and favored under their former dictator's leadership. Buhriz's residents also included a significant number of former Iraqi intelligence and army officers. Their loyalty to Saddam and to the Ba'ath party made for an easy transition into criminal or terrorist activities. It was not known at the time, but elusive and charismatic personalities, including the duplicitous mayor of Buhriz, Mayor Auf, had all perfected the art of fusing criminal and terrorist activities—the art of using ideology when it was profitable.

The people of Buhriz were also the scapegoats for Iraqis from every other district in Baquba. When an Iraqi anywhere in Baquba was questioned regarding the people involved in attacks or anything else that may have been negative, the people of Buhriz were blamed almost as much as the Iranians. The culpability of the citizens of Buhriz was mainly due to the resentment that many of the Shiite citizens felt against the high Sunni population in the district. Although Baquba was situated within the so-called Sunni Triangle, the population in Baquba was generally far less monolithic with respect to religious sects. With a population within the urban area of roughly 280,000 people, 60 percent were Sunni and 40 percent were Shi'ia. Even if they were just vindictively blaming their former oppressors, all indications should have made clear that Buhriz was more than a sleepy little hamlet.

Aside from its sectarian diversity and troubles, Baquba also had a significant agriculture industry and was the provincial seat for the Diyala province, one of Iraq's eighteen provinces. Baquba was known throughout Iraq for the expansive date palm groves that line the Diyala River, which meanders through the city. The river provided the irrigation necessary for vegetation to thrive on its banks and up to three kilometers to its east and west. Most of the date palms that forested the groves grew to heights of two to four-story buildings. Thick, waist-high grass and un-pruned bushes that seasonally produced pomegranates and oranges hampered the movements of anyone seeking to negotiate a path beneath the palms. Independent farmers owned nearly all of the groves, and some built mud-brick walls to enclose their property. For the most part, however, nothing separated one Iraqi's orchard from another.

It would take a significant amount of time after the 588th Engineers departed for everyone in C Company and throughout the task force to grasp the nuances and intricacies of the city. The formal transition with the engineers was relatively brief, beginning on March 12 and ending on March 18. During this short period, C Company learned as much as possible about the southern half of the city, while the soldiers of B Company focused their efforts on learning about the northern half of the city.

On the first full day of the transition period, C Company leaders joined the soldiers of the engineer battalion on a patrol through the city. Engineer platoon leaders played the role of tour guides while meandering through the traffic congestion along the poor city roads tattered with piles of trash and flowing slit trenches. Their drivers also demonstrated that the streets remained easily manageable for a convoy of humvees with machine-guns mounted on them. According to the engineers, seventy-five percent of the population loved the Americans.

The engineers passed along what information they could in the curtailed week before they left. Time and time again they warned that IEDs were the biggest threat in Baquba. The new officers and non-commissioned officers listened closely while they described how to navigate through the sector, which roads were passable and which were not, how they dealt with the children who would swarm their vehicles, and how they would handle detainees.

All of this information was far from obvious and quite valuable, as it certainly shaped much of the incoming unit's own initial read on the city. The leadership in Task Force 1-6 began to formulate the impression that the enemy situation in Baquba would be fairly unimpressive. Neither the engineers nor the artillerymen-turned-riflemen realized that Baquba had been quietly developing the necessary foundation for an insurgency since the declared end of the ground war. Although an engineer patrol had not been directly engaged in three months, the insurgency had been feverishly building for the previous two months and did not have the capacity yet to stage massive attacks.

On March 13, during the transition with the engineers, C Company received its first opportunity to react to an IED. At a moment's notice, the company commander assembled as many of his platoon leadership from the four platoons as he could muster and told them that they were going with an engineer platoon to cordon an IED so that the Explosive Ordinance Demolition (EOD) team could detonate it in place. Upon arriving at the site of the possible IED, the lieutenants watched the procedures intently. After hearing so many horror stories over the course of the previous few months about IEDs, they were all a bit anxious to see how one looked and how someone on the ground would react to it.

Situated on Highway 2, near the western edge of the city, the lieutenants watched as the engineer platoon established blocking positions on opposite sides of the highway to prevent an unassuming civilian from driving by the roadside bomb. Other soldiers searched 300 meters of highway stretching on either side of the bomb to ensure that a secondary device did not exist on the road. Once soldiers secured the area the EOD team could clear the bomb. From an observation point with the northern cordon, Caleb, Greg, and Kirby could see the IED, comprised of a 155-millimeter artillery round wired to a battery and garage door opener conspicuously placed on the side of the major highway. With binoculars they watched the EOD robot drop a charge of plastic explosives on top of the artillery round before backing away. It all seemed so nonchalant. Aside from the loud explosion of the device, which was planned and controlled, the only disturbance to the mission was a mentally handicapped Iraqi man who was wearing purple snow boots and probing the security perimeter.

The following afternoon Greg and 1st Platoon Leader Lt. Jim Gifford accompanied Lt. Gary Phillips on a patrol of Baquba and Buhriz. The two C Company platoon leaders rode in Gary's open-top humvee as the engineer platoon first drove into Shifta. Bouncing along a dusty road, the lieutenants monitored radio traffic alerting patrols to be on the lookout for a blue flatbed truck transporting refrigerators. According to a recent informant, criminals were smuggling weapons through Baquba in refrigerators. Like an all-points bulletin for cops in a city back home, army platoons were expected to respond to the information received from their battalion headquarters. Gary instructed his driver to detour out of Shifta so that the platoon could establish a vehicle checkpoint by the central bridges and search for the wanted truck.

It was not so much a vehicle checkpoint that the platoon set up as it was a meter-maid operation, with soldiers walking on the sidewalk alongside the highway to search for the blue truck. The Twin Bridges functioned as one of only three crossing points over the Diyala River in Baquba, and traffic crossing the bridge during the afternoon rush hours slowed to a crawl or complete idle. It would be impossible for anyone outside of the U.S. military to pull out of the traffic jam to evade capture. The platoon parked their humvees in the median of Highway 5 on the east side of the Twin Bridges. Gary ordered half of the soldiers to guard the vehicles, while the other men walked along the side of the highway. Greg and Jim joined the walking patrol as they inspected the three lanes of east-bound traffic. A couple of teenage girls laughed, then blushed as the lieutenants passed the sedan in which they rode. School children in a minibus pressed their faces against the glass to gain the officers' attention.

Beyond the inquisitiveness of the Iraqi youth, most drivers on Highway 5 did little more than curtly acknowledge the soldiers' presence. After fifteen insignificant minutes of walking beside the traffic, Gary ordered his soldiers to regroup at the humvees and prepare to move out. A radio update reported that the brigade commander's personal convoy had located and stopped a blue flatbed truck carrying a load of refrigerators. The engineer platoon needed to assume responsibility for searching the cargo.

The platoon found the commander's column of three humvees parked near Qusay Hussein's stables in the district of New Baquba on the west side of the Twin Bridges. No sooner did Gary receive the details from the colonel's driver about the suspected truck than the commander's vehicles departed. The lieutenants observed the middle-aged truck driver while Gary interrogated the man through his translator. Where was he going? Who did he work for? Did he carry anything inside the refrigerators? Without hesitating, the Iraqi provided straightforward answers to each question.

"OK, let's take a look for ourselves," Gary said.

One of the platoon's sergeants motioned to the suspect to open all of the refrigerators. This proved to be a challenge due to the creative method used to stack about twenty full-sized units atop one another on the flatbed. In the United States, this driver would probably have been jailed for endangering other drivers by stacking refrigerators four high and then tying them together with an old rope. However, this was Iraq, where national and provincial regulations were sparse with respect to safety of any kind. The lieutenants watched in admiration as the man nimbly climbed on top of the third level of refrigerators and lowered the fourth set of units to the ground.

One by one the man opened each unit for the soldiers to inspect. Thirty minutes later all of the refrigerators stood on the street, and Gary reported with authority to his headquarters that they had stopped the wrong Iraqi. This individual was not carrying a cache of weapons after all. Gary thanked the man and told him he could take his merchandise and continue on his business.

Gary instructed the platoon to remount their humvees so that he could show Greg and Jim Buhriz before dark. The most direct way to Buhriz from Baquba was to travel south along the eastern shoulder of the Diyala River. However, Gary wanted to show the lieutenants the back route, which took them east of Camp Gabe and south along an asphalt road running through farm country. It was the first time of the day that they escaped the incessant beeping and congestion of the city traffic.

As the humvees sped towards Buhriz, Gary explained that Buhriz was the only part of their sector that his battalion did not patrol by foot. Twice in as many months, Iraqi civilians had stepped onto anti-personnel mines in Buhriz. While it was unclear whether the mines were set for U.S. forces or for a particular Iraqi, the 588th Engineers were convinced that they could complete their mission without unnecessarily endangering soldiers by dismounting from their vehicles. Exceptions were only when operating on the main Canal Street or when it was essential to the mission.

Entering from the southern entrance to Buhriz, the lieutenants initially found the town unremarkable compared to the districts of Baquba seen so far. Cars cluttered the streets; women walked to market vendors, and men sipped chai under tea shop awnings. The platoon veered off of Canal Street and into a residential neighborhood. Just as in Tahrir and Shifta, children ran from their homes to wave to the Americans and ask for chocolate. Adults continued about their business, and not a single person made an obscene gesture towards the Americans.

At the end of a cul-de-sac the driver of the platoon leader's humvee attempted a sharp U-turn. Despite months of navigating the streets of his company's zone, the driver got the humvee stuck in the slit trench running through the gravel road. "Try to stay clear of the trenches," Gary warned the lieutenants, "they don't look like it, but some of them are more than two feet deep."

Soldiers dismounted to secure the area while the driver struggled to pull out of the trench. Children pointed to the humvee and giggled at the situation in which the Americans found themselves. An Iraqi man approached the front of the humvee and motioned to the driver which way to turn his steering wheel in order to escape the trap. A couple of minutes later the humvee found the required traction to successfully return to the road. The civilian who offered directions smiled as the children surrounding the patrol clapped. Meanwhile, the lieutenants heard the humvee driver mildly curse as he wiped from his face the sewage that had splattered on him through his open window. Jim and Greg laughed out loud at his misfortune.

As the patrol returned to Canal Street, Gary told his driver to stop his humvee. An Iraqi man was walking in front of the platoon with a shotgun slung over his shoulder. Gary approached the man with his translator as his soldiers secured the road. The man explained that he was returning from a hunting excursion in the palm groves. He did not realize that it was against the new laws to carry a weapon in public. Gary explained the law, which allowed each household to maintain one rifle *within* their home for security, but not to take the weapon outside.

Two Iraqi policemen approached the patrol and assured the platoon leader that they would handle the situation. Without finding the man or his shotgun to be a serious concern, Gary was content to leave the man with the police. The platoon continued on its way out of Buhriz and returned to Camp Gabe. The C Company platoon leaders admired Gary's style in the sector and his interaction with the local populace. Both officers decided that patrolling their sector and handling the nuances of daily life would not be too difficult for themselves or for their men.

When the formal transition period concluded, everyone in the company, from the platoon leadership to the youngest soldiers, believed they understood what Baquba would be like. After all, it was not just satellite imagery and intelligence reports that they had to base their analysis on anymore. Now they had actually been in the sector, seen live Iraqis, and observed how other American soldiers responded to the scenarios as they unfolded.

Perhaps more than any other event during the transition, the IED clearing operation on March 13 developed a false sense of security in everyone from C Company who observed the "routine" mission. The situation was so easily controlled and the device was so easily destroyed that no one thought twice about the dangers of a 155-millimeter artillery round set to detonate and destroy everything within its immediate surroundings.

The days that followed the changeover only hardened this sense of security in the soldiers. The 588th Engineers departed Baquba for Fort Hood, Texas, after a transfer of authority ceremony on March 18. With the departure of the 3rd and 4th Infantry Divisions, OIF II formally began. The city officially belonged to Task Force 1-6 immediately after the ceremony, and the platoon leaders eagerly started conducting various independent missions throughout the city. Confidence in the sector and the mission were building as the platoons reacted to whatever came their way. There was still a degree of uncertainty, but most wondered if this was all that counterinsurgency warfare consisted of.

This perception was promptly shattered forever for the men of C Company on March 25. Exactly one week after Task Force 1-6 had officially taken over the city of Baquba, Lt. Christopher Lacour led the 2nd Platoon of C Company into New Baquba to cordon an IED. One of Chris' squads established a blocking position more than 300 meters from the primary device. While the humvees blocked the road, soldiers searched the area for hidden secondary devices before assuming security positions in alleyways and side roads. Then a mortar round lying beneath one of the dozens of trash piles along the road detonated only a few meters from Spc. Adam D. Froehlich. The explosion instantly killed Specialist Froehlich and injured two of Chris' other men.

From the point of Adam's passing, the façade of the harmlessness of IEDs and the tranquility of the city disappeared. An IED would not always be a conspicuous object that locals would identify for their police or a U.S. patrol. The enemy had a cunning side and the ability to demonstrate tactical patience. Rather than detonate the device against a passing humvee, the triggerman, with his reconfigured cell phone or garage door opener, chose to remotely detonate the bomb at the moment that Specialist Froehlich positioned himself on the ground as part of the dismounted cordon.

The men of C Company were now certain of whom their enemy was. They also realized that they would not always be able to identify the combatant before he blended back into the civilian populace on the bustling streets of Baquba. For the cynics seeking a meaning to the war, they now had one. The true believers added another justification to their list of reasons to persevere. With the heartbreaking loss of their brother in arms, C Company, Task Force 1-6 was ready to make the year count.

PART 2
the easter offensive

chapter 3
INSURGENCY: A PRIMER
Lt. Greg Tomlin, 3rd Platoon Leader, C Company

beginning in early April, nearly one month after Task Force 1-6 began to arrive in Baquba, the distinction between frivolous and important questions started to become abundantly clear. Time and experience in the city began to illuminate and refine what soldiers would really need to know. Along with the time and experience in such an environment, the massive, week-long offensive staged against the U.S. and Iraqi forces during Easter Week, 2004 provided a rather intensive course regarding the insurgency and the capabilities of the enemy.

The week began with a sense of expected normalcy. For the period immediately following the transition of authority for Baquba with the 588th Engineer Battalion, Jim Gifford and I were ordered to provide security, with our platoons, for the Iraqi Police at the Diyala Provincial Police Headquarters in downtown Baquba. Upon returning to Camp Gabe on March 30, 2004, Jim's platoon began a stint as the battalion's escort platoon, with responsibilities for taking Lt. Col. Steven Bullimore, our battalion commander, to meetings in the city, and completing distant logistical missions outside of the brigade area of responsibility. Meanwhile, 3rd Platoon anxiously fell into a robust patrol schedule.

Our static two weeks at the police headquarters, while relatively safe and secure, hardly sufficed in keeping at bay my platoon's eagerness to execute their training. Finally, back at Camp Gabe and with a patrol schedule in hand, the sector was ours. The twenty-four members of 3rd Platoon began conducting patrols that included establishing impromptu vehicle checkpoints and walking patrols to speak to the local populace. Twice a day for three-hour blocks, we mounted our five humvees to investigate the security situation in one or two city districts.

These patrols lasted for one week, and they were colored by amusing encounters with truck and donkey-cart drivers, as well as conversations with local shop owners and one former Iraqi prisoner of war who had

Inquisitive children line a side street in Khatoon while 3rd Platoon conducts a dismounted patrol. (Gregory Tomlin Collection)

spent fifteen years in Iranian captivity. At every stop along our unpredictable route, children ran to the roadside to ask for candy, restaurant owners invited me and the platoon's interpreter into their establishments for tea, and homeowners itemized infrastructure complaints for the American government to resolve.

During our patrols, the soldiers of 3rd Platoon stuck to the fundamentals we had learned from our training in Germany and Kuwait, and I focused on the small unit leadership I had learned from the classroom, as well as my experience in the Army to date. The soldiers maintained security encompassing 360 degrees of our position wherever we moved; they reported all suspicious activity to me, and they treated the local populace with dignity and respect. Before we left the gates of the camp for a patrol, I issued a thorough mission order and conducted a map reconnaissance with my squad leaders, Staff Sgt. Bogdan Burduselu and Staff Sgt. Wade Hunter. During the safety briefing held prior to every patrol, I quizzed soldiers on the names of the Baquba suburbs or the Buhriz road network that we would visit. While some found it trivial to properly pronounce Sebat Nisan or Mualimeen, I felt it was important for all of us to be able to mentally picture the layout of our sector, in order to prepare ourselves for the times when we would be deluged by confusion and frustration.

Within a week of patrolling, most of the men managed to learn all the significant Arabic names of the seven districts in our sector, and their respective direction from Camp Gabe. Concluding each patrol, we gathered around the hood of my humvee to identify techniques we needed to improve in future patrols, recognize what we did well outside of the gate, and recall any notable civilians observed during the mission. The formality we initially observed and the methods we practiced would become less rigid in the future due to these initial discussions, but in the first weeks of our ownership of the city, we executed our missions with an almost vigilant adherence to the military doctrine we received before our arrival.

Because of the seriousness of our mission, we anticipated this sort of rapid development of models and procedures. What I did not anticipate was the security situation drastically changing after only a week of patrolling. On April 7, I was called to the battalion headquarters just as I sat down for lunch in our mess hall, shortly after noon. Maj. William Chlebowski, the battalion's operations officer, told me to disregard my scheduled patrol for 2:00 that afternoon, and get into Baquba as soon as possible. A 600-man crowd, previously assembled in front of the provincial capitol building, had moved into Old Baquba, apparently protesting what they felt were existing government inadequacies. The group might converge on the Civil-Military Operations Center (CMOC) for the Diyala Province.

Guarded by a platoon from our task force's B Company, the CMOC housed the offices of members of the Coalition Provisional Authority (U.S. civilians) and Army Civil Affairs officers. Positioned in the center of Baquba, the CMOC location was ideal for Iraqi civilians and public servants of the transitional government to meet with American officials. Its location also posed a higher security threat to its inhabitants than if they resided at Camp Gabe, or in the brigade headquarters at Camp Warhorse to the north of the city.

Third Platoon received the mission to determine whether the crowd had dispersed, and if it had not, to confirm reports that members in the demonstration carried weapons. Because we had to rush out an hour earlier than our scheduled 2:00 P.M. departure, we could not get the platoon's fifth humvee out of the maintenance shop in time from its scheduled automotive service, so I left behind a fire team of five soldiers. For the first time since beginning our patrols of the city, I did not travel with my entire twenty-four-man platoon. Our four-vehicle convoy meandered through the streets of Old Baquba, a district not within our company's sector, for thirty minutes without observing any large groups of men or any unusual activity. Unassuming patrons surrounded the kiosks of the old city's large open-air market, and the typical vehicular congestion filled the major boulevards. I radioed this report to the battalion headquarters and we began to drive west toward the river to conduct our originally scheduled patrol.

Only a couple minutes after receiving our change of mission order, the CMOC reported on our battalion radio frequency that an unknown number of men had just launched multiple rocket-propelled grenades (RPGs) at the compound from alleyways and rooftops in Tahrir, the suburb of Baquba immediately to their south. My planned patrol route would take 3rd Platoon directly in front of the CMOC in fewer than three minutes, so knowing that Old Baquba was peaceful, I altered our route from the highway, electing to go through a number of residential streets, and await further guidance. This time, as we traveled through Old Baquba, soldiers in the trail vehicles of our patrol noticed shops beginning to close, and the lively activity that we observed only ten minutes earlier in the same area had disappeared.

The CMOC reported that they began to receive additional RPGs from the northwest in Old Baquba, and rooftop observation posts at the provincial police headquarters announced that a mass of people were moving to the CMOC from the north. As I scanned my map in the lead convoy vehicle to figure out if I needed to change our route again, Pvt. First Class Jason Lynch hollered, "RPG!" from the rooftop hatch of our humvee, where he manned a .50-caliber machine gun. Private Lynch had observed three men with RPGs walking toward us from a perpendicular alleyway only thirty meters away. Most likely, the trio was headed for the CMOC because we were only a couple blocks north of the compound. My vehicle passed the narrow passage too quickly for Private Lynch to engage the enemy with his machine gun. I broke through the battalion's radio traffic to provide my location, to alert the drivers of my other three vehicles who monitored the same frequency. If not positioned directly in front of the narrow alley, it would be impossible for anyone to see the hostiles.

The three rockets were fired in quick succession before any of the machine gunners in the humvees could respond to the three civilian-dressed men, who were probably as surprised by our presence as we were by theirs. At least one of the grenades hit a vehicle, but for a couple moments, we were unsure who was hit. Sgt. Barry Poynter, traveling in the third of our four vehicles, observed smoke to his rear, and reported that the last vehicle had been hit. In the second humvee, Sergeant Burduselu saw smoke to his rear, and reported that Sergeant Poynter's vehicle had been hit. Receiving the brief reports, I envisioned that we would have to salvage two immobile vehicles as an unknown number of hostile men continued to gather in my vicinity—and we were short a humvee's complement of soldiers! There was simply no training real enough to prepare anyone for the sudden violence and confusion of one's first firefight.

Spc. Jesse Garcia, my driver for the entire time that I served as 3rd Platoon leader, stopped our humvee at a traffic circle several hundred meters north of the attack site. I looked behind me to see two other humvees file into the roundabout, the second of which was on fire, but there was no sign of the trail humvee. I attempted to reach Sergeant Hunter on the radio, but he was not responding. Without being able to speak with him on the radio, there was no way for me to confirm whether his vehicle was also damaged.

As my gunner shouted at civilians to get off of the street directly in front of my humvee, I grabbed my M-16 and began running toward the damaged humvee. With the exception of rooftop gunners, everyone dismounted from their vehicles to provide security around the traffic circle and search for more potential attackers. Should the enemy choose to engage us again, I knew we had substantial firepower, and while limited in numbers, my squad continued to maintain 360-degree security.

When Private Lynch initially screamed, "RPG," my heart began racing, but not nearly as bad as when I ran to the side of Sergeant Poynter's burning humvee at the traffic circle. Each heartbeat pounded against my eardrums. Additional RPGs, small arms fire, and hidden insurgents did not concern me. What I dreaded most was approaching the burning vehicle to find casualties. I was not sure whether I was prepared to see one of my own men covered in blood, suffering from a gaping wound.

Sergeant Poynter met me by his humvee, and although I stood only a meter away from him, he screamed to me that no one was injured in his burning vehicle, which was, of course, good news. A small trickle of blood emanating from one of his ear canals, however, proved that his statement was not exactly true. The RPG that exploded just behind Sergeant Poynter's seat in the humvee had obviously caused some sort of hearing damage. Surveying the damaged humvee, however, I knew it would not leave Old Baquba by its own power. One of the RPG warheads managed to strike exactly between the vehicle's floorboard and the base of the right-side passenger door. Continuing on its course, the projectile detonated inside the central fuel cell, causing a fire that disabled the humvee's steering column and melted flat two of its tires.

With the fear of seeing one of my men severely injured quashed by Sergeant Poynter's update, my mind could more calmly focus on the unknown location of Sergeant Hunter's vehicle. No one from the platoon who was assembled at the traffic circle could tell me where the last vehicle went. No one knew whether it remained in the kill zone, or if it had turned onto a different side street in Old Baquba. Several agonizing minutes later, while soldiers extinguished the fire and we continued to scan our sectors for future attacks, I managed to gain contact with Sergeant Hunter on the radio in my humvee.

Sergeant Hunter reported that his humvee was not hit. The smoke that Sergeant Poynter reported seeing to his rear emanated from his own vehicle. Based on how Sergeant Poynter's vehicle was hit, and due to its rising smoke cloud, Sergeant Hunter had stopped his vehicle fifty meters short of the alleyway, thinking that an improvised-explosive device (IED) had detonated and immobilized the vehicle to his front. This was exactly the technique we had agreed to use in such situations. By the time the smoke cleared, the fourth vehicle sat alone in the middle of the street, and with heavy radio traffic on the battalion frequency, he could not reach me to ask for the platoon's location. Finding himself isolated, Sergeant Hunter judiciously directed his driver to move south to the CMOC, a known location in the same area that we had all identified during the previous week.

Once I understood that the soldiers in the fourth vehicle were fine, and using the CMOC as a rally point, I requested for battalion to dispatch another platoon to help us recover our broken vehicle. Being a fire team short even before we left for the mission, and with the fourth vehicle at the CMOC, we were sitting in central Baquba with only a squad and two operational vehicles—a total of thirteen soldiers including myself and an interpreter.

The battalion, however, had a larger concern on its hands. Just as I approached the traffic circle, I observed a Kiowa helicopter fly over my mangled platoon, heading for the CMOC. While I was attempting to reach Sergeant Hunter on the radio, the bullets of an AK-47 damaged one of the helicopter propellers, forcing it to make a hard landing in a field between the CMOC and the district of Tahrir. Rooftop guards at the CMOC observed locals continuing to shoot at and attempt to approach the Kiowa. Task Force 1-6 now had the priority mission of securing the downed helicopter and its U.S. pilots before a wild hoard engulfed the aircraft. With a touch of dark humor, I silently wondered whether 3rd Platoon would be forgotten as production for the sequel to *Blackhawk Down* unfolded a kilometer to our south.

Fortunately, the battalion did not forget us, and pushed another platoon to our location as the helicopter rescue began. Lt. Paul Lashley and his 1st Platoon from B Company arrived to reinforce our security arrangement at the roundabout, and tow Sergeant Poynter's humvee back to Camp Gabe. Several soldiers preparing the vehicle for towing ceased their efforts after taking a closer look at the right-side passenger door. The propellant pipe of the RPG warhead was still wedged between the door and the floorboard of the humvee. With our limited experience at that point with RPGs, neither Paul nor I could confidently decide whether the warhead had exploded. The vehicle fire had melted the seat and other items to such an extent that we could not judge if the warhead remained intact, and I was not about to open the door to find out.

With all the other threats in the sector and two sizable crowds newly forming off of two spokes of our traffic circle, we could not wait for the Explosives Ordinance Demolition (EOD) team from Camp Warhorse to travel to our location and investigate the damaged humvee. Soldiers from both platoons attached the smoldering vehicle to the back of an up-armored humvee—a stronger, more powerful version than what we had—so we could tow it back to Camp Gabe, where EOD could safely examine the vehicle.

As the men attached the tow bar, an IED detonated 200 to 300 meters up one of the traffic circle's spokes, adding a bit more confusion to the already intense situation. Perhaps someone thought we had stopped at the location of the detonation, but we did not have any interest in prodding up that particular road. Once the smoldering humvee was securely connected to one of Paul's vehicles, we headed to the CMOC, so Sergeant Hunter's vehicle could join our convoy for the return to the base camp. As we passed the CMOC, Lt. Kirby Jones's platoon, the single Infantry platoon attached to our battalion, complete with four Bradley Fighting Vehicles, could be seen securing the helicopter's crash site as a military wrecker prepared to haul the Kiowa back to Camp Warhorse. It seemed that everyone was getting a chance to learn about the complexities of urban warfare that day.

Upon pulling off the highway and onto the dirt road that led to Camp Gabe, finally able to think instead of react, I replayed the entire episode in my head, and realized for the first time just how surreal the entire situation was. Third Platoon suffered no injuries, save for Sergeant Poynter's mild hearing loss, which he acknowledged only after our medic, Spc. Stewart Eubanks, insisted that he receive an examination at the battalion aid station.

I realized that all the training worked. Notwithstanding the initial panic, the chaotic radio traffic, and the continual detonation of live explosives, the platoon instinctively responded with fundamentals ingrained since basic training and the advanced techniques practiced in Germany and Kuwait. Security remained the primary focus at all times. A lost sergeant relied on a rally point, and somehow I was providing coherent orders on the ground while also providing situational updates to battalion on the radio.

In preparing for Iraq, most of us wondered whether we would be able to effectively lead under fire. On April 7, 2004, we discovered that while it was by no means easy, our will to protect our fellow comrades and complete a mission superseded any perceived shortcomings. Each soldier of 3rd Platoon, from the youngest private to the most experienced squad leader, demonstrated his ability to perform in the face of real danger. Over the next week, I would witness them continue to develop their capacity for judiciously applied violence, time and again.

As Spc. Garcia drove the final dusty stretch of road back to our camp, I also realized that miracles do occur. Since 3rd Platoon had to rush out of the gate and leave a humvee and fire team of five soldiers behind for the first time in Iraq, I had one empty seat in one of the four vehicles in the convoy. That empty seat would burn to ash after the RPG penetrated the tiny space between the armored door and the floorboard of Sergeant Poynter's humvee. Had I taken the entire platoon, all twenty-five seats would have been occupied.

We found EOD waiting for us just inside the camp's gate to remove the potentially armed RPG. The ordnance soldiers stared in amazement at the protruding propellant pipe and confirmed that the warhead had detonated. "No one was sitting there, were they, sir?" one sergeant asked as he took a digital photograph for his report. Indeed, it was truly amazing that the seat, the only empty seat in the convoy, was vacant when 3rd Platoon became the first Task Force 1-6 element to be involved in a direct-fire engagement.

As adrenaline was replaced with relief, small indicators, such as distant explosions in the city and the lack of traffic on the streets, left an eerie feeling for some in the platoon. Visiting the battalion operations center, the battle captain shared with me reports that flourished throughout the city about groups of black jumpsuit-clad insurgents moving into Baquba. Local informants said that an estimated 200 members of the Mahdi Army, zealots of the Shi'ia Imam Muqtada al Sadr, had trekked north from Baghdad's Sadr City to Baquba with plenty of weaponry. With presence patrol missions on hold, I issued a movement to contact order to the platoon for the next day's trip outside the gate. In other words, our mission was to find the enemy, and once we made contact, our duty was to destroy them.

chapter 4
ALL THINGS CONVENTIONAL
Lt. Greg Tomlin, 3rd Platoon Leader, C Company

"I never thought we'd shoot artillery in the city. I never thought we'd drop bombs in the city. We did both."

LT. COL. STEPHEN L. BULLIMORE, COMMANDER, TASK FORCE 1-6,
LIEUTENANTS' BREAKFAST, AUGUST 2, 2004, CAMP GABE, BAQUBA, IRAQ

On April 8, my platoon prepared to participate as a component in a battalion-sized raid on the al Sadr Party headquarters in Old Baquba, which happened to be located exactly where the improvised-explosive device (IED) detonated while we prepared to tow Sergeant Barry Poynter's humvee. However, later that night, intelligence sources confirmed that al Sadr sympathizers recently vacated the building. Despite issuing a platoon order and conducting rehearsals at the squad level, we would not conduct the anticipated raid.

Since there had been limited contact since the afternoon attacks on April 7, Major William Chlebowski adjusted 3rd Platoon's mission to instead conduct a movement to contact along Highway 5, along which the key provincial government buildings were located. Specifically, we were concerned about the security of the police headquarters, the capitol building, and the Civil Military Operations Center (CMOC). It was Baquba's own little "Green Zone." However, so as to impress upon the insurgents that Task Force 1-6 meant to annihilate any opposition to its presence or to the transitional Iraqi government, the operations officer directed my platoon to travel in our tracked Field Artillery Ammunition Supply Vehicles in lieu of our humvees.

While ammunition tracked vehicles, or "armored barns," as members of our Infantry platoon sometimes referred to them, may look intimidating, they do not share the Bradley Fighting Vehicle's firepower, reactive armor, or speed. Fully knowing the limitations of the ammunition track, my squad leaders and I were a bit leery about leading the battalion's, and quite possibly the U.S. Army's, guinea pig ammunition track combat patrol in the urban environment.

The Bradley is the premiere infantry fighting vehicle of the U.S. Army. The ammunition track was designed to transport 155-millimeter artillery shells and bags of propellant to self-propelled howitzers. A Bradley has a rotating turret, thermal sights, and a 25-millimeter main gun. Its rear ramp falls downward to rapidly provide eight infantrymen with an obstacle-free path onto enemy terrain. Were a Bradley to receive enemy contact, the turret gunner could provide an impressive base of suppressive fire, while a squad of soldiers could dismount to flank the enemy and assault their position.

The ammunition track, however, was never designed for close combat. In contrast to the Bradley, it does not have a turret, and its gunner mans either a .50-caliber machine gun or a MK-19 automatic, 40-millimeter grenade launcher. The rear door to an ammunition track opens upward, and it is so narrow that soldiers must exit slowly, one at a time. During previous wars, ammunition tracks were employed miles behind the front lines, where they required less armor and offensive capabilities. The question remained: Would the enemy appreciate the difference in capabilities, and be less intimidated by a patrol of ammunition tracks?

Just after midnight on April 9, 3rd Platoon drove out the gate of Camp Gabe, with three ammunition tracks, and my humvee positioned between the first and second tracked vehicles. For command and control purposes, I still needed a humvee, because I could not monitor two separate radios from the gunner's hatch of an ammunition track. We also reintroduced MK-19 grenade launchers to our inventory, which we had not carried during presence patrols since arriving in Iraq. Interpreters shared with me that Iraqis hated the MK-19, referring to it as the "big fat gun," because of its shape and immense firepower. So with two mounted .50-caliber machine guns and two MK-19s, we headed toward the CMOC.

With an 11:00 P.M.–4:00 A.M. curfew in effect, we traveled along desolate streets. As we passed the city's large stadium that sits on Highway 5 between Old Baquba and Camp Gabe, an IED detonated ten to thirty meters to the front of our last ammunition track, driven by Pvt. First Class Richard Roman. Perhaps the explosive would have damaged a humvee, but Private Roman's ammunition track suffered no damage, and we continued on our patrol.

During earlier patrols conducted in April, I took care to rarely travel the same road twice during the same mission. However, this was a movement to contact, and we were looking for trouble. I began doubling back on popular roads and revisiting Baquba neighborhoods only minutes after an earlier tour. Not surprisingly, this technique proved highly successful in drawing the desired attention to my platoon.

We drove through the suburb of Tahrir, which sits immediately south of Highway 5 facing the Green Zone. As we exited the district by way of Highway 5 to travel somewhere new, a rocket-propelled grenade (RPG) exploded about 100 meters short of the trail convoy vehicle. At night an RPG makes a spectacularly bright explosion when it impacts against an asphalt or concrete surface. Sgt. Winston Martinez served as gunner in the last vehicle, but he could not see the location of the launch because there were too many fluorescent lights on the street, limiting the effectiveness of his night-vision goggles to less than fifty meters. Without a target to engage, Sergeant Martinez did not return fire, and we continued our patrol. I became concerned that if the electricity plant did not turn off the city power to the street lights, we would never be able to scan very far, making it a challenge to "own the night," as we were expected to do with our expensive night-vision devices.

Thirty minutes later, the platoon again ventured into Tahrir. We approached a key intersection by a Sunni mosque maintained by an imam known for his anti-American sentiment. Sergeant Poynter, who was traveling in my humvee, noticed an old man sitting on the street corner by the mosque with a box in his hands. This was very odd considering it was 2:00 in the morning and the city-wide curfew began at 11:00 P.M. each night. As my humvee cleared the intersection, and I began to caution the gunners of the two tracked vehicles behind me through the radio about the man on the corner, another RPG exploded 100 to 200 meters away from the ammunition track traveling behind me, as it passed through the same intersection.

Staff Sgt. Burduselu, who manned an MK-19 as the gunner of the tracked vehicle directly behind my humvee, could not identify the location of the launch, due to the same limitations of his night-vision equipment that plagued the other gunners. The last ammunition vehicle continued through the intersection without drawing any contact. Seconds later, the CMOC reported receiving small arms fire from Tahrir originating a block north from our position. Because we were nearby, I told Staff Sergeant Wade Hunter in the lead vehicle to make a U-turn once we reached the next intersection, to allow us to search for the people taking potshots at the CMOC. Returning to the mosque intersection where the most recent explosion occurred, Spc. Charles Copp, who sat behind me, noted that the old man had disappeared.

So far, we had experienced a patrol of near misses. We continued moving through Tahrir at about five miles per hour with our enormous "armored barns," adjusting our breathing and heart rates to the situation at hand. None of the seemingly random attacks had been close enough to the convoy to cause damage to soldiers or equipment, but they were all close enough to keep us alert and expectant.

Hearing sporadic small arms fire nearby, the convoy turned west in search of the source. Just as all four vehicles completed the turn to the west, a rocket exploded fifty meters in front of the lead ammunition vehicle, flashing brilliantly against the asphalt. While that was the only RPG I observed, all four vehicle gunners reported hearing the very distinct sound of four RPGs sail over the entire convoy. The first ammunition vehicle stopped momentarily, but I told its gunner, Sergeant Hunter, to continue moving west at our standard speed of five to ten miles per hour. While I did not intend for 3rd Platoon to act as a sitting duck, I did not want to speed away from the engagement area, either.

As the first vehicle resumed moving, the sound of AK-47 fire erupted, as "contact" reports squawked over my radio speaker. For the first time, the enemy directed their small arms fire at us from the rooftops of buildings shouldering the street. In spite of the night-vision restrictions, it did not take long to determine the location of the rifle shots. As I looked straight out of my passenger seat window, I saw at least two different flash sources from the roof of the building twenty meters from the humvee. We were sitting directly under the enemy, and unlike previous reports, where soldiers from the 588th Engineers assured us that insurgents shot wildly into the air, the multiple flashes I saw were definitely directed downwards, and very much toward our vehicles.

Continuing to move at a deliberately slow speed, the crew-served gunners of the three ammunition tracks focused their fire toward the rooftop and questionable alleyways. Spc. Will Douglas, who manned the MK-19 in my humvee from the rooftop hatch, returned fire while shouting details to me of what he saw from his perch. Dropping both hand mics— one for the battalion radio frequency and one for the platoon's—I aimed my M-16 out of the window and squeezed the trigger. Never before had I tried to kill a man, but there was no hesitation in my mind that this was justified. The two insurgents on the roof wanted to kill my men, and I had to do what I could to deny their success.

Tahrir is only two kilometers wide, and we were positioned in nearly the center of the district when the firefight began. The kilometer we traveled west to exit the suburb seemed to stretch on for several kilometers as we scanned for more insurgents, and heard more shots fired from the rear of the convoy. It was difficult not to just accelerate as fast as possible to leave the danger area. While such a decision would have been safer, it would not have allowed us to complete our mission of destroying the enemy in the area. Because we were traveling in ammunition tracks, it was impossible to unload the squads from the compartments, organize them into raiding and security teams, and clear the civilian houses usurped by insurgents. Conducting a drive-by shooting seemed to be the only effective measure for us to take in our present vehicular configuration. Without physically clearing the building, we at least confirmed that if the rooftop gunmen were not killed, they were seriously wounded, and no longer posed a threat.

Upon exiting Tahrir, I confirmed with the gunners that no one was injured, and that all vehicles were functional. We returned to Camp Gabe shortly thereafter, and during the platoon post-mission brief, we agreed that ammunition vehicles might be useful in the daytime, but should not be used again at night. Without thermal devices, my gunners could not scan beyond fifty meters in urban terrain. In addition, it was impossible to concentrate fire from the platoon's four crew-served weapons while still providing 360-degree security to the platoon. Only two soldiers could see outside of an ammunition vehicle, and one man cannot remove his hands from the steering controls. In contrast, soldiers traveling in humvees could shoot out the windows, as the members of my vehicle did, to provide additional fire against an enemy positioned as close as twenty meters away.

When I sat down with the battalion planner, Capt. John Bushman, around 4:00 that morning to rehash the patrol in detail, he seemed convinced that 3rd Platoon had disrupted an attack planned against one of the government buildings. Perhaps the IED by the stadium was designated for the humvee platoon that would later rush to reinforce the Green Zone during an attack against the three compounds. Perhaps the RPG that exploded as we left Tahrir the first time was intended to dissuade us from returning to the district that night. Possibly, the second RPG was also intended to convince us to leave Tahrir. However, Captain Bushman and I agreed that the insurgents did not think we would be crazy enough to go straight back through the same area of Tahrir for a *third* time. The next four RPGs shot at our convoy, that miraculously missed each time, were most likely intended for a larger attack against the police headquarters or the CMOC. Seeing us return, however, the attackers made us the immediate target. Third Platoon's fires and enormous ammunition vehicles might have influenced other insurgents to hide in local houses and stow their RPGs for another day; that is one of the infamous benefits of fighting for an insurgency.

Even if 3rd Platoon's actions did not disrupt a larger attack, our early morning patrol on April 9 would serve as the prelude to a very busy day of synchronized insurgent operations throughout Baquba. By mid-morning, various sources confirmed that a plan existed for a coordinated attack on the Green Zone, but the time and direction of the assault were unknown to our informants in the city.

Lieutenant Colonel Bullimore, the battalion commander, wanted to be a bit more proactive, rather than wait for the enemy to strike first. With the reports of informers in mind, 3rd Platoon was ordered to conduct another movement to contact along Highway 5 and neighborhoods that included Tahrir. Lieutenant Colonel Bullimore wryly explained to me in the battalion operations center that because my platoon was so good at attracting attention, perhaps we could rout the insurgents out of their hiding places.

So, with three ammunition tracks and my humvee, 3rd Platoon left Camp Gabe at 1:00 on the afternoon of April 9 to search for more enemy contact. The entire platoon was beginning to feel the strain of our recent missions. Since the attack on April 7, we had been constantly either preparing for or executing missions for more than forty-eight hours. Just as we left the gate, the battalion radio operator called on the radio to notify us about a flier surfacing around mosques in Baquba and Tahrir, stating that today would be the last day Americans occupied Baquba. I turned towards Specialist Jesse Garcia and quipped, "Oh, great; this is just getting better and better." Although I doubted the truth of the propaganda, I did not doubt that the enemy would try to make it a reality.

We found the streets of Baquba to be eerily quiet. When I reported the lack of vehicular or pedestrian traffic, and the fact that few stores were open, the radio operator explained that April 9 was a Shi'ia religious holiday. We drove around Mufrek Traffic Circle on the west bank of the Diyala River, and found our first evidence of city life, in a mosque that was so packed, at least 200 men were praying in the dirt outside the main en-

Third Platoon conducts a movement to contact with their Field Artillery Ammunition Supply Vehicles to destroy enemy forces during the "Easter Offensive" on April 9, 2004, as smoke billows from the Blue Dome in the background. (Provided with permission by Will Douglas)

trance. A voice from the minaret's speakers blared harshly, and even without an interpreter, I could tell that it was not the melodiously sung Qu'ran passages normally heard during the afternoon call to prayer.

Returning east across the river, we patrolled Tahrir, and I initially gained comfort in finding more Iraqi policemen on the suburb's main street than I had found at any other time in Baquba. However, when we passed the Sunni mosque at the street corner of our early morning attacks, we observed another large group of men assembled in front of the mosque. With the imam's voice booming over the speakers, prostrate men raised their heads in unison to watch our every movement.

Unbeknownst to us at the time, the minaret's speakers directed the faithful to kill Americans, incredibly, as my platoon drove by. Normally, I would have received an instant translation, but on this day, no interpreters showed up for work at Camp Gabe. We would later understand that this "sick day" phenomenon signaled a coming attack. We completed another pass along Highway 5, from the river to the eastern stadium, without incident before receiving orders to patrol several kilometers of Highway 5 east of Camp Gabe, to confirm reports of groups of insurgents with RPGs walking down the highway towards Baquba.

An hour after beginning our patrol, we found the eastern portion of the sector, which alternates between undeveloped fields and farmland, to be serene, with no signs of insurgent activity. After reporting this observation to battalion, the operations center instructed us to return to Camp Gabe. As we turned west, shortly after 2:00 in the afternoon, the three main provincial governments reported receiving multiple RPGs from Tahrir, Old Baquba and surrounding palm groves. As the platoon entered the camp gate, Major Chlebowski ordered us to return into Baquba to protect the Green Zone with our crew-served weapon systems.

Relaying the instructions on the platoon frequency, we passed once again through the force protection barriers, and returned to Highway 5. The battalion radio traffic told me that this situation would be different. This time we would encounter more than a handful of insurgents. Evident by the blistering tone of soldiers reporting over the radio, as well as the distant explosions, I knew that the enemy had finally commenced their decisive inner city attack.

I inhaled sharply, and felt like I was about to jump into a cold lake. It was the same sensation that I felt as a Boy Scout, preparing to jump into the freezing waters of my summer camp reservoir. I knew that the experience would not be pleasant, and I could anticipate my body freezing up. The only thing was that if my muscles did freeze, I would sink, and then fail the swim test. Twelve years later, and seven thousand miles away from the California Pico Blanco Scout Reservation, I knew that my mind could not freeze up. I had to think clearly, react to enemy fire, and provide coherent directions to my platoon. Nevertheless, it would not, much like jumping into the lake, be a pleasant experience.

As I concentrated on the radio reports about the location of RPG fire, our platoon was ambushed by five to seven RPGs and small arms fire from both sides of Highway 5, in the vicinity of the city stadium. From the same location where an IED exploded near our convoy shortly after midnight, I broke through battalion radio traffic to report that 3rd Platoon had been ambushed. I did not have to tell the gunners to return fire; that happened automatically.

Amid my reports, I found myself looking out the open window and into the face of a man laying prone, shooting at us from the top of the stadium thirty meters away. Wearing all black, he remained undeterred as Specialist Copp and I shot at him. Direct .50-caliber shots provided by Sergeant Martinez, however, killed the men on the top of the stadium, and Specialist Douglas lobbed two MK-19 grenades into the stadium soccer field from my vehicle, to silence possible reinforcements. No soldiers were injured as we passed through the kill zone, but one RPG hit the rear ammunition vehicle. Fortunately, the RPG did not have an anti-armor warhead, and the impact did little to deter Sergeant Martinez from using his .50-caliber machine gun to tear apart the top level of the stadium concealing the insurgents.

We continued down the highway towards the CMOC, as I tallied the number of RPGs striking the government buildings, based on radio reports: twenty against the police station, fifteen against the capitol building, and twenty against the CMOC. Feverish reporting described the condition of wounded personnel in the buildings, an interior fire that trapped soldiers on the roof of the capitol, and a prison riot at the police headquarters. The city was under a major attack, and we were all pretty certain that we were driving straight into the middle of it.

Major Chlebowski instructed my platoon to pass the capitol, to eliminate insurgents in a palm grove who were responsible for targeting both the police headquarters and the capitol building. As we passed the CMOC, flames rose from a neighboring house inadvertently hit by an RPG. Despite all the chaos, what threw me off the most was a Special Forces sniper calling over the battalion radio frequency for an artillery fire mission, on the palm grove situated in the middle of Baquba. Here we were, pitted against an enemy nestled in a city, and now we were preparing to use field artillery assets? The battalion's A Battery, that had not converted to a motorized rifle company, had a platoon on Camp Gabe that was used to shoot artillery in response to incoming mortars, but the 155-millimeter rounds always impacted against targets well away from the city.

The battalion leadership, not sure if artillery should be used in the urban environment, denied the fire mission at this time, and 3rd Platoon was instructed to launch the grenades of our MK-19s into the same palm grove from the highway. Not wanting to remain static during this mission, I told the gunners to slow their tracked vehicles to a patrol speed of five to ten miles per hour, and make a 200-meter loop around a portion of the highway north of the walled palm grove. After two complete loops, we had depleted our cases of MK-19 ammunition, and observers from the police station and capitol confirmed that the grenade detonations effectively silenced the attacks from at least five insurgents.

We then received a new mission: to provide area security for Lt. Paul Lashley's platoon, while they searched a house in the district of Shifta that was a suspected launch site for RPGs against the police headquarters. Upon completion of this support mission, which occurred without either platoon receiving any enemy contact, my platoon returned to the same palm grove to search for more insurgents. An observer from the capitol building requested that I send an ammunition vehicle to the seven-foot wall separating the palm grove from the highway, and eliminate remnants

Members of 1st Squad, 1st Platoon perform a security halt in Tahrir. (Caleb Cage Collection)

of the enemy with .50-caliber fire. Their request came too late, though, as I was told by the operations officer to hand the mission to Lt. Kirby Jones's Bradley platoon, which was to link up with us in a couple minutes.

Major Chelbowski's primary concern rested with my platoon's ammunition status. While we still had half of our .50-caliber rounds, being empty of 40-millimeter MK-19 grenades placed us at a disadvantage should an enemy surge occur. The only way Sergeant Burduselu could protect his vehicle would be with his M-16. We needed a replenishment of our ammunition soon. I provided Kirby with a radio situation report as our convoys passed each other in front of the capitol building. As 3rd Platoon headed back to Camp Gabe, Kirby directed a Bradley to crush a hole in the wall of the palm grove, and his men cleared hidden insurgents from the orchard. A Bradley mounted infantry platoon was ideal for this mission.

At around 3:30 in the afternoon, we returned to Camp Gabe without further incident. This time, I kept the vehicles and men standing by, in anticipation of a follow-on operation. Indeed, there would be a follow-on mission. The tremendous attack left U.S. platoons protecting the government buildings with a precariously low supply of a variety of necessary munitions. Hunched over the battalion conference table in a room adjacent to the operations center, the battalion executive officer, Maj. Arthur Weeks, the ammunition officer, Capt. Michael Michaud, and I ran through the math, to determine the quantities of a dozen different munitions required for each location, before Captain Michaud coordinated an ammunition drop-off by my platoon.

Anticipating another attack, we also re-supplied our platoon ammunition cases, and stocked a generous surplus in each vehicle. Other soldiers conducted elementary vehicle and weapons maintenance, while waiting for us to store the ammunition. Ironically, the ammunition vehicles would serve their original purpose, resupplying munitions to others. Throughout the logistical operation, my humvee passengers excitably provided battle details to the other soldiers, who gained a minuscule appreciation for the day's activities from the windowless compartments of the ammunition vehicles. It was, after all, not 3rd Platoon being aggressed in a city district this time, but a full scale assault on the city's government and security facilities.

During the first year of the U.S. occupation of Iraq, such attacks, especially in Baquba, were unheard of. Now, the insurgency had clearly organized, and rethought its approach. The platoons in our battalion were quickly gaining a new perspective of the insurgency capabilities. Indeed, we would see the same methods used in city-wide attacks throughout the rest of our yearlong deployment.

At 5:00 in the afternoon, as our platoon returned to the sector to transport ammunition to the Green Zone, we observed a trickle of civilian traffic on the highway, and handfuls of people standing outside of their homes, showing us that even in Iraq, the events of this day were somewhat new and unusual. Shops remained closed, but Baquba was no longer the ghost town we traveled through four hours earlier. The fire department had also managed to send personnel to extinguish fires at several locations, a degree of municipal organization I believed to be impossible up until then.

We completed the resupply mission of the Green Zone quickly, and began our trek back to the camp yet again. Upon returning to Camp Gabe, the platoon was told to remain on standby for yet another mission, which was not impossible but seemed unwise. I warned Major Chlebowski that 3rd Platoon had been in sector for more than eight hours, with combat operations for that day beginning at midnight. While the circumstances required every available soldier, I asked if we could stand down for at least six hours to complete much-needed maintenance and get a few hours of sleep. Major Chlebowski granted this request, but the entire platoon knew that it was but a brief reprieve before we would head out again.

Even after completing maintenance and consuming a Meal Ready to Eat (MRE), the uncertain situation made it difficult to sleep. Shortly after 11:30 that night, the shock waves of three 155-millimeter rounds being hurled from our camp's Paladin howitzers reverberated off of the aluminum door of my room. The tremors of Bradleys and Abrams tanks passing my barracks, sent from brigade to reinforce our task force, shook my bed well past midnight. I equated those sounds with the obvious reality of little sleep, and more missions on the horizon. Indeed, around 1:30 in the morning of April 10, a soldier from C Company woke me, and told me to report to the battalion headquarters.

Major Chlebowski provided me with an update of what had occurred during my fitful slumber—events that I comprehended entirely, but still could not believe were occurring in real life. Kirby's platoon left the palm grove by Highway 5, where I had passed them hours before to conduct a movement to contact in Buhriz, the town immediately south of Tahrir. As they approached the town, the Bradleys began to receive small arms and RPG fire. Kirby led a dismounted squad to man a house rooftop. However, each time the lieutenant attempted to lay down a base of fire to allow another one of his squads to flank the enemy, which was a standard and effective infantry tactic, his men received RPGs from a different direction. At every turn, the infantrymen were out-maneuvered by an enemy force certainly larger than his forty-man platoon. Insurgents also attacked from random houses overlooking Kirby's fighting vehicles, and by shooting from deep inside nearby palm groves. The squad manning the rooftop reported destroying squad-sized elements of black-clad insurgents, suggesting more clearly than any of the indicators before that we were not just fighting the locals, but an enemy that had been trained and brought in from elsewhere.

A pair of Abrams tanks, detailed to Task Force 1-6 from Task Force 2-63, my old armor battalion who was responsible for a sector of Diyala province adjacent to Baquba, arrived to focus fire on the palm groves, while the infantry concentrated on the streets of Buhriz. The intense firefight lasted until 6:00 that evening, and cost the life of one infantryman, Spc. Allan Vandayburg of Kirby's Punisher Platoon. An RPG hit a transformer connected to an electrical pole, which sent shrapnel into the turret of a Bradley. The torn metal ricocheted inside the close quarters of the compartment before going into the soldier's abdomen. Specialist Vanday-burg died from severe internal bleeding in the Bradley as the vehicle raced toward the Camp Warhorse trauma center.

Just after dark on April 9, informants sighted groups of about thirty Mahdi Army guerrillas blatantly carrying RPGs, congregating around vari-ous traffic circles throughout the city of Baquba. In response, our brigade split the Task Force 1-6 urban sector into two halves, east and west, assign-ing everything west of the Diyala River to Task Force 2-63. This allowed my battalion to concentrate on clearing Old Baquba, Tahrir, and Buhriz, and reinforcing the critical provincial government buildings. At 9:30 that night, intelligence confirmed that more than eighty insurgents were at the Mufrek Traffic Circle. Reconsidering the popular notion that artillery was a useless entity in urban warfare, our battalion fired three high-explosive artillery rounds into the circle, which triggered the U.S. counterattack in the city. Task Force 2-63 then sent armor platoons down Highway 2, the major north-south route in western Baquba, to kill additional insurgents and locate IEDs. The next task of the tanker platoon was to secure both the Mufrek Traffic Circle and the Twin Bridges, connecting the two halves of Baquba. Enemy efforts did not dissipate, however, with the arrival of the tanks, and insurgents continued their sporadic attacks from small alleyways spurring off from the highway.

Shortly after midnight on April 10, Kirby's platoon went into Baquba to raid the Al Sadr headquarters we were originally supposed to raid the previous night. After dismounts removed several computers, a tank ar-rived to roll through the building, taking out most of the support beams, and leveling the structure. Not only did the building crumble, Task Force 1-6 sent a clear message to the population that with our newfound tank support, homes harboring insurgents might also be totaled.

Kirby's platoon returned to Camp Gabe as Major Chlebowski ex-plained all of these developments to me. With Bradleys loudly passing outside of the operations center, I received new orders for 3rd Platoon. My platoon would conduct a movement to contact in Tahrir and Old Baquba, a mission to which we were all accustomed at this point, and the opera-tions officer wanted us to again use our ammunition tracks. At that mo-ment, there seemed to be no more ludicrous plan in the world than trying yet again to successfully outmaneuver an enemy of any size with the "ar-mored barns." Major Chlebowski could tell from the expression on my face that I was a bit apprehensive, so he reassured me that he had positioned an additional B Company platoon at the CMOC, standing by to assist 3rd Platoon should something go awry.

When I assembled the platoon for the safety brief and intelligence update prior to our mission, one of my soldiers asked for clarification of the definition of "movement to contact." This was an innocent question, considering that these soldiers, including me, were trained very quickly in the art of maneuver. When I explained that we were looking for someone to shoot at us so we could shoot back, he replied sardonically, "So they're dangling us out there like a piece of red meat." At this bit of gallows humor, everyone laughed, and I could not help but agree with his interpretation of our situation. Because we had been so good at conjuring the enemy during the last few days, we all agreed that we were probably the right platoon for the job. So with the spirit that often accompanies dangerous jobs, the men of 3rd Platoon took this realization as a compliment, and a testament to their abilities as warriors.

My usual caution to my soldiers, to remain vigilant in observation and in providing security, was made redundant by the activities of the day, which eliminated any degree of complacency that might have begun to mature in their minds. These basic military actions were, after all, a matter of life and death. At 2:00 in the morning on April 10, we departed Camp Gabe and began our patrol, moving into Tahrir through a far eastern access road.

Fewer than 500 meters into the suburb, two successive RPGs exploded thirty meters in front of my humvee, both aimed at the track of Sergeant Hunter's ammunition track, which again led the platoon patrol. The insurgents launched the rockets from a second-story rooftop no more than fifteen meters from the ammunition vehicle, the closest RPG attack yet. Both grenades exploded against the pavement, only inches short of hitting the track, leaving a spray of shrapnel marks on the right side of the vehicle that we would not notice until later in daylight. We were almost certainly heading into an ambush, because the insurgents were attempting to immobilize the lead ammunition vehicle by breaking its tracks. This left us with the options of either continuing toward the ambush in the slow, lightly armored vehicles full of my soldiers, or taking an alternate route, to see if we could gain a better view of the attackers. The simple fact that I recognized the obvious disparity between the two options proved to me that we had progressed considerably from an artillery mindset.

If I had given the order to proceed through the ambush kill zone, the outcome could have been dire. I pictured having to send Sergeant

Burduselu's ammunition track in front of Sergeant Hunter's destroyed vehicle. Then, as the dismounted soldiers worked on connecting a cumbersome tow bar, a sizable attack would commence from all directions. We were too close to the highway entrance to not turn around. However, as the lead ammunition vehicle made its U-turn, Specialist Douglas, who was still manning the open hatch in my humvee, noticed the silhouettes of two insurgents on the rooftop. Using his MK-19, Specialist Douglas aimed two shots at the roof, but we were too close to the target for the grenades to arm themselves and detonate. Luckily, behind us in the second ammunition vehicle, Sergeant Burduselu took aim at the two attackers with his infrared laser sight, and dropped both men with an entire magazine of bullets from his M-16.

After I radioed the attack to headquarters, battalion did not want to commit another platoon just yet. I did get permission to stay out of Tahrir that morning, however, as it made better sense to employ Bradleys or humvees in the neighborhood, than to further prod with our ammunition tracks. We continued to patrol the highway and Canal Street, the western boundary road of Tahrir that led into Buhriz. The gunners scanned palm groves to the west, that shouldered the Diyala River, and Tahrir to the east, from various road intersections and canal bridges. Because the tanks and Bradleys had rolled through Old Baquba only a couple hours earlier, we also began prodding the neighborhoods north of the CMOC for contact. The remainder of the patrol proved uneventful, presumably because the heavy armor movement in Baquba had dissuaded insurgents from conducting additional attacks that morning.

My platoon participated in several more movements to contact in Tahrir and Buhriz between April 10 and 14 without receiving contact. On Easter Sunday, April 11, the imams from several local mosques directed their followers to not attack the Americans on their holy day. This was hardly a gesture of pro-coalition support—these were the same imams who encouraged violence during Holy Week. The peace on Easter Sunday was more a manifestation of the incredible power wielded by the imams. It also indicated the imams' apparent lack of a sense of irony.

We narrowly missed a massive firefight in Tahrir on April 12. That night, we patrolled the suburb from 9:00 to 11:30, while two Abrams tanks simultaneously patrolled Old Baquba. Tahrir seemed peaceful; some locals patronized tea shops and corner grocery stores prior to the 11:00 P.M. curfew. However, a number of men whom we observed, assembled around a pickup truck parked on a side street, did not sit well with me, or with the

A child sporting an Adidas cap and dishdasha poses during a 3rd Platoon patrol in Shifta. (Gregory Tomlin Collection)

passengers in my vehicle. When the group of twenty-something-year-old men scattered after seeing our convoy 150 meters down the road, I ordered warning shots to be fired in their direction. Other men quickly ran from the street in separate ways. A number of vendors and tea shop frequenters scarcely looked in our direction; such was their disdain for us, or for the insurgency, or both. If they believed themselves innocent, all the men would have run into the building closest to the truck. As we returned to Camp Gabe from our patrol, the tanks pulled in behind us, also returning from their patrol in the city.

As if on cue, the CMOC reported receiving mortar fire as 3rd Platoon entered the gate. Soldiers manning observation posts on the CMOC roof reported that the indirect fire originated from Tahrir, only 100 meters east of the location where 3rd Platoon earlier fired warning shots at men who scattered in various directions. Paul Lashley's platoon from B Company departed the CMOC in an all-humvee convoy, to investigate the possible mortar site. They ran directly into a terrific ambush as soon as they entered Tahrir. I stood outside of my barracks, brushing my teeth, only two kilometers east of Tahrir, just as Paul's platoon arrived by the mortar launch site. Hundreds of tracers streaked through the sky, as soldiers fought insurgents shooting from rooftops. The broad, white flashes erupting across the night sky told me that the enemy was shooting RPGs at Paul's platoon. Paul's men caused a lot of damage to the enemy in Tahrir that night, but two of his soldiers received shrapnel wounds in their legs. Had the tank section not been in Old Baquba during my platoon patrol in Tahrir, it is likely that the same insurgents would have ambushed us during our night patrol.

On April 14, 3rd Platoon received orders to relieve Lt. Chris Lacour's 2nd Platoon protecting the capitol building. Arriving at the governor's compound, with its static regimen of guard duty, I seriously reflected on what we recently experienced. Over the week of Easter, 2004, the riflemen of C Company, as well as we, their platoon leaders, furthered our education in unconventional warfare.

The most valuable lessons we learned had very little to do with the way in which the enemy attacked us. They were fighting with guerilla tactics, and had the advantage of being able to melt into the local populace. Our earliest and most important lessons were in regards to how we would fight them. Our confidence grew as we tailored our weapon systems, tactics, and vehicles, to successfully destroy our unconventional enemy.

During our year in Baquba, we employed weapon systems of every size, even though we were told prior to our deployment that we would find their bulk and heavy capabilities prohibitive in urban terrain. The soldiers carried their personal M-16, a notoriously middling weapon designed during the Vietnam era, with them on every mission. The armored humvees never left the gate without powerful .50-caliber machine guns or MK-19 automatic grenade launchers attached to their roofs. Abrams tanks and Bradley Fighting Vehicles, though built like armored condominiums, proved to be nearly unstoppable and highly effective tools when the level of violence escalated to warrant their use. Even our Paladin howitzers, which had a questionable future even before the war in Iraq, demonstrated incredible capabilities, although artillery fire missions were judiciously limited. Most importantly and impressively, the soldiers, some with only a few months of training for their new task, proved to be highly capable of adapting and using these old-world weapons in such a new way.

Thrown in willingly and voluntarily, we sought to adapt conventional tactics to win on a noncontiguous battlefield. We were facing the reality of discerning the underlying principles that would keep us alive. The policymakers were struggling with the same issues at their level, but being so entrenched in the tradition of the black and white, good and evil paradigm of the modern world, their fight was harder and is ongoing today. Conventions known to the foot soldier in Baquba and the political advisor in Baghdad changed in usage, but they did not change in essence. The same was true for every convention we encountered during our time deployed. From engaging the enemy, to dealing with a local populace often skeptical of our sincerity in wanting to improve Iraq, conventional wisdom changed underneath our noses, and we fought as hard as we could to adapt and overcome.

PART 3
june

chapter 5

INSURGENCY: A PRACTICUM

Lt. Caleb Cage, 1st Platoon Leader, C Company

t hrough March and April, 2004, the first two months of our stay in Baquba, I remained as the executive officer for our company. The executive officer is commonly referred to in the military as the "Extra Officer," and as unflattering as that term might be, it is often true. It was especially true in our company, where our commander sought to minimize opportunities for real leadership as much and as often as possible. My days, for the first two months, consisted of a 12-hour night shift in our company command post, several logistics meetings throughout the morning and early afternoon, and whatever else the company commander or the battalion executive officer needed at any given time.

The job had a relatively regular sleeping schedule, and excellent shift-mates, Spc. John Akridge and Staff Sgt. Josh LeValley, but little else to recommend it. Because I worked the night shift, I had to listen helplessly as the platoon leaders and sergeants barked warnings and orders to their subordinates over the radio, often over the obvious sound of gunfire and explosions. The long silences that occurred when the platoons switched from the company frequency to their platoon internal frequencies were a regular source of nervous debate and conjecture in the operations center, as we waited to hear the speakers crackle with updated information.

As an officer who had been preparing for a leadership role in combat for the past five years, working an administrative job in a combat zone was torturous. I immediately began to live vicariously through the other platoon leaders. When Greg would return from a basic patrol, or from a firefight to which I listened nervously, we would share a bowl of early morning cereal and decompress over the details of how his platoon responded. Lt. Kirby Jones, my roommate and the infantry platoon leader, would stop by after particularly exciting missions and fill me in on the details I had missed in their radio conversations. This was as close as I got to the real thing in the first few months; I had not left the wire of the camp since our first week in Baquba.

I enjoyed living vicariously through the other platoon leaders more at the end of April, and not simply because the platoons were getting dangerously better at their jobs. Kirby's platoon, the Punisher Platoon, had been ordered to the outskirts of Najaf by the brigade commander, after the so-called Easter Offensive in April. For the time that they were there, the infantrymen sat behind a berm, frustrated at the political decisions echelons above them that would not allow them to engage Muqtada al Sadr's militia in the city.

Shortly after Punisher Platoon returned from Najaf, Kirby's infantry battalion announced that Kirby would be replaced as platoon leader. Kirby had led the platoon for over a year, and it was time for him to return to his regular battalion, following the normal progression from platoon leader to executive officer. Walking down to the Punisher living area, I was surprised and blown away to see my old friend from college, Lt. T. J. Grider, standing there, being introduced to his new platoon for the first time. He and I were friends, through one of my roommates, but we had fallen out of touch. I knew him to be incredibly intelligent—book smart and street smart—and an excellent athlete. Seeing him mingle with his new platoon, I assumed that we would pick up immediately where we left off, and that he would be an incredible leader. I was happy to be proved correct on both counts.

Over the next week or so, T. J. shadowed Kirby on familiarization patrols in Baquba, gaining competence in his new job. He also became my roommate, personalizing my vicarious experiences even more, getting me closer to the action, but still living on the outside looking in. By the end of the week, T. J. was officially platoon leader for the Punisher Platoon, and was already gaining credibility within the task force.

On May 2, only his third official day as a platoon leader, T. J. became fully established and a known quantity. While I listened to their radio transmissions in the company command post, T. J. and his platoon entered Buhriz. It was the first time that anyone had returned to the city since Kirby had endured the all-day firefight, and everyone was anxious to see the town's reaction. Unsurprisingly, unless you happened to be the driver of the lead Bradley, T. J.'s platoon rolled into several near-ambushes that night, fought back, and brought everyone home to discuss everything I had heard over the radio. T. J. came by the company command post after the mission, and we smoked as we discussed the fight. I did not yet know

The majority of 1st Platoon, C Company, Task Force 1-6 on a weapons qualification range on Forward Operating Base Gabe, in June 2004. From left to right (standing): Spc. Thomas Zaragoza, Sgt. Eric Girasia, Spc. Jon Cochran, Spc. Marcus Garrant, 1st Lt. Jim Gifford, Sgt. Aaron Hokenson, 1st Lt. Caleb Cage, Staff Sgt. Thomas Bramer, Spc. Jorge Pineda, Pvt. First Class Garret Larsen, Sgt. Jason Brownlie, and Pvt. First Class Ismael Quiroz. Left to right (kneeling): Spc. Michael Griffin and Sgt. Javier Vega. This was the closest the platoon ever came to taking a group picture. (Caleb Cage Collection)

it, but this would be the last time I would be inside the wire while one of my friends was stuck in danger in the city.

A few days after T. J. and I rehashed his first firefight, Maj. Arthur Weeks approached me after one of our logistical support meetings. Walter, as Major Weeks was called—because his disposition was much like that of John Goodman's character in the film *The Big Lebowski*—caught me in front of the task force operations center and told me the news: I would be taking over as the platoon leader for 1st Platoon, C Company the next day. When I expressed my gratitude for the move, but suggested that I would have liked to have had more of a heads up, Walter gruffly threatened to give it to someone else, as was his nature. Technically, moving from executive officer to platoon leader is a step down in position, but no one in their right mind would consider the move as anything but a promotion. Over the course of the next two weeks, the majority of my time was spent learning my new job from Lt. Jim Gifford, the outgoing platoon leader.

Walter continued in his abrupt and colorful way through the rest of May, while I became more acclimated, and T. J. became the critical workhorse for that task force. One night in late May, Walter finished briefing a mission that was planned for T. J.'s platoon. The mission was a fairly standard sort, briefed in a standard way, complete with Walter's catchphrase closing: T. J. was to go forward and "do good things to bad people." The rest of us had heard the phrase many times before from Walter, and the response was generally an internal smirk at such a clichéd sentiment, and an external affirmation of the good major's remark.

T. J. came back to the room we shared in the old Republican Guard barracks, and brought up his confusion with the statement he had just heard for the first time. What could that mean, he asked, laughingly. For several hours, we dissected the statement into its base terms. We were pretty sure that we knew who the bad people were: they were the guys in the proverbial "black pajamas," who were bussed in, courtesy of Al Qaeda, to attack us. Or, they could even be the homegrown terrorists, who planted the roadside bombs that would kill many more of their own neighbors than they would Americans. We were pretty certain, in both cases, that the persons in question were the bad people of whom Walter spoke. The confusion rested in why we were to do good things to them. And what constituted a good thing? Should we give them boxes of paper and pencils, as we had planned to do for the school children? Should we help them fix a flat, as they happen to be trying to get away from Coalition Forces? These facetious possibilities were certainly out of the question.

Even while we were discussing this conundrum, we were both pretty certain as to what his statement meant: we were supposed to go into our sector and shoot bad people if we saw them. But we were enjoying the confusion of the phrase too much to either admit that we understood it, or to just drop it altogether. We were enjoying the moral murkiness of the statement too much to let it die peacefully.

It occurred to us later that by saying "good things," Major Weeks was looking at it from our perspective. To shoot an insurgent was no doubt an undeniable good in our eyes. They were the ones setting improvised explosive devices (IED), killing local civilians and coalition troops, and staging monthly attacks in the city against our soldiers. One fewer of "them," we gathered, meant one fewer who could shoot at one of our guys. Such "other"-ing has been true with every war. Our confusion, though sarcastic and faux, was based on another perspective altogether: the perspective of someone not in our shoes.

It did not matter whether Walter's remark was clichéd, or if our commentary was real. What mattered, we quickly learned, was that the the month of June would give many of the platoons in Task Force 1-6 ample opportunities to do good things to bad people. We learned in April that Buhriz would be our most challenging area, and June would further prove this theory for us. Baquba began to appear more frequently in the news. It was ranked the most troubled city in Iraq, as things seemed to be calming down in Samara, and the ceasefire in Fallujah had yielded some semblance of peace in that troubled area. In the 3rd Brigade Combat Team sector, Baquba was by far the least compliant area.

Buhriz was clearly a haven for insurgents, evident in the fact that its civilian populace would leave before a major conflict, and only the fighters would remain. At the same time, inter-tribal fighting confused the security situation in the town, and we often could not tell who was fighting whom, if activity was due to a resurgence of the insurgency, or another bland tiff between local tribes or criminal entities. Buhriz fell under the jurisdiction of C Company, and it was our job to ensure that it did not turn into a "Fallujah East," as many worried.

The insane operational tempo that would accompany the month of June actually began May 28, and lasted for almost two months. There were nearly two months of constant disruptions, sporadic fighting, and general unease with the security situation in the city. The most probable reason for the two months of attacks was the national Transfer of Sovereignty that was scheduled for June 30. The insurgents obviously believed that if they could derail the transition by demonstrating that security was not under control in Baquba, then they could prevent the progress the Americans desired in the Iraqi political situation.

The battalion had been receiving indications that the insurgency planned to stage an attack in Baquba around the time of the transfer, in order to show the inability of the U.S. to provide stability and security within their city, and to break what they deemed as the delicate façade of the Iraqi Security Forces (ISF). Since the fighting in April, aside from a few ambushes that T. J.'s platoon endured, and regular IEDs against everyone, Baquba had been calm and quiet. From the end of May, however, it became increasingly clear that more than the local Jihadists were in town, and more were on their way to join the impending brawl.

On May 27, two nights after T. J. and I had our final discussion about

Crossing the Tigris River on a military bridge while conducting a logistics run to Logistical Support Area Anaconda outside of Balad. (Caleb Cage Collection)

Major Weeks' confusing phrase, my platoon had been given an overnight escort mission from Baquba to the Balad airbase, a logistics hub about an hour to our northwest. We were carrying a group of the soldiers taking mid-tour leave, and picking up those who were returning. It was an administrative nightmare, especially for the first solo mission of a brand-new platoon leader, but when I returned to Camp Gabe, my management problems seemed rather shallow.

As we approached Baquba from the north on May 28, my radio began to be in range of the other radio transmitters in the city, and I was partially able to hear what was going on in Buhriz. Both Greg's and T. J.'s platoons were in enemy contact in the town. This was surprising to me, because it was early afternoon and most attacks occurred during the hours of darkness, with the exception of the Easter Offensive. T. J. was having serious mechanical issues with two of his Bradley Fighting Vehicles. There was also no company-level commander on the ground to coordinate fire between the two platoons, which went against basic reason and task force policy. According to the radio traffic, the soldiers of 3rd and 4th Platoons had taken rocket-propelled grenade (RPG) and small arms fire, from alleys and rooftops near the dense market area located in the heart of Buhriz. Even without a commander on the ground, Greg and T. J. managed to coordinate their fire and efforts with great success.

As my platoon entered the gate of Camp Gabe after our mission to Balad, it was pretty obvious that we would be a part of a larger operation in Buhriz later that day. What I did not know was that four minutes after our return to Camp Gabe we would be escorting the company commander

Task Force 1-6, with enhanced firepower from the 82nd Engineer Battalion's "Ice Platoon," begins movement into Buhriz on May 28, 2004 following a coordination meeting. (Caleb Cage Collection)

to a location just outside of Buhriz, where Greg's and T. J.'s platoons would consolidate after withdrawing from the city, to replenish their ammunition stocks expended in their forty-minute firefight.

We took a southeastern, roundabout route that dropped my platoon in the middle of an open field south of Buhriz to meet other elements preparing to reenter Buhriz. Greg's platoon was already on the scene, and his soldiers were collecting more ammunition from Lt. Lance Magill's motorized platoon from B Company, also in our task force. A specialty hybrid platoon was positioned by the field. The platoon consisted of two tanks and two Bradleys attached to the 82nd Engineers, led by Lt. Christian Boggiano. They were known as Ice Platoon. Eventually, T. J.'s platoon was able to manipulate their transmission problems enough to pull into the field. The brigade commander arrived to see how the re-engagement plan developed.

The new plan consisted of Ice Platoon tanks taking the lead, followed by my platoon, T. J.'s platoon, Greg's platoon, then two Bradleys from Ice Platoon. Together, we would travel into Buhriz from the southern end of town, via Canal Street. In urban combat, it is near impossible to place a formation of vehicles abreast to each other to mass fire power. Instead, everyone has to filter into the battle area on the limited two-lane road network that leads through Buhriz.

Lieutenant Boggiano's lead tank was to pull past the market area bridge in the most wide open area of the town and provide northern security, while T. J. and I took our platoons across the bridge, and stopped in the area where he had been attacked earlier. Greg, and the remainder of Lieutenant Boggiano's platoon, were to stay on the western side of the canal, to secure our opposite flank.

As our ad hoc task force entered Buhriz, we noticed many curious people out and about that afternoon. They had just endured yet another firefight in their community, and now we pulled back in with more firepower and even aviation assets overhead, to beg the bad guys to again come back out. Once our vehicles were set in positions where our mounted machine guns would prove most useful, several of T. J.'s and my soldiers secured key rooftops for observation, on buildings stretching down about 200 meters of road.

Meanwhile, Greg busied himself with setting sectors of fire to our west and south, to complete our 360-degree security perimeter. Soldiers from 3rd Platoon also marveled how clean the street was where a significant portion of their earlier fighting happened. Every U.S.-made ammunition casing, from the tiny M-16 bullet to the beer bottle-sized Bradley 25-millimeter round, had been cleared from the street while C Company reorganized on the outskirts of the town. If the locals did not intend to recycle the brass, they might have wanted to pretend the firefight never took place. This act, however, could do little to convince visitors, as smoke continued to billow out of the windows of several houses on the west side of Canal Street.

While he was establishing his security perimeter, and appointing fields of fire for his platoon, Greg was beckoned to fetch the interpreter traveling with 3rd Platoon, so the commander could buy a bag of onions from a local vendor on the side of the road. Watching the scene from the opposite bank of the canal as the captain walked back to his humvee with a large bag of onions was certainly surreal at the time, but most of us realized the gravity of the situation and returned to our responsibilities. Every soldier carefully watched his sector of fire, awaiting some poor fool to take a shot at us. Of course, we were the fools for believing that such a thing could happen. The enemy would not attack such a large force, but would rather await the next lone platoon that would inevitably venture into the town on patrol in the weeks to come.

We waited in the market area in that one-sided staring contest for about an hour, before we remounted and headed north through Buhriz, and then into the city of Baquba. There was no contact left to be had in the town. True to their definition, the insurgents who had shot rockets and bullets at Greg's and T. J.'s platoons had hid their weapons, and melted back into the community. The drive out through the two northern kilometers of Buhriz was intense, as we anticipated another attack. However, again, nothing remarkable occurred.

The next two weeks or so were relatively calm, and normal patrols, as well as a smattering of special missions, occurred successfully. Sniper teams shot several people attempting to plant IEDs under the cover of darkness. Additionally, our efforts to use government money to fund projects for the local communities was starting to take hold under Lt. Jim Gifford's supervision as the newly appointed task force civil-military affairs officer.

On June 12, Lt. Chris Lacour's and T. J.'s platoons conducted an early morning dismounted reconnaissance of a section of palm groves along the Diyala River in southern Buhriz. While Chris's men secured the road, T. J. took the majority of his platoon into the growth to reconnoiter the route. A couple of T. J.'s men reported observing two locals moving by fishing boat to the opposite side of the river, which was unusual because it was so early in the morning. The infantrymen restrained themselves enough to allow the strange sequence of events to develop a bit before they took action.

Within a matter of minutes of the boat coming ashore on the opposite bank, T. J.'s platoon began to receive small arms fire from the west bank of the river, a wild palm grove primarily used as a date farm. After engaging the enemy with great success for awhile, the soldiers realized that the secondary use for the grove on the opposite side of the river was as a weapons cache site. His men determined this as they launched their grenades onto the opposite side, and saw that the impacting explosions were much brighter and more deafening than that of a standard high-explosive M203 grenade. Quickly, a fire grew in the palm grove, and the enemy's hidden munitions continued to erupt violently long after the infantrymen stopped firing.

News of this skirmish received Arab media attention immediately. For the second time in as many weeks, Buhriz gained international notoriety in skewed stories presented to the Arabic-speaking world, where U.S.

soldiers wreaked havoc in a commercial center, but also suffered significant casualties at the hands of skilled "freedom fighters." While we recognized the accounts as exaggerated, if not blatantly false, the reports posed
a real danger to increase hostilities in the Baquba area. Like a moth drawn
to a flame, certain groups of extremists watching the fantastic stories on
television, or reading about them on the Internet, became enraged and
motivated to help their brothers in their struggle against the occupying
army. Indeed, intelligence reports suggested that busloads of Al Qaeda-
trained and affiliated insurgents were working their way toward Baquba
from Fallujah and other well-known hot spots. They just used the word
"insurgents" as a euphemism for "bad people."

chapter 6
IEDS: THE MENACE BENEATH
Lt. Greg Tomlin, 3rd Platoon Leader, C Company

he events of May 28 and June 12 convinced many of us that a complex enemy attack in Baquba would be inevitable in the near future. The size of the enemy forces engaged in Buhriz was not the typical car full, responsible for seeding local roadways with improvised explosive devices (IED). This enemy was much larger, and comparatively better organized. Although Arab news agencies noted the hostilities in Baquba, Western sources, at that point, had only tucked a couple lines about Buhriz into larger Iraq security pieces. The complexities and determination of insurgents in the Baquba area were not yet appreciated. A series of IEDs, hidden on the northern road leading into Buhriz on June 15, finally caught the attention of Western media, and even more Arab media, toward investigating and reporting about what was going on in the city.

If "go do good things to bad people" meant destroying enemy forces, nothing became more aggravating to soldiers in Baquba than dealing with IEDs, because we rarely squared off with the responsible bad guys. During a movement to contact mission, or in reacting to a direct fire ambush, soldiers have an idea of where the enemy is located. Men in a humvee-mounted platoon can shoot back, and leaders can competently coordinate fire between smaller units to ensure the elimination of enemy forces. However, a well-concealed IED on the side of a road, perhaps camouflaged beneath a pile of rotten produce or a heap of building rubble, presents an unknown danger to passing convoys and dismounted patrols.

An IED can be as small as a cigar box packed with TNT, or as large as a pair of meter-long, 155-millimeter South African artillery rounds, wired together and encased in a block of concrete. Soldiers initially arriving in Iraq in 2004 convinced themselves that they would easily identify a conspicuous roadside mound, but such optimistic certainty quickly dissipated upon finding the abundance of garbage littering alleys and highways. The loss of Spc. Adam Froehlich to a well-concealed IED on March 25, that no one realized he was virtually standing on, also reminded all of us how vulnerable we were to the insurgents' favored weapon.

Often, the bombs exploded without causing damage or injury to Americans, because the triggerman, a civilian standing nearby with a remote or wired detonation device, miscalculated the speed of approaching vehicles. On occasion, searing, jagged shards of steel, torn from a piece of ordnance, caused damage of varying degrees of severity to vehicles and their passengers.

During our deployment to Baquba, the number of triggermen killed or apprehended by Task Force 1-6 could be counted on one hand. Normally, the triggerman stood inside a building overlooking the site of the IED, or blended into a crowd of pedestrians. From time to time, a soldier reported spotting a suspected triggerman fleeing the scene of an IED explosion, but the actual culprit always escaped detainment. Sniper teams attempted, on dozens of early mornings, to find those individuals responsible for emplacing the IEDs, and several times they accomplished their lethal mission.

The remainder of the time, we primarily relied on local citizens reporting suspected IEDs to the police, which accounted for locating only about fifty percent of the IEDs. For the other half of the roadside bombs, we had to find the devices on our own. Indeed, the reluctance of the Iraqi populace to provide information about the location of hostile threats was a frustration shared by U.S. forces throughout Iraq. In particular, the unwillingness of Iraqis to call their police, or talk to U.S. patrols about the specific position and composition of IEDs, especially agitated soldiers anytime a hidden device detonated near their convoy.

A man walking around the corner with a rocket-propelled grenade (RPG) is not going to be seen by the general populace until the moment he aims his launcher at a U.S. patrol. However, three men toting a shovel, artillery round, and remote detonation device to a spot adjacent to a neighborhood should attract the attention of someone living in that community. More Iraqis knew about the activities of the enemy than they often admitted to their police, much less to U.S. forces.

On the occasion that an IED was reported to the local police, the police sent their own Explosives Ordinance Demolition (EOD) team to the site, in an attempt to defuse the device with the meager equipment they carried. With a grappling hook, a Russian-made sniper rifle, a pair of binoculars, a Leatherman multi-tool, and a flashlight, a trio of policemen did their best to remove discovered bombs. Whenever they found the IED to be too complex to defuse, the Iraqi EOD team requested U.S. support.

Every platoon in the battalion conducted a multitude of IED cordons, and supported a highly skilled U.S. EOD team in dismantling or destroying reported IEDs. Each counter-IED operation placed EOD soldiers in imminent danger of losing their lives, and for those of us providing the cordon, another opportunity to realize how frustrating it was to find the bad people in Iraq.

At 7:00 in the morning on June 15, a soldier from the company woke me, asking me to get 3rd Platoon ready for a mission, and to personally report to the battalion operations center. Inside the headquarters Capt. John Adams, the battle captain, ordered my platoon to cordon an IED, and then wait for U.S. EOD to arrive on site to clear it. Local residents reported to police that morning that three wired rockets lay next to the major road in northern Buhriz.

Captain Adams saw the concern in my eyes as I plotted the IED on the map: insurgents planted the bomb in Buhriz. Besides our last visit to Buhriz on May 28, when twenty-odd locals attacked 3rd and 4th Platoons, I was fully aware of Lt. T. J. Grider's more recent riverside attack. Everything about the location of the suspected IED told me that someone wanted to draw U.S. forces into Buhriz that morning. The blatant device sat on the western side of the north-south Canal Street, one kilometer into Buhriz, on the primary road leading into the narrow and congested market area. Our procedures for blocking an IED required us to establish a cordon 300 to 500 meters on opposite sides of the suspected device, meaning my southern cordon of two humvees would be isolated deep in Buhriz.

I recommended establishing a northern cordon with the two humvees in Staff Sgt. Bogdan Burduselu's 1st Squad, while the three remaining humvees in the platoon would travel along the east side of the canal to the town police station. With the assistance of an interpreter, I could describe the bomb and its location to the police, and ask them to provide a southern cordon. Staff Sgt. Wade Huntert's 2nd Squad would travel with me to establish an observation post (OP) atop a dominating house near the police station, to watch over the west side of Canal Street, while also scanning farther into the town for suspicious activity. Captain Adams found the plan agreeable and called brigade to coordinate the EOD team with 3rd Platoon in northern Buhriz.

While briefing the plan to the squad and team leaders, from a map covering the hood of my humvee, a company runner approached, saying that the company commander needed to see me. After finishing the brief, I entered the command post, where the captain told me that he would lead the mission, and a Bradley section would come along. It was clear that he had not talked to the battle captain about my plan, because he began to lay out an entirely different operational concept.

Although I felt that the risk of being attacked in Buhriz was fairly mitigated by conducting face-to-face coordination with the Buhriz police, as well as by emplacing an OP on a prominent rooftop, the commander did not want anyone near Buhriz. Instead, we would sit more than a kilometer to the north of the IED, while the police secured the southern cordon. I asked what if EOD needed to get closer to the IED, and learned that "We'll creep forward if necessary." As to how we would coordinate with the police, he replied, "They'll take care of it."

Still puzzled about who "they" were, I found T. J. to refine the plan, because he would be with the Bradleys participating in the mission. Before returning to my platoon, I also stopped by the battalion headquarters to inform Captain Adams that I would no longer be the patrol leader for this mission, because the company commander was coming along. The battle captain was surprised by this information. He was even more surprised when I told him that I would no longer be visiting the police station, because my limit of advance was the burnt-out governor's mansion sitting north of Buhriz, and 800 meters away from the IED. He asked me what the difference was between having the battalion headquarters call the provincial police headquarters, that would then call the Buhriz police station, and having the platoon on the ground visit the same station. I responded, "Sir, please direct all questions to the commander."

With two Bradleys leading the way into southern Tahrir, we found the police poorly attempting to redirect traffic near the dilapidated governor's mansion, that sat on a bluff overlooking the Diyala River. The police knew the location of the threat, but their patrol cars were positioned where my platoon needed to be. Upon arriving on site, we learned that there was not a triple rocket threat. Instead, there were two IEDs, both long South African 155-millimeter artillery rounds separated by 500 meters. Both were on the east bank of the canal. No one knew what I was talking about, when I inquired about the location of three rockets on the west side of the canal. While the infantry dismounts climbed onto the mansion's roof, and Sergeant Burduselu's squad moved west to the bank of the river, the EOD team arrived. Because the commander elected to establish a command post 500 meters farther north of the mansion with my

2nd Squad, I flagged the EOD vehicles to the location of my humvee, by the police pickup trucks and Bradley parked by the mansion.

I pointed out the location of the two IEDs to the EOD team's Sgt. First Class Gregory Miller, with whom we had worked during a tedious six-hour IED clearance operation in late May. He asked why traffic continued flowing north by the devices. I explained that the police needed to establish a southern cordon, because our limit of advance was the governor's mansion. He looked at me incredulously. A cordon, as I well knew, was supposed to be established prior to the arrival of the EOD team. His team unloaded two robots, which traveled by remote control to examine IEDs with their cameras, snip wires if appropriate, and place blocks of C4 explosives on top of the IEDs for controlled detonations. Utilizing both robots, Sergeant Miller wanted to complete the clearance operation quickly, but the absence of a complete cordon would slow his progress. Without stopping all traffic, a passing car might crunch the pricy robot under a tire, or an unsuspecting local could suffer mortal wounds from being too close to a controlled detonation.

I approached a police sergeant and told him to go into Buhriz to stop traffic from the south. Upon returning from the gaggle of police, I saw a woman, dressed in civilian clothes, step out of one of the EOD team humvees, while another civilian began photographing us. Introducing herself as Gina Cavallaro, an *Army Times* reporter, she took my name, and began asking questions about the IED mission, the plight of dealing with IEDs, and then about our unit's larger operations, as we waited for the police to establish a tight cordon.

Fifteen minutes later, with the cordon still not set, Sergeant Miller began to become impatient. He asked me again why, with five 6.5-ton humvees and two Bradleys, I could not venture 500 meters into Buhriz to stop traffic. I pointed to the distant commander's vehicle, and told him to talk to the commander. He shook his head, and told me he intended to voice an official complaint against the captain with brigade once he returned to Camp Warhorse. Then he politely gave me ten minutes to establish a southern cordon, before his team would pack up and leave for another mission.

Passing the police sergeant, I found his lieutenant, and asked why his men would not go into Buhriz. He answered that his men worked in Tahrir, the district directly north, so Buhriz was not their responsibility. He had radioed the Buhriz police station, but could not explain why the Buhriz police would not do their job. I warned him, "In five minutes, the

U.S. EOD team will leave if a southern cordon is not set. Then, I'm going to General Whalid's office, and tell him to fire *you* because you left a bomb in Buhriz today."

On mentioning Major General Whalid's name, the provincial police chief, the lieutenant's eyes widened. He anxiously yelled at two of his officers, who jumped into a blue and white pickup truck along with the lieutenant, and sped off into Buhriz. Less than five minutes later, traffic stopped moving north, and the robots began their methodical work.

Both IEDs were destroyed with C4, although one robot had to drop a second block atop the southern most 155-millimeter round, as it was dug well into the soil next to the asphalt road. The journalist took many notes as we talked, and I provided Gina with names, locations, and specific dates of serious IED attacks and insurgent operations in the Baquba area over the past three months. Her interest suggested that she might write a story on our efforts, so I spoke of the entire company's efforts and not just 3rd Platoon. Her IED story did appear in the August 2nd edition of the *Army Times,* with a photo of one of the bombs detonating in northern Buhriz, and a detailed account of the duties of Sergeant Miller's EOD team. With this photo and story, the message was sent out to the rest of the world that the insurgents were in town, in force.

Once the EOD team packed away their gear, I radioed the commander to report that we could leave when he wanted. At this time, my humvee and a single Bradley were on the east side of the canal with the EOD vehicles, while the rest of our men remained on the west side. The captain told me to travel north on the eastbound lane, and linkup with the other vehicles in the company as they crossed to the east side, on a bridge two kilometers to the north of our present location. The mission was a success, and it was time for us to return to our camp.

Taking the lead, my vehicle did not get 400 meters away when a tremendous explosion shook the humvee. A third 155-millimeter round detonated between my vehicle and the Bradley behind us. No one had seen the well-hidden device, not even the police who drove in front of us as we departed. As panicked civilians near the road ran into houses and shops, I told Spc. Jesse Garcia, my driver, to turn onto a smaller residential road with our humvee, so we could scan for additional devices. Looking up, I yelled to Pvt. First Class John Akridge, my rooftop gunner for the mission, to see if he was injured. Fortunately, no shrapnel flew his way.

On the radio, the captain ordered T. J. and me to locate the triggerman. However, as Specialist Garcia returned our vehicle to the main road, my concern shifted to the EOD team trailing the Bradley. I asked, on the company radio frequency, whether anyone could see the EOD vehicles from the west side of the canal, and whether their occupants were all right. The commander ignored my question, and directed us to continue scanning for the triggerman, as dozens of locals continued fleeing the scene in search of protection from possible secondary devices or American bullets. Still, I pressed the issue concerning the safety of the EOD team, and after my third request via radio, Sergeant Miller came onto the company frequency to report to me that his team was fine.

Pleased that we could all return to our respective camps in one piece, I turned my attention to the ludicrous task of finding the triggerman. After ten minutes, as T. J. and I dispersed our men, inspected a roadside grocery stand, and searched a broken-down taxi, the commander permitted us to reform into a convoy formation and return to Camp Gabe. We did not locate the triggerman, because he had disappeared from the street, window, or rooftop he stood on the moment he pressed the button on his reconfigured beeper, cell phone, or garage door opener.

We had not anticipated the third IED, and after two successful controlled detonations, we believed we had destroyed a bad man's munitions before he could strike us. Despite the relief in knowing no one was injured, we remained frustrated that we could not do anything "good" to him. I wondered, on the return drive to Camp Gabe, how three large artillery rounds could be planted so well without anyone in Tahrir or Buhriz noticing. Additionally, most of the intricate IEDs were normally placed on the highways that served as our major supply routes. These three well-hidden rounds could only be intended for preventing a convoy from entering Buhriz. Perhaps the locals noticed diligent masked men with shovels, but just as they choose to ignore the RPG teams trailing my platoon in their town on May 28, so too did they overlook the insurgents digging alongside the road sometime around 4:00 in the morning on June 15.

The Transfer of Sovereignty to the Iraqi Transitional Government, scheduled for June 30, would certainly attract the attention of the insurgency we wished to destroy, and there would almost certainly be violence. The fighting from April had sent out several messages that would change the nature of our existence in Baquba. To the insurgency, the Easter Offensive said that we were not willing to allow them to gain a foothold in the city, and that we would use every weapon at our disposal to keep them from doing so. To the enemy, this would mean that if they were planning to attack us in June to disrupt the Transfer of Sovereignty, the attack would have to be on a grand scale.

To the media, the fighting in April said that Baquba was not Najaf, where U.S. soldiers were kept at bay outside of the city, and at times could not return fire if they were being fired upon. If the insurgency rose up to fight us, we would move to destroy them, which is always more palatable and marketable than watching America's sons and daughters being kept from doing their jobs for political reasons. The series of IEDs in Buhriz served as another sign that the insurgency had taken our hint from April, and they had returned in force to pick a fight. Gina and her photographer were some of the first reporters to arrive in the city, and many more would flow in over the course of the weeks ahead.

chapter 7
A CITY UPON A HILL: THE URBAN MORASS
Lt. Greg Tomlin, 3rd Platoon Leader, C Battery

throughout the first half of June, the insurgency remained non-committal. The enemy appeared to want to stop our progress, and remove our established position in Baquba, but they did not yet want to exhaust their relatively limited resources of personnel and munitions. We were all fairly certain that the transition from the Coalition Provisional Authority to the Iraqi Transitional Government, at the end of June, would bring increased attacks, and we knew that the increase we had felt thus far was due to the influx of insurgents and weapons that had been flowing into Baquba in preparation for the fight.

We assumed the enemy would stage a spectacular attack on one of the local governmental buildings. Most likely, they would target a police station, which seemed to be the tactic of choice throughout the country at that time of the war. In fact, we could operate with near perfect knowledge of what was coming, because every U.S. combat unit in Iraq was preparing to respond to the exact same sort of attacks. It was not a secret that the Transfer of Sovereignty would be exploited by the enemy in order to slow our momentum, as well as to depict the U.S. and Iraqi Security Forces as incapable of keeping the streets of Iraqi cities secure.

Because all of the security forces in Iraq, both foreign and domestic, seemed to be holding their breath, awaiting the attacks that would undoubtedly come, the media presence in Iraq had also been informed, or had figured out what to expect. Presumably, stuck sitting in hotel rooms in Baghdad's Green Zone, or covering Coalition units in other cities for the first couple of weeks in June, reporters were all anticipating the attacks, so they could go to where the story was. The earlier attacks in June brought in the first reporters who had been in Task Force 1-6's sector since we took over in February. As the Transfer of Sovereignty got closer, and the attacks became larger, more well-known news agencies began sending their journalists and photographers into Baquba.

The increased media presence in Baquba brought with it more than the possibility of seeing reporters whose names we recognized from the news. It brought with it, as well, a degree of hope and possibility for Iraq. Maybe more than in any other war, information beamed via satellite to every citizen of the world, in and out of Iraq, could very much complement the military combat power in winning against the insurgents. Obviously, if the mainstream media reported only the sensational, and the American public did not see the actual progress being made daily in Iraq, support for the war could wane, and our enemy would be closer to winning.

A much fiercer battle ensued inside the Arab media, not for Nielsen ratings, but rather, for the Muslim mind. Media organizations, such as Al Jazeera, fought with every other media outlet in existence for the power to influence members of the Arab world. The media outlet with the largest viewing audience would be granted an opportunity to shape the popular opinion in much of the Middle East, a crucial component in determining the overall success or failure of the much larger struggle in the turbulent region.

Unfortunately, the journalists and photographers trickling into Baquba by the middle of June did not intend to examine how well the Diyala government was appropriating its half billion dollar coffers in improving the province's infrastructure. The reporters arrived in the city when they foresaw the impending attacks in our city, or as soon after the attacks started, to catch up on explaining the violence.

The increasing presence of the media over the month was of little concern to us in June, and getting to know reporters and their intentions seemed to have little value to us. The trends of violence in Baquba indicated that the expected combat was imminent, which left us working doubly hard to prepare. Also, the trends themselves, the menacing hit-and-run tactics of the insurgents, continued to consume large amounts of our time while we waited. We needed to continue in our combat role and let the media focus on telling the story, in whatever fashion they preferred to report it.

Long since weary of taking a defensive posture against the insurgents of Buhriz, Lt. Col. Steven Bullimore, the Task Force 1-6 commander, tasked his operations officer to create a plan where the task force would establish a temporary fire base in Buhriz to force the enemy to move to our location, versus allowing insurgents to ambush us at locations and times of their choosing. It was time for our battalion to maintain a presence in the town that would last longer than a three-hour patrol, to ensure that we could kill them on our own terms as much as possible. Accordingly, the battalion published Operation Smack Down as a solution.

To assist the task force with accomplishing this aggressive plan, the brigade attached its reconnaissance troop to Lieutenant Colonel Bullimore's command. A company-sized cavalry element, mounted in humvees and Bradleys, the Brigade Reconnaissance Troop traditionally serves as the eyes of the brigade, conducting missions several kilometers ahead of the brigade tank and Bradley formations. In Iraq, the reconnaissance troop served as a reserve element for the brigade, and was often attached to different battalions for specific missions requiring more soldiers than were otherwise available.

If the mission went as planned, it would begin with a raid on the house of Hussein Ali Septi, one of two principal organizers and financiers of terrorist activity in Buhriz. Immediately upon seizure of his house, the three platoons of the reconnaissance troop would occupy a building in central Buhriz, fortify it, and "attrit" the enemy, by engaging whoever fired against the unit over a twenty-four hour period. Next, on the following morning, C Company would occupy a different structure in Buhriz, with two rifle platoons and Lt. T. J. Grider's Bradley platoon, for another entire day. Soldiers would conduct dismounted patrols from their strongpoint, once the situation in the town stabilized.

Upon destroying the homegrown insurgency in Buhriz, the next phase of the operation would include Civil Affairs soldiers working to improve the infrastructure and quality of life for the good people of the town. Third Brigade would pour millions of dollars into projects to renovate mosques and schools, and to construct another bridge across the Diyala River to improve the flow of commercial traffic into Buhriz. Platoon leaders would explain, in subsequent patrols, that U.S. forces did not like to shoot in their neighborhoods, and that it is necessary to enhance the cooperation between the people of Buhriz, their provincial government, and U.S. security forces. The Buhriz operation could become the model for eliminating organized resistance, and building a shining community inside of a developing Iraq.

The trigger for launching Smack Down would be the next direct attack by rocket-propelled grenade (RPG), or small arms fire against U.S. forces in Buhriz. According to the order, T. J.'s and my platoons would move to kill or capture Ali Septi, and seize his house. While both of our platoons had conducted predawn raids in Buhriz in May, on those occasions we had the luxury of driving directly up to the houses that were located on streets that accommodate humvees. This mission would differ, because Ali Septi's house sat aside a narrow path bordering the palm groves, a 300-meter walk from the market street where we would park our vehicles.

Lieutenant Colonel Bullimore ordered my company commander to visit Mayor Auf of Buhriz on June 16, in his office in the northern portion of the town. Lt. Christopher Lacour's 2nd Platoon from C Company would provide the escort for the captain. I would also go along, to conduct a route reconnaissance for the impending mission. As the captain met with the mayor, 2nd Platoon would drive me into the market area, where I would look for the most suitable location to stop a wheeled convoy, and identify which alleyway would lead towards the target house.

This plan fell apart, shortly after our arrival at the mayor's office at 9:00 in the morning on June 16. In order for us to be able to leave the commander at the office, the battalion Civil Affairs team would meet us in Buhriz to secure the mayor's building. However, upon our arrival at the office, the Civil Affairs captain was climbing into his humvee, intending to leave because he had arrived early, and completed his meeting with the mayor ahead of schedule. Chris's platoon would now need to remain at the mayor's office until the commander completed his meeting. The reconnaissance would have to wait until the meeting adjourned.

After conducting missions in Buhriz for more than three months, it was common knowledge in the company that if you stayed on the ground for more than an hour in the town, you would outlive your welcome. As we stood outside the mayor's office while the captain met inside, I continuously looked at the hands of my watch, and observed civilian traffic on the street. A carpentry shop stood open next to the lead humvee in the security formation, in which I was traveling with Chris. I entered the structure to look at large wooden doors that two teenagers were refurbishing. People continued to walk along the streets, including, strangely for Buhriz, a twenty-something-year-old woman in western apparel.

I looked at my watch to see that we had been stationary for fifty-five minutes. Seconds later, the first rocket-propelled grenade (RPG) slammed into a telephone pole near the rear of the convoy. Two additional RPGs exploded, as I watched the now-exasperated young woman hurriedly seek refuge in the woodshop next to my humvee. Soldiers positioned around the rear humvees of the convoy returned fire towards the smoke trails, but it was unclear what other contact would be coming. Regardless of further enemy efforts that day, this attack would trigger commencing Operation Smack Down.

The commander ran from the mayor's office to his humvee, where Chris provided him with a situation report. The captain then ordered the convoy to complete a U-turn and return to Camp Gabe. I recommended moving just a little deeper into Buhriz, to take an alternate road back. As it was only the day before when we discovered three improvised explosive devices (IED) on Canal Street, other bombs might be waiting for those imprudent enough to travel the same route twice during the same mission. Supporting the recommendation, the captain told Chris to follow my directions.

As we turned at the next bridge crossing the canal, I noticed a large two-story building on the opposite side of the canal that stood taller than most houses in the area. It also had a walled-in parking lot, offering significant standoff distance from other structures in the neighborhood. A large sign on the front of the building identified it as a Department of Agriculture office. I thought that this would be an ideal location for a strongpoint, should we have to return to Buhriz for a twenty-four hour period.

The captain stated earlier that if we had to create a strongpoint, he intended to occupy the mayor's office, a mere single-story building with limited fields of fire, shouldered by taller structures, and offering very restricted room for parking a column of humvees. On returning safely to Camp Gabe thirty minutes later, I discussed the tactical advantage of using the agriculture building. The captain informed battalion that his company would utilize the agriculture building in lieu of the mayor's office if the company had to establish a strongpoint in Buhriz.

T. J. and I then turned our attention to the details of how we would locate Ali Septi. The raid on Ali Septi's house would be the most dangerous phase of Smack Down, but we could maintain the element of surprise provided we moved quickly. In our discussion, we shared two major concerns. First was the requirement to walk 300 meters in the dark, along a street lined with two to three-story houses, where enemy personnel could easily shoot downwards or toss grenades at us. Intelligence reports already warned us that Ali Septi employed bodyguards.

Second, and just as disconcerting, was the requirement to leave two platoons of vehicles on the market street for two and a half hours, with only the drivers and rooftop gunners to guard them. Lined with the tallest buildings in the town, the narrow street made it impossible to arc the vehicles' machine guns effectively toward the rooftops. Should the vehicles come under RPG attack, an extremely probable enemy course of action considering the extended duration of our stay, the vehicle detail would have to hold their ground until the main body of both platoons could return to their location from the target house.

Because the company commander would be with 2nd Platoon, in a reserve position at the southern limit of Buhriz, T. J. and I would control movement on the ground to the target houses. Two houses, in fact, had to be raided, Ali Septi's and his aunt's. His relative's house was located another fifty meters down the footpath. Sources suggested he might hide at his aunt's if he realized we were coming to grab him. With the infantry platoon taking its Bradleys, it made more sense for my platoon to take the lead, as humvees maneuvered better on the narrow market street.

Turning our attention to our organization for the mission, we agreed that I would travel with one of my fire teams and an infantry squad to the aunt's house, and T. J. would follow with another of my fire teams, and one of his squads. The 3rd Platoon fire teams would secure the outside of the two houses, while the infantry squads raided them. My raiding element would take the lead, because the aunt's house was further down the road. In this manner, should a firefight ensue, my element would not have to cross in front of the fire from T. J.'s men at Ali Septi's house to get to the aunt's home.

Staff officers, commanders, and platoon leaders, including commanders of the reconnaissance troop and an attached National Guard Bradley company, assembled for a Smack Down rehearsal early on the evening of June 16 at the battalion headquarters. We all stood over a terrain board, or a miniature version of the Buhriz street and building network, so that we could each explain our tasks for the mission. This would be our last opportunity to synchronize our efforts face-to-face, because the operation would begin the following morning.

With limited time to prepare soldiers for this rather long and deliberate operation, the handful of platoon leaders were anxious to return to their men, to complete orders and rehearsals, and to verify vehicle load plans. T. J. and I also wanted our squad leaders to join us in watching unmanned aerial vehicle (UAV) footage of the meandering paths of Buhriz, so we could better understand how to get to the houses. This was especially important for Staff Sgt. Wade Hunter, who would serve as the point man for our mission. Following our preparation, we tried to get a few hours of rest prior to departing camp at 1:30 the next morning.

Task Force 1-6 members exit Camp Gabe for another mission. (Caleb Cage Collection)

In the first hours of June 17, riding in the lead humvee of the convoy, my first task was to travel down a highway several kilometers east of Buhriz, and select a suitable location for an assembly area. This is a staging area, where the company and the battalion forward command element could park their vehicles, for final checks prior to executing the mission. In the daytime, such a task was fairly simple, but when using night-vision devices, it becomes easy to drive a humvee into an impassable depression, due to degraded depth perception. Locating a field that did not look too well plowed, I directed my driver Spc. Jesse Garcia, to turn off the road. To prevent getting stuck, I sent two soldiers ahead of us to ground guide our vehicle a couple hundred meters into the field. By 3:00 that morning, nearly two dozen wheeled and tracked vehicles created a massive wagon-wheel formation.

Stopping at each of the five humvees in my platoon, I visited with the soldiers and checked weapon systems. At 4:10 A.M., T. J.'s and my platoons departed the assembly area, traveling farther south, before exiting the highway to head into Buhriz. As we entered the town limits, the community appeared inactive, with the exception of several mosque minarets blaring the early morning prayers. From the market street, I located the alleyway spurring off towards the target houses. I was a bit relieved that I did not miss it, because I never had the opportunity to conduct the reconnaissance the day prior. Throwing an infrared chem light out the humvee window to mark the alley's entrance, I instructed Specialist Garcia to stop our vehicle once we moved as far as I thought we needed, in order to fit the humvees and Bradleys of our convoy on the market street.

Once the fire teams and squads assembled on the street, the first soldiers prepared to head down the alley. As the lead team began to move, however, a magazine of AK-47 rounds poured from deep in the alley we were about to travel. Now, everyone in town knew we were there. As we stood in the darkness, moving to the sides of the street for protection, it was absolutely silent. For a moment, everyone stood quietly, peering through weapon scopes and night-vision devices, nervously scanning for someone to shoot. To expedite our movement, Staff Sgt. Daniel Neal, the infantry squad leader traveling with my element, sprayed the alley, as well as rooftops to our front and sides, with a machine gun.

Despite the suppressive fire, movement was hesitant as soldiers scanned doorways, windows, and roofs for possible attackers. No one wanted to admit it, but most of us began to miss the armored vehicles, .50-caliber machine guns, and Bradley main guns that we left behind. The alley was not straight or free of intersections. At the first T-junction, according to our UAV video, we needed to take a left. Turning right at the second T-junction, Sergeant Hunter took two aimed shots around the bend. Sergeant Neal and I could not see what Sergeant Hunter was shooting at, and we asked for details. He responded that there were men in the alley, and one held an AK-47.

Moments later, when I took the right turn myself, I saw two men in their twenties, lying prostrate on the ground. A third man, possibly in his fifties, lay on his back with an AK-47 nearby. Removing my night-vision goggles to take a better look, I unconsciously clenched the pistol grip of my M-16 a bit tighter, after seeing a pool of blood enlarge under the older man's dishdasha. Soldiers from my platoon's fire team, who were under T. J.'s control for the mission, remained with the Iraqis while the rest of us ventured farther down the path. We had to keep moving, because there were still more than a hundred meters remaining between us and the first target house. If we all stopped, Ali Septi might flee to the palm groves, if he had not done so already.

Passing the next right turn became impossible, when the point man reported that a grenade sat in the middle of the path to Ali Septi's house. Following this dimly lit and unpredictable trail brought back high school memories of reading Joseph Conrad's *Heart of Darkness*. The deeper Charles Marlow traveled down the river in search of Georges-Antoine Kurtz, the more daunting his venture became. Fighting to keep my nerves calm, I was unsure of what still lay ahead in our search for Ali Septi. I continued to remind myself that if I was scared, then there were certainly younger soldiers more scared and more vulnerable than me who were looking to T. J. and me for purpose and direction. As platoon leaders, we had to press on with the mission.

Sergeant Neal sent one of his men forward with another grenade. Seconds later, the U.S. grenade rolled to a stop next to the pre-positioned one, blowing both up with a piercing bang. While we were waiting for the obstacle to be cleared, my rear fire team approached the three unidentified personnel to take the single weapon, attempt to stabilize the wounded man, and detain the other two as prisoners.

Several minutes later, we finally passed Ali Septi's house, and my element turned left at another T-junction, closing in on the aunt's house. While the infantry squad prepared to break into the relative's house, T. J.'s element fired upon two men with weapons, standing on a rooftop near Ali Septi's house. Before Sergeant Neal's squad entered the aunt's house, I received a report on my radio that Ali Septi had been detained, but we needed to continue the search of the aunt's house. Both target houses were cleared rather quickly, and T. J. led a squad into the neighboring palm grove to search for possible weapons caches.

While standing outside the aunt's house, with the palm grove search ongoing, Lieutenant Colonel Bullimore approached my objective house on foot with his driver. The battalion commander told me that the old man shot on the street by Sergeant Hunter was Ali Septi. An air medical evacuation would fly him to the U. S. trauma center at the Balad airfield. If he lived, his interrogation could yield much valuable information.

The man's chances of living, however, did not look good. He suffered from two gunshot wounds, one through a lung and another in the abdomen. Sgt. William Joy from my fire team working with T. J., tried to put three intravenous needles into Ali Septi's arm, but the old man obstinately pulled out each one. Sergeant Joy struggled to put the fourth one in as the veins collapsed. Our platoon medic, Spc. Stewart Eubanks, arrived from the vehicle convoy to put the high-profile insurgent on a litter.

Although alive for the helicopter flight, Ali Septi would not live through the night.

After almost an hour of securing the aunt's house, my team consolidated at Ali Septi's house with those soldiers not searching the palm groves. We remained at the primary target house until T. J.'s soldiers returned from their investigation of the thick vegetation. They found nothing of significance in the groves. Reorganizing into our original dismounted formation, we began the walk to our humvees in the bright sunshine of the 7:00 morning hour. As we withdrew from Burhiz, T. J.'s Bradleys took the lead this time, and 3rd Platoon provided rear security for the egress route. Despite being on the ground for nearly three hours, the enemy did not engage us in Buhriz, other than the defiant old man who stood near his home, prepared to fight to the death. In a region where guerrillas preferred hit-and-run tactics against uniformed security forces, Ali Septi's obstinacy was anomalous for the archetypal insurgent leader.

Even though our convoy was oriented north, we would not travel through Buhriz to return to Camp Gabe, based on the likelihood of a string of IEDs waiting for us, much like what we saw two days earlier by the dilapidated governor's mansion. As we traveled the southern route out of town, U.S. helicopters screened our route overhead, while inquisitive families began to come out of their homes to see what the Americans were doing in their town. During our departure, I did not see any signs of hostility or agitated locals scowling at us, which gave me hope that the reconnaissance troop would see little action that day. Perhaps C Company would not even have to establish a strongpoint the following day in Buhriz.

Was Ali Septi truly the high-valued target that intelligence suggested? I began to imagine that with the loss of his personal direction and finances, the town's insurgency would lose its motivation to continue. Our Civil Affairs team could begin the transition to the reconstruction phase of Operation Smack Down before the week's end. The next mission of 3rd Platoon to Buhriz would have nothing to do with monitoring imams talking through minaret speakers, or raiding homes in predawn hours. We would be escorting Civil Affairs officers with bags of money to the mayor's office, or taking Army doctors to assist in the local clinic. Of course, this optimism was grounded less in the reality of the tactical situation, and more from the immediate relief enjoyed in completing the raid.

chapter 8
A CITY UPON A HILL: THE HIGH GROUND

Lt. Greg Tomlin, 3rd Platoon Leader, C Company

From the market bridge in the center of town, I watched the brigade reconnaissance troop's scout platoons and an armored 5-ton truck drive onto the grounds of a large single-story secondary school on the east side of the canal. The strongpoint they seized stood adjacent to where Lt. T. J. Grider's and my platoons fought for forty minutes on May 28. As we passed the outskirts of the town, I saw that the battalion's forward command element had moved closer to Buhriz, with recovery vehicles and the field ambulance that had driven Ali Septi to a makeshift helicopter landing zone only a couple hours earlier.

Shortly after noon on June 17, having completed a platoon after-action review of the morning's raid, and having taken a nap, I went into the battalion operations center, to see how the reconnaissance troop was faring in their Buhriz stronghold. On a plasma screen, a live feed from an unmanned aerial vehicle (UAV) proved that my estimate for a peaceful day in Buhriz was incorrect. The battle captain and I watched small groups of men with weapons running through alleyways, hunkered down on rooftops, and moving through the western palm groves. Indeed, the reconnaissance troop was surrounded, and its commander reported receiving heavy RPG and AK-47 fire since about 10:00 that morning. Soldiers on the school's rooftop destroyed multiple enemy teams, including one attempting to set an IED less than 300 meters in front of the school. The battle was manageable, according to a radio transmission from the reconnaissance troop commander, and if his men ran low on ammunition, his Bradleys would push through the town to provide a resupply.

Returning to the platoon bay in the old Iraqi barracks, I delivered an order to the squad and team leaders so they could prepare vehicles and go to sleep. At 4:30 in the morning on June 18, C Company would move into Buhriz, to establish a strongpoint in the agriculture building for a twenty-four hour period in order to "attrit" enemy forces. T. J.'s Bradleys would lead the way, to clear the two roads we would travel of IEDs; my platoon would follow, with Lt. Chris Lacour's 2nd Platoon in the rear. Third Platoon would clear the building and man the roof, while 2nd Platoon would secure the parking lot and man weapons mounted on humvees from behind the brick wall. The Bradleys would secure the four corners of the building, maneuvering as required to combat more distant enemy elements. Concluding the order, I fielded suggestions from the platoon leadership. Staff Sgt. Bogdan Burduselu suggested using a sledgehammer to make holes in the wall surrounding the roof, to ensure that the tripods of our larger weapons could be used on the rooftop. This idea proved to be very useful in establishing our machine gun positions.

While squad orders were being issued, I found T. J. running to his platoon bay. The infantry platoon had received new orders to return to Buhriz immediately, to reinforce the reconnaissance troop. During the afternoon hours, the reconnaissance troop commander called for his company's Bradleys to bring more ammunition and water to their strongpoint. While the tracked vehicles were en route to Buhriz along a secondary road, RPGs disabled one of his Bradleys. The other two Bradleys pushed ahead to conduct the resupply before returning to tow the third out of town. Enemy contact had not subsided during the afternoon, and the newest reported threat was a sniper whose aim was improving as the day progressed.

The enemy had also shot down one of the battalion's UAVs, and a picture of three masked men holding AK-47s and the broken UAV appeared on Al Jazeera and CBS news later that same night. T. J.'s platoon needed to travel to the reconnaissance troop strongpoint from the south, take an additional resupply of water and ammunition to the existing strongpoint, and then seize a house on the west side of the canal. The two strongpoints would limit their weapon fire to their respective sides of the north-south canal, and continue to engage the enemy through the night.

With our company's Bradleys going to Buhriz for the night, C Company would receive another attachment to provide the armor we would need for the following day. The 82nd Engineer Battalion that shared Camp Gabe with Task Force 1-6 maintained a platoon consisting of two Abrams tanks and two Bradleys. This platoon, known as "Ice Platoon," would accompany Chris's wheeled platoon and my platoon the following day.

Meeting in the battalion headquarters with Maj. Arthur Weeks, my company commander, and the Ice Platoon leader, we reviewed the company plan. The biggest concern was how to rotate the four-man tank crews out of the 120-degree heat over the twenty-four hour period. The Bradley crews could rotate with the squad of dismounts each carried, but the tankers did not share that luxury. This problem remained unresolved, as we reviewed the route and engagement criteria.

The Ice Platoon leader did not know the city of Baquba, let alone Buhriz, as it was not a sector in his battalion. Fortunately, our drive included only two turns, one from Highway 5 in Baquba to Canal Street, and one from Canal Street into the agriculture building's parking lot. The two tanks, followed by the Bradleys, would lead the convoy, and as the lead Abrams approached the appropriate turns, I would radio a warning to the first tank commander.

After ensuring 3rd Platoon was packed and ready to go, I went to bed at 9:00 that night to catch five hours of sleep. The prospect of sitting in Buhriz for an entire day should have terrified me, but for some reason I slept soundly. Considering the previous engagements in the town, and the fact that a fight continued to ensue while I rested, I should have been dreaming about bullets and RPGs zipping by, a sound with which my platoon had become all too familiar.

Perhaps it was the prospect of holding the high ground for the first time that steadied my nerves. Part of me was actually looking forward to the mission. In all of our previous urban combat operations, the enemy always held the high ground, shooting at us from positions on buildings that our vehicle-mounted weapons could not accurately range. Even when we cleared buildings floor by floor, we rarely apprehended the individuals we sought, because they fled upon hearing the distinct sound of our humvee engines. Also to our advantage this time, we were approaching from the north, prior to the reconnaissance troop's exit in the south. There was a chance that the enemy would be unprepared for a company-sized element to take over a building a kilometer north of the reconnaissance troop's strongpoint. However, since the enemy vainly tried to emplace an IED only 300 meters from the first strongpoint in broad daylight, we would most likely see an IED the following morning.

Waking at 2:00 in the morning on June 18, I walked outside to observe soldiers struggling to get our humvee radios to talk to the Ice Platoon radios. Radio problems, a constant Army quandary, delayed our departure from Camp Gabe until about 4:45 A.M. . With the Abrams and Bradleys leading the way, we turned off from Highway 5 and onto Canal Street, toward the old governor's mansion. Two sights along the route concerned me. First, why were three teenage boys standing along Canal Street? Second, as we approached the ruined governor's mansion, I saw the crater of the surprise IED that detonated near my humvee three days earlier.

No more than a few hundred meters from the crater, a thunderous explosion sounded behind my vehicle. At the same time, I saw a flash of light from the old mansion on the opposite side of the canal, as an RPG headed in our direction. The chemical smell of the propellant was so potent that I thought the RPG must have barely missed us. I reported the contact to the commander, who traveled with Chris's platoon, before calling the vehicle behind me for a status report. SSgt. Wade Hunter, who rode in that vehicle, stated that they had been hit. No injuries were incurred, but the humvee could not drive as fast as before. Only later that morning would I learn from the driver of that vehicle that an IED had exploded against the left side of their humvee, flattening three tires, and leaving several nasty shrapnel holes in the side armor.

The company convoy continued moving toward our destination, a kilometer farther south. Certainly, the explosions from the north would announce to any insurgents in Buhriz who were interested that another U.S. element was entering the town. It would be only a matter of time before they would close with us. As Ice Platoon passed the agriculture building, I radioed them to stop heading south. Telling my driver, Spc. Jesse Garcia, to turn into the parking lot, we saw that a large metal gate with a padlock secured the only opening in the two-meter-tall wall surrounding the lot. For a brief moment, I imagined the opening credits of the *A-Team,* as I told Specialist Garcia to step on the gas and drive through the gate. Still attached by the lock, the two metal sheets fell under the front wheels of the humvee as we drove over them.

Third Platoon pulled directly to the front of the building. The platoon's building breach team of four soldiers positioned themselves with their battering ram next to the front door, but they would not break in the door until the room clearing team, another group of four soldiers, was stacked against the opposite side of the door. Finally ready, they broke the door open, and the clearing team returned shortly from inside, with two men to hand over to the designated detainee handling team. Neither Iraqi carried a weapon, but both appeared shaken by our forced entry.

Once the first floor was clear, I had the detainee team take the Iraqis into a room, until the company commander determined what he wanted to do with them. As the clearing team continued their efforts on the second floor, other members of the platoon began stacking crates of ammunition, and the crew-served weapons for the roof, by the entrance. Sgt.

Barry Poynter, the clearing team leader, radioed me from the roof, saying that the building was clear. With this news, other men rushed upstairs to emplace the weapon systems, and establish their corner observation posts (OPs).

As with nearly all Iraqi government buildings, locals looted the agriculture building in Buhriz after the 2003 invasion. The existing interim government had refurbished the first floor, but the second remained cluttered with trash. A hallway ran the width of the ground floor, with rooms on each side. Sgt. First Class Marvin Walters and Staff Sgt. Jason Bacon, 3rd and 2nd platoon sergeants, respectively, spent the day on that floor, seeing that soldiers ate, drank, and slept, however briefly, during their hour-long breaks.

Simultaneously, Chris' soldiers drove their humvees into a semicircle in the parking lot, orienting MK-19 automatic 40-millimeter grenade launchers and .50-caliber machine guns toward Canal Street and the tallest neighboring buildings. One of the two Bradleys, in an effort to find the most ideal spot for observing the area, came under RPG attack from the north. Using thermal sights in the early light of dawn, the gunner in the vehicle killed one RPG team. Shortly after the Bradley stopped firing its heavy machine gun, odd booms began emanating from the roof of the agriculture building. It took only a moment to realize that Sergeant Burduselu was knocking holes with the sledgehammer on the western side of the building to accommodate the two tripods for our crew-served weapons.

With early daylight increasing visibility of our surroundings, I climbed to the roof about twenty minutes after our arrival. The building truly was an ideal place to establish a strongpoint, much taller and larger than the mayor's office about one hundred meters west of our location. The north-south Canal Street sat in front of the parking lot, an ideal route for resupply and medical evacuations. At the southwestern corner of the agriculture building, a bridge, sturdy enough for a tank to cross, provided access to the west side of the canal. A dirt road west of the canal ran parallel to the water. Buildings, including the mayor's office, stretched west from the unimproved road for only 250 meters prior to reaching the palm groves that banked the Diyala River.

A three-block residential community was north of the agriculture building, and north of those houses, a smaller palm grove. An alley ran immediately along the east side of the building. Without an additional wall, an insurgent could potentially throw a grenade through a rear first-floor window of the agriculture building. However, this was unlikely, because anyone approaching the alley would be observed very quickly from a rooftop OP. Past the east side alley, there were three additional rows of houses, then a small 200 by 200 meter palm grove. Separated only by a road, houses bordered the southern wall of the agriculture building, and continued densely into the center of Buhriz.

More than likely, enemy reinforcements would work their way to our location from the western palm groves and through the neighborhoods from southern Buhriz. The enemy could potentially make their way to the second story of the houses encircling our strongpoint by maneuvering through the palm groves. Based on what I identified as the most probable threats, I wanted seven men on the roof at all times. Taking a black marker, I walked to specific locations on the rooftop and drew a big letter, A through F, on the wall so that soldiers would know from what OP to call when reporting.

Defensively, the largest problem for men on the roof was the lack of cover. The wall around the edge of the roof stood between eighteen and twenty-four inches tall. Most rooftops we visited when clearing houses or when working at the provincial government building were three to four feet in height. At the agriculture building, soldiers needed to squat, kneel, or even lie prone while on guard if they wanted to protect any part of their bodies above their calves. During the heaviest of the fighting that day, we would find ourselves high-crawling to OPs.

The reconnaissance troop had an *Army Times* photographer embedded with them during their stay in southern Buhriz, and his published photos of the school rooftop with its four-foot high wall told a different story about the threats of operating from the top of a building. Along with the *Army Times* photographer, the reconnaissance troop had a CNN cameraman with them on the roof during the majority of the fighting. Several minutes of the fight could be downloaded from the Internet, thanks to this gentleman's camera and presence. Although these were the only two members of the Western media in Buhriz that day, their reporting drew dozens of other journalists to Baquba in the next week, some specifically requesting to accompany platoons on patrol to Buhriz.

As the reconnaissance troop withdrew from southern Buhriz around 6:00 in the morning on June 18, C Company began to receive sporadic gunfire from two or three locations to the west of the agriculture building. At least one of the enemy riflemen had a decent aim, based on the bullet

Spc. Jesse Garcia mans a .50-caliber machine gun on the roof of the Buhriz Agriculture Building on June 18, 2004. By noon, the tar sealing the cement tiles on the roof melted in the 120-degree heat, coating every soldier's uniform as men crawled across the roof to their security positions. (Gregory Tomlin Collection)

that pitted the wall only a foot from Spc. Will Douglas's position at OP D. This was the first direct attack against the strongpoint, and everyone with a weapon oriented west, from the roof to the street, returning fire with tremendous zeal. Our fire concentrated on the sources of the AK-47 fire, but it seemed excessive for the caliber of the enemy's weapon system. However, because we just arrived, perhaps it was not a bad idea to demonstrate to the enemy that we meant to destroy any insurgents who ventured into our vicinity.

Ten minutes later the situation calmed down again, allowing everyone to work on position improvement. Infantrymen dismounted from Bradleys and searched houses neighboring the agriculture building, and soldiers from 2nd Platoon attempted to pull small trees out of the parking lot with automatic humvee winches. On the roof, Sergeant Burduselu and Sergeant Hunter sent for more ammunition and scrounged up makeshift cushions for men to sit on at the OPs. We quickly established a battle rhythm for the rooftop. Soldiers knew the probable threats, the weapon systems they would use, and the location they would be defending for hour-long intervals until we were able to leave the next morning.

Around 8:00 that morning, I stood in the doorway of the stairwell on the roof. The staircase rose to the roof in a small room that stood taller than anything else on the roof, like the conning tower on a ship. For enemy personnel, this made a great distant aiming point. I found this out personally when we heard a loud crack and saw a bullet hit the wall several feet to the right of the doorway. Sergeant Burduselu suggested that it would not be wise for me to stand in the doorway anymore.

Over the next thirty minutes we continued to hear the same crack originating from the northwest. Some of the bullets found a home in the walls of the strongpoint. The rooftop spotters could not find who was shooting, but we were fairly certain that there were at least two enemy riflemen, because pairs of shots came too quickly after one another, and from slightly different directions, to have originated from the same gun. The weapons were not AK-47s, and Sergeant Poynter proved this by digging a bullet out of the stairwell wall. The fired round was smaller than the 7.62-caliber round of the popular Kalashnikov rifle.

Sergeant Poynter and Sgt. William Joy, along with Spc. Justin Nichols from 2nd Platoon, were excellent marksmen. For the next four hours, they volunteered to play a cat and mouse game with the two unseen snipers. While the initial shots came from the northwest, the two enemy personnel began to move directly north of us, then northeast. The snipers had to be shooting from inside second-story rooms, away from the windows, so as to evade being spotted. We eventually killed one of the shooters in the northeastern area. The second remained a menace, even moving to houses south of our position that were no more than 200 meters away from the agriculture building.

While the sniper was in the south and operating at a very close range, his accuracy continued to improve. I squatted underneath a window outside of the stairwell room on the roof to look south. Sergeant Joy and Specialist Nichols observed the scene from inside the same window, while Sergeant Poynter shot toward the suspected sniper from a southern OP. After every enemy rifle crack, one of the spotters standing inside the stairwell room announced a probable direction to the sniper for Sergeant Poynter, who would return fire. Then the sniper would shoot back.

Initially, the sniper aimed for Sergeant Poynter's position on the roof. Bullets crept up the wall in front of his OP, and one bullet chipped the top of the wall, sending small splinters of concrete into the sergeant's eyes.

Eventually the sniper shifted fire to the window of the stairwell room. The first shots impacted against the wall a meter east of the glassless window frame. Then one bullet flew a couple feet over my head and hit the wall four inches from the window. I told the spotters to get away from the window, and the duo moved to the second floor to find another window. Still crouched beneath the window, I heard the next bullet go over my head, and through the window.

The sniper to the south became the bane of our operation. As the task of eliminating him carried us to high noon, infantry dismounts tried spotting for us from houses to the south, but to no avail. I even coordinated to have a Bradley travel repeatedly east to west on the alley just south of our building, and use its heavy machine gun on rooftops and windows where we thought the sniper hid. Sergeants Poynter and Joy and Specialist Nichols guided the Bradley gunner to the suspected targets by shooting tracer rounds from our rooftop. However, we continued to hear the sharp crack of the enemy's rifle after the machine guns ceased firing.

Around noon, Sergeant Poynter asked me if he could use an AT-4 antitank rocket, assuring me that he knew exactly where the sniper was located. After I crawled to his position against the wall, he showed me a barred window on a house two blocks away and explained that our small arms fire was not getting through the metal bars. Although normally an excessive weapon for killing a single enemy combatant, I approved the use of the AT-4. Sergeant Joy and Specialist Nichols moved to locations by second floor windows to provide over-watch for Sergeant Poynter and lay down suppressive fire. After I moved to the northern side of the stairwell to stay clear of its blistering back-blast, the AT-4 roared toward the window to make an accurate impact. We never heard from the sniper again that day, but we never physically saw the elusive man, either. Perhaps the anti-tank weapon claimed his life. Perhaps its massive concussion frightened him into shrinking back into southern Buhriz, to fight another day. The uncertainty was a frustrating experience, witnessed numerous times during the war.

While the three-man counter-sniper team worked through the morning, the men at the other OPs also remained gainfully employed. Although tracking the sniper activity, I was acutely aware of three to four other on-going skirmishes. Patrolling north and south along Canal Street, the two tanks found two additional RPG teams and destroyed them with the powerful coax machine gun contained in the Abrams' turret. AK-47 fire occasionally rose from along the western side of the canal. The MK-19 arched its grenades into the western palm grove as the .50-caliber machine gun tore through buildings, and M203 grenades detonated on rooftops.

In addition to the rooftop fire, I talked to Chris on a handheld radio to explain where his fire would be most effective. With an advantageous vantage point enjoyed by being on the roof, I verbally adjusted the humvee gunners onto their targets. It was like being a direct fire support officer: coordinating MK-19 and M203 grenades into palm groves, running tanks along the surrounding road network, and concentrating M-16 and other personal machine gun fire against enemy teams. The tanks also shot thirteen main-gun rounds over the course of the mission, through houses where the enemy remained stubbornly entrenched. Because the company commander never visited the roof, he did not fully appreciate our available fields of fire, so it rested mostly with the Ice Platoon leader out in front and me up on top to coordinate the fight. Chris greatly assisted by passing my recommendations onto the Ice lieutenant via secure radio.

Sporadic fighting continued throughout the early afternoon, mostly in the shape of RPG teams or individuals with AK-47s firing in our direction. The source of enemy fire also shifted to hiding positions in the east. The eastern houses were much too close for an enemy to engage us, so I knew that fire originated from the small palm grove immediately behind them. The rooftops to our east obstructed our view of the entire palm grove, where enemy elements could retreat after firing from behind the protection of the brick wall surrounding the grove.

I instructed the M203 grenadier to launch a lateral north-to-south spread of grenades across the palm grove anytime we received contact from the east. The M203 is a grenade launcher affixed to the barrel of an M-16. By using its special sight, a grenadier can accurately lob grenades several hundred meters away. Every time we received contact from the east, three or four grenades would explode in the grove, silencing enemy activity. My platoon's three grenadiers, Spc. Charles Copp, Spc. Frankie Cortes, and Pvt. First Class Richard Roman, proved to be expert shooters of the grenade system that day.

Hunkering down at a western OP around 2:00 in the afternoon with Sgt. Jarrod Matthews, I heard automatic fire from the southwest, coming in our direction. Normally, enemy shots flew high. The roof had been the favored target, with its conspicuous stairwell room, and we had already heard two inaccurate RPGs sail overhead, in addition to the sporadic bullets. This gunfire, though, was different. Based on the sound of it zipping below the western wall, I knew it was aiming for the gunners mounted on the humvees in the parking lot. One of the Bradleys found the source very quickly and returned fire with its 25-millimeter cannon. Once this particular spray of AK-47 fire ceased, I heard over my handheld radio that a humvee gunner in the parking lot had been hit and required urgent care.

One of the AK-47 rounds found its way into the back of Pvt. First Class Jason Lynch, just below the protection of his body armor, while he faced the north with his MK-19. Until only a couple weeks earlier, he had been a member of 3rd Platoon before being selected to become the company commander's gunner. He was not even hit while in his own vehicle, but rather, in a 2nd Platoon humvee, which he mounted to help that platoon man rotations. I had seen Private Lynch's smiling face only a couple hours prior. He was resting in the main hallway of the building we fortified, casually sitting in a chair. I sardonically asked him if he was having any fun yet, and still smiling, Private Lynch answered, "Yes, sir."

While our medics, Spc. Stewart Eubanks and Spc. Michael Miranda from 2nd Platoon, tried to stabilize Private Lynch in the first floor of the building, an Army ambulance with Military Police (MP) escort began moving to our location from the Diyala Provincial Police Headquarters. As the evacuation convoy made its way south on Canal Street, an IED exploded, targeting the ambulance in lieu of the two up-armored humvees. Despite the attack, the patrol continued its drive to Buhriz. The company medics placed Private Lynch into one of the Ice Bradleys, which would link up with the inbound ambulance at the governor's mansion, a casualty exchange point halfway between our two locations. However, by the time Private Lynch became stable enough for movement, the ambulance convoy arrived at our location. The medics transferred Private Lynch into the shrapnel-marked ambulance and sped off to Camp Warhorse, about twenty minutes away. Watching from the roof as the humvees sped north, we told ourselves that Private Lynch would be fine under the care of the brigade's surgeon.

Shortly after handling the evacuation, 2nd Platoon, B Company arrived with a resupply of water and ammunition for us. The men welcomed the cases of cool water. While we already maintained a plentiful supply of water at our strongpoint, our stock had gone lukewarm. Cases of MK-19, .50-caliber, and rifle ammunition were shared between the ground and roof platoons. I made sure, however, that the hundreds of new M203 grenades went directly to the roof for my expert grenadiers.

Speaking briefly with Lt. Richard Szczurowsky, the visiting platoon leader, I learned that UAV coverage at Camp Gabe depicted dozens of men moving up and down the western palm groves of Buhriz, using the vegetation as a logistical route from southern Buhriz to our strongpoint. While men with weapons moved north, other insurgents carried the wounded south on makeshift stretchers along the insurgent's very own Ho Chi Minh Trail. Although causing plenty of damage to the town, it was unclear how well our attrition effort was working. Rich's platoon returned north on Canal Street within thirty minutes of their arrival.

Since we had been hit by an IED three days ago, shot at with RPGs two days ago, and fired upon while looking for Ali Septi the day prior, I wondered aloud, with gallows humor to Sergeant Douglas, whether we would be mortared at the strongpoint. The answer arrived around 5:00 in the afternoon, when six 60-millimeter mortars came our way. The indirect fire originated from the small palm grove northeast of our location. Due to the high angle firing of the weapon system, the rounds moved so slowly through the sky that from the rooftop we followed the descent of the first two like foul baseballs before they impacted near the tank and Bradley positioned by the bridge southwest of the building. Two more mortars landed short of the building, impacting north on Canal Street

The fifth sailed towards the northeast rooftop OP, where the MK-19 gunner, Pvt. First Class Wesley Waggoner, was lobbing grenades in the direction of the hidden mortar tube. As Private Waggoner stumbled to get up from his firing position, the mortar hit the wall next to his gun. Sergeant Joy happened to be standing by Private Waggoner when this occurred. From another OP, just twenty meters along the wall from them, I watched the surreal scene. The mortar impacted just after both soldiers had turned their backs to the wall, scrambling for the protection of the stairwell room. As they began to run, chunks of concrete and yellow brick pelted them. Both men ran into the stairwell, and I heard Sergeant Joy yell to Private Waggoner, "Am I hit? Am I hit?" They patted each other down to look for holes deeper than the ones the concrete made in their desert camouflage uniforms, and assured each other that they were fine. Seconds later, Private Waggoner returned to his MK-19 and began reengaging the northeast palm grove.

Private Roman, the M203 grenadier at the northwest OP, sitting only fifteen meters away from the MK-19, remained at his post during the entire mortar barrage. He continued launching grenades into the palm grove and onto a rooftop where another insurgent hid with an AK-47. A sixth mortar flew our way and exploded in the air. I thought it had a time fuse, something we had not yet seen in Baquba. I ran down the stairs to plead with the commander for an artillery fire mission into the palm grove to our northeast to put an end the mortar fire. Later I learned from members of the platoon guarding the northern half of the roof that the mortar did not detonate in the air because it had a time fuse. Rather, Private Roman inadvertently hit the mortar with a grenade he had launched toward a distant rooftop to the north. It was the kind of absolute chance occurrence that could only happen in war.

The commander's vehicle was parked parallel to the agriculture building, with the passenger doors only a couple feet from the wall. The captain spent nearly the entire twenty-four hours in his vehicle, making reports to battalion. I wedged myself into the space next to his door, told him that I just watched a mortar hit the roof, and that we needed an artillery fire mission to the northeast immediately. He said he was working on it, but instead he called for a fire mission on the palm groves west of our location.

Before returning to the roof I found two more casualties in the makeshift aid station on the ground floor. The first was an Iraqi man, probably in his fifties, who approached the southwest bridge by the Bradley between the mortar attacks. Two of our bullets hit him amidst the chaos, and our medics treated him as best they could. The second was Sgt. Winston Martinez, one of my fire team leaders. A piece of brick from the rooftop explosion hit him in the groin while he manned a northern OP. Examining him, Specialist Eubanks recommended that he be evacuated immediately. This time, the two Ice Bradleys drove the two casualties directly to Camp Warhorse and returned an hour later. The elderly man died before reaching Highway 5, and to this day, no one knows why he was out in the open as the fighting ensued. Sergeant Martinez flew to the U.S. Army Hospital in Landstuhl, Germany the following day, where he would enjoy a full recovery.

Returning to the roof, I found that our MK-19 had begun to jam, most likely from when mortar shrapnel hit it. Private Roman continued to launch grenades toward the presumed position of the mortar tube. Several minutes later, radio traffic warned us that our A Battery howitzers would fire artillery at our targets. The map grid location announced would place the 155-millimeter rounds to our southwest, meaning they would not hit the mortar men. Lt. Peter Guellnitz's platoon of Paladins began to boom from Camp Gabe five kilometers away. Everyone on the roof scampered from their OPs to use the second floor for protection until we heard all six rounds impact 400 meters to our southwest. Then we hurried back to our positions, waiting for more mortars.

Those mortars never came. The MK-19 and M203 fire from the roof might have destroyed the mortar team. Perhaps the artillery rounds, although impacting nearly a kilometer from the mortar tube location, intimidated the mortar men from shooting again, fearing our next fire mission would pinpoint their exact position. The possibility also existed that the mortar team depleted their supply of available rounds. One way or another, it was quiet again, and all of us on the roof began to realize just how vulnerable we were to mortars—even on the high ground.

Like the climax in a powerful drama, the scene of exploding mortars served as the most intense action of the day. From that point on, we played minor roles in the falling action of our bizarre little play. Although we engaged several more riflemen and one RPG team during the early evening hours, enemy activity subsided. By dark, a hush fell over Buhriz. The reconnaissance troop experienced a similar situation the previous night. Most likely, the enemy realized that our night-vision and thermal capabilities provided us with a lethal advantage that to some extent made it easier for us to engage them in the dark than in the daytime—especially if electrical power was cut. Around 11:00 at night, Specialist Copp, who sat at a southern OP with his M203 grenade launcher, saw through his night-vision goggles a strange shadow in a southern alleyway. As I squatted next to him, I watched in amazement as he accurately launched a grenade into the alley shouldered by two-story buildings. It would be the last shot fired during the mission.

My squad leaders kept asking me when I would go downstairs to rest. Throughout the day I required soldiers to rotate every hour and move to the first-floor hallway to rest. However, when I was not on the roof I sat at the top of the staircase so I could move to an OP at a moment's notice. Shortly before midnight I walked downstairs. With the adrenaline finally waning, I felt tired for the first time that day.

I approached Chris's humvee parked in the semicircle to see how he was faring. His face was grave as he told me that he received a text message on the Blue Force Tracker computer in his humvee. It stated that Private Lynch died around 6:00 that evening. "I'm sorry, man," he said, placing his hand on my shoulder for a moment.

For some reason I did not know how to respond. The convoluted mixture of rushing adrenaline and forgotten physical exhaustion prevented me from feeling any real sense of loss at that time. It just did not

click with me that a member of my platoon would not rejoin the fight—
that he was dead. After three months of near misses, I was delusional
enough to believe that we would return from our deployment unscathed.
Walking back inside the agriculture building, I realized that I not could
share this devastating news with anyone in 3rd Platoon, at least, not until
we returned to our camp. We had to stay focused on the mission at hand
until we returned to Camp Gabe.

Returning to the first floor main corridor after talking to Chris, I
looked at the men from my platoon, nodding off in chairs and lying on the
dirty floor. Dimly illuminated by the glow of a few scattered flashlights,
they were all covered with black tar. Looking at myself, I realized that I
was, as well. The rooftop was constructed with a spread of two-by-two-foot
cement tiles sealed together with a very cheap tar. By 11:00 that morning,
as the temperature rose to nearly 120 degrees, the tar melted into a sticky
paste that smeared over our knees, backsides, and elbows. I made a mental note to speak with the company supply sergeant about exchanging the
entire platoon's uniforms for new ones when we returned to camp.

As I paced the hall, the only soldiers I found awake were in the
makeshift aid station. Working out of a small room, the two medics attended to members of one of the tank crews. Over the course of the day,
the medics stuck over fifty IVs into dehydrated soldiers, mostly members
of Ice Platoon who rarely escaped the suffocating heat of their Abrams
and Bradleys.

After dozing in a chair for about an hour, I heard a faint explosion
at around 3:00 in the morning on June 19. Moving to the roof, the OPs reported observing a bright flash three kilometers to the north, most likely in
Tahrir. According to radio traffic, a RPG exploded near Rich Szczurowsky's
platoon as they returned to Camp Gabe from an early morning patrol.
Thirty minutes later, another explosion resonated in Tahrir. The radio immediately filled with anxious requests for a medical evacuation for two
soldiers wounded in a RPG attack against an MP patrol moving through
the center of Tahrir.

The C Company commander decided that we needed to leave earlier
than our battalion-directed departure time of 5:00 A.M. Leaving his humvee to find me, he ordered the expedient removal of all materiel from the
roof. While I had given a timeline for the methodical collapse of rooftop
defenses to the squad leaders at about midnight, we now had less than
thirty minutes to pack the humvees and ensure all ammunition and sen-
sitive items were out of the building.

With all equipment finally accounted for and the company ready to move, the company began heading north just before 4:00 A.M. The two Bradleys led the way, followed by 2nd Platoon, 3rd Platoon, and the two tanks. In every vehicle, soldiers waited anxiously for contact. Some anticipated another IED explosion on Canal Street, while others expected an RPG attack originating in Tahrir. Fortunately, the ride back was as uneventful for the company as the night had been at the strongpoint.

At 4:30 A.M., we arrived at the main gate to Camp Gabe to clear our weapons. I approached Sergeant Burduselu to tell him that Private Lynch, a member of his squad, did not survive. For the first time, reality struck me, and the grief I refused to acknowledge while at the strongpoint washed over me. Minutes later, the platoon huddled around our humvees outside the platoon barracks. Several jubilant soldiers joked about completing the surreal mission or about one of their perfect rifle or grenade shots. Normally, we conducted a post-mission brief, but this morning everyone needed sleep. I commended them for their unbelievable performance over the course of twenty-four hours. Pausing, I explained that we did not all make it back: Private Lynch died from his wound at 6:00 P.M. on June 18 at Camp Warhorse. There was nothing more I could say. All airiness dissipated once I broke the shattering news, and soldiers solemnly unloaded their humvees before finding their way to their bunks.

Walking alone into the battalion headquarters, the battalion intelligence officer and battle captain wanted a debriefing. After seeing my haggard face and tarred uniform, however, Maj. William Chlebowski told me to return in the afternoon. I would not have long to sleep, though. At 1:00 in the afternoon, platoon leaders and commanders needed to attend a rehearsal for the next phase of Operation Smack Down. Similar to the Easter Offensive, this mission did not seem to have an end. Exhaustion and personal emotions had to be stoically hidden as we awaited the next order. Before returning to my room I returned once more to my platoon bay. Several soldiers could not sleep, and they sat quietly outside the barracks, saying little. Walking through the bay, I passed Private Lynch's bunk. A U.S. flag lay over the mattress as a memorial to our brother-in-arms.

Several hours later we learned that no one was going into Buhriz on June 19, but that several companies would conduct a house-to-house clearing operation of Buhriz on the morning of June 20. During the afternoon's rehearsal, where I worked hard to stay awake, I learned that 2nd and 3rd Platoons from C Company would establish a blocking position south of Buhriz while the reconnaissance troop, an engineer company, and an infantry company would search every house in the northern half of Buhriz. With a departure time of 4:00 in the morning on June 20, I quickly prepared a mission order for the squad leaders so they could prepare vehicles with concertina wire and other necessary items to establish an all-day vehicle checkpoint. Leaving the sergeants to prepare the platoon, I returned to the battalion operations center to describe events at the strongpoint with the intelligence and assistant operations officers.

At 5:00 that evening the battalion headquarters announced that Col. Dana Pittard, the brigade commander, cancelled the June 20 phase of the operation. After attending our rehearsal that afternoon, the colonel drove to his capitol building office, where the mayors of Baquba and Buhriz met with him and the Diyala governor. Mayor Ra'ad of the city and Mayor Auf from the southern town assured the most powerful military and political leaders in the province that as mayors, they could get Buhriz under control with Iraq police and Iraqi Civil Defense Corps assistance, providing that the Americans stayed out of the town for awhile. With the national Transfer of Sovereignty occurring in fewer than two weeks on June 30, the municipal leaders wanted time to improve their own independence and political footing. Colonel Pittard acquiesced, and hence, to the relief of many men in the reconnaissance troop and C Company, Operation Smack Down concluded.

For years prior to the fall of Saddam Hussein's regime, the people of Buhriz prided themselves in operating a Mafioso-like town where a popular sinister attitude and widespread organized crime snubbed the efforts of Iraqi police to maintain proper order in the town. This shared amorality turned common thugs into insurgents during the U.S. occupation of their country, and they seemed determined to prevent U.S. forces and the new Iraqi police from regulating behavior in Buhriz. Hence, every patrol that spent more than an hour on the ground in the town between April and June received enemy fire. Sheiks, former military officers, imams, and shopkeepers did little to dissuade the guerrillas. In fact, we knew that many pillars of the community quietly encouraged and financially supported the criminals fanatical enough to take up arms against the Western occupiers.

Considering his town's history, Buhriz Mayor Auf stated something rather striking in his conversation with Colonel Pittard. He intended to establish order in a wayward community where he formally served as the first citizen but where he spent the past year ignoring his people's impunity. Perhaps he saw the national Transfer of Sovereignty looming

ahead as something more than the handover of political power to a democratic Iraqi regime, away from a foreign army or a ruthless despot. Perhaps he envisioned June as the opportunity to unite community leaders
in an effort to eliminate organized crime, drive out foreign insurgents and
take advantage of the U.S. Army's generous coffers to provide economic
and social advantages for his constituency. Perhaps, without appreciating
early American history, Mayor Auf intended to be the John Winthrop of
his community in a land previously ruled by savages and tinkered with
by distant authorities. On the other hand, perhaps the mayor only wanted
to prevent the eventual siege of his town by the U.S. forces determined to
rout out the hardnosed enemy.

C Company, the reconnaissance troop, and the engineers' Ice Platoon went to Buhriz with orders to "attrit" enemy forces operating in the
town. Based on the number of confirmed kills, UAV real-time imagery, and
reports made by local residents, each unit proved successful. This accomplishment can only be attributed to the commendable performance of the
soldiers who pushed through the streets of Buhriz and held their positions
atop roofs and the gunner's hatches of vehicles, engaging the enemy until
the adversary's guns fell silent.

True mission success, however, could not be measured purely by
attrition warfare, which can callously be compared to the fair game of
Whack-a-Mole. Long-term success required more than the swift pounding
of a mallet wherever an insurgent emerged. Stability for Buhriz—as in all
Iraqi towns and cities—required improved government and security cooperation and an honest dialogue between Iraqi and U.S. leaders. If the citizenry did not see progress, be it social, economic, or security, they would
resume their passive or active support of an insurgency that would eventually surface its ugly head again.

In the weeks following Operation Smack Down, whenever conversation at Camp Gabe shifted to discuss Buhriz, most people who were
not on the roof or even in Buhriz told me that holding the strongpoint on
June 18 must have been the most daunting mission to date. I disagreed.
While the efforts of the snipers and mortar men proved harrowing, 3rd
Platoon finally held the high ground. I thought back to the early morning hours of April 9, when six RPGs and small arms fire from rooftops
flashed around our convoy in the streets of Tahrir. On that occasion, I felt
much more helpless in coordinating fire as fluorescent lights washed out
our night-vision devices, and I could not effectively dismount my soldiers

from our cumbersome ammunition tracks to clear the buildings occupied by the insurgents.

Perhaps the tankers and infantrymen who operated in the Abrams and Bradleys outside our strongpoint held a differing opinion. Chris's men certainly had a different vantage point from mine. However, I personally left Buhriz with a clear understanding of how to conduct defensive operations, and throughout the rest of my military career I will carry with me the vivid memories of leading my platoon from the high ground.

PART 4

good things, bad people, and the pictures to prove it

chapter 9
THE MORAL FIGHT: PHOTOGS
Lt. Caleb Cage, 1st Platoon Leader, C Company

recall sitting in a mandatory class at West Point sometime during my junior year, before September 11. The one-hour class, immediately following lunch, was a part of a professional development series that took place twice a month. I usually dreaded these classes because the audience of cadets was generally very small — under twenty people — and catching a post-meal nap was generally out of the question.

The class, one of the few that I remember, discussed the nuanced relationship between the military and the media. The instructor, an Army major who normally taught economics, provided a relatively concise history of the interaction between the two institutions from World War II forward. Based on his emphasis of the troubled Vietnam era, there was no mistaking his point: while reporting during the Vietnam war was starkly different than the positive and personal missives from the Ernie Pyle era that began the discussion, it had also changed considerably since Vietnam.

The instructor knew his audience. He knew that the small group he was teaching, young students who had chosen a military path out of high school, was most likely to be the children of veterans of Vietnam, or at least the children of those who likely questioned the media's approach to that war. From the discussion that followed, he was correct. There was a degree of enmity assessed toward the media from the group. There also was a degree of unquestioned certainty that the media was in direct competition with the military. In a post–Cold War world, where defining an enemy for the world's sole superpower proved increasingly difficult, the instructor made a tremendous effort to ensure that the cadets did not choose the media to fill that void.

Operation Desert Storm, the instructor said, resulted in an enormous change in the way the military dealt with the media, and in the way the media covered the military. It was hardly a friendly relationship, but it was also not as adversarial, either. The media often complained about a lack of access during the invasion, but much of the animosity had been reconciled. The instructor pointed out that, given our age, almost everything we as cadets knew about Operation Desert Storm came from live coverage from one major news agency or another.

The lesson took place before the attacks on September 11; the instructor had no way of knowing how much the relationship had truly changed. In the ramp-up to the invasion of Iraq during Operation Iraqi Freedom (OIF), the Pentagon announced their broader embed program, where reporters with credentials could actually join units on the front lines and report the war from the front. It proved to be a wise decision. With the exception of information that would give away battlefield positions or tactical procedures, the embedded journalists were generally given the opportunity to report anything to which they had access. More than a mere manifestation of good faith on the part of the military leadership, this program clearly expressed the belief that this war would be fought in the media as much as anywhere else.

Reporting during OIF prior to our task force's arrival in Baquba was sensational, but not necessarily with the negative connotation of the word. Reporters willing to endure the harsh conditions of combat captured images of a massive modern force rapidly moving north, capturing Baghdad, and liberating a people from a dictator. Human interest stories of soldiers and Iraqis alike put an almost immediate human face on the story for the world to see. Although there was some negative press, the general media response proved to be highly positive during the initial invasion.

The emotional scene from April 9, 2003, of the Saddam Hussein statue being toppled in Baghdad's Fardus Square was, possibly a significant turning point in the coverage. Images of Iraqis scaling and beating the statue, but failing to topple it without the help of the U.S. military crane became an instant metaphor for the war. A Marine climbed the statue to place a U.S. flag over the face of the statue. This evoked an immediate and obviously diplomatic question: "What kind of message does that send?" The cameras then caught footage of the embarrassed Marine climbing the statue a second time to remove the flag. The message was extremely clear that the actions of the military in Iraq were immediately and closely watched.

Indeed, the period after the "end of major combat" on May 1, 2003, and the formation of the insurgency resulted in a changed military approach as well as a dynamic media reassessment. Just as the military struggled to categorize its observations about the enemy situation in Iraq, the media developed a systematic approach to their reporting. As the insurgency slowly began to inflict casualties during its incubation period, a long list of adjectives were developed to associate with troubled areas. Cities like Najaf, Baghdad, and Mosul carried constant monikers such as "restive," "troubled," or "war-torn," while the relatively peaceful cities of Basra and Kirkuk were often described as "oil-rich." To the careful observer, the connotation of these adjectives was not lost.

When we arrived in Baquba, our city did not have its own adjective. It was always qualified as being a part of the "tumultuous Sunni Triangle," a nod toward the growing Sunni insurgency in the heart of Iraq. Our battalion's Operation Smack Down in mid-June raised awareness of the fragile security situation in Baquba. From this operation, both the insurgency and the U.S. forces proved that they could orchestrate periods of heavy combat if they so desired. The higher echelons of command above the battalion level certainly realized this and understood that such a situation, a situation with the potential of easily escalating out of control, could justify more serious media attention for our city. Although increased news coverage was almost a given, no one could really decide if it was a good or bad thing.

One of the objectives of Operation Smack Down was to disrupt the enemy's effort to exploit the much touted Transfer of Sovereignty for their own gain. The Transfer of Sovereignty was the formal ceremony in which the Coalition Provisional Authority, headed by L. Paul Bremer, handed over responsibility of the country to the Iraqi Interim Government. It was perceived as a hugely important diplomatic event that would show that the U.S. did not wish to colonize Iraq, and it would also show progress towards democratization. The insurgency realized this, we assumed, and would do everything it could to ensure that we would not meet our goal. With the Transition of Sovereignty nearing quickly and the proof of a heavy insurgent presence that the recent fighting provided, journalists began arriving in Baquba.

Although journalists representing every possible medium would flow in and out of Camp Gabe and Baquba regularly throughout our remaining days there, the first group to arrive after the fighting in mid-June was primarily made up of photojournalists. There were a couple of print journalists along as well, but apparently the news industry believed that nothing told a story faster and better than a picture. Baquba during the Transfer of Sovereignty would likely provide plenty of photographs worthy of publication.

Purely by luck, my first roommate, Lt. Kirby Jones, recommended that I read a book by Anthony Lloyd entitled *My War Gone By, I Miss it So,* an account of Lloyd's time as a photojournalist in war-torn Yugoslavia and Chechnya. After reading the book earlier in the deployment, I considered the role of the war photographer for the first time. In my mind, I likened Lloyd, an Englishman who wished to find manly honor through military service in Desert Storm, to the protagonist from an Evelyn Waugh novel. Lloyd, it seemed, needed more than the rigid formalism of the grand scale, sanitary, controlled conflict that he faced in the Middle East in the early 1990s, and turned to war photography.

In reading his book, I was continually dismayed by the war photojournalists' craft in the way Lloyd refused to take a moral stance throughout his travels in troubled regions. Because of this, I was unable to relate directly to Lloyd's journey and memoir. The possibility of being able to take such a morally detached stance professionally was too incredibly foreign to me as someone in a position where my moral judgments would directly affect the lives of Iraqi civilians and of my own soldiers. Lloyd followed the bloodbaths that pitted Bosnian against Serb or Chechen against Russian, and allowed his immediate feelings to dictate right and wrong. This, of course, eventually led to his sense of nihilism about the whole undertaking.

He referred openly to his whorish morals as he watched the oppressed underdogs, the Muslims of Yugoslavia, participate in violence that forced the observer to forfeit any notion of sensitivity to their plight. In order to stay there and continue to land himself in interesting situations yielding provocative pictures, he had to suspend judgments of right and wrong, good and evil. In time, I realized that his beliefs about the inherent good or evil in what he was witnessing did not matter, and could only unjustly influence the photos he took or those he chose not to take. To his credit, he was quite open about his moral position. He was there to cover the carnage of a war he did not start, not to directly take part in stopping it.

When the photographers arrived I was a platoon leader, and the moral questions became more complex. Seeing the expensive equipment slung over their shoulders and around their necks, I knew that I could very well be the subject, an active participant, in their craft. Would I perform my job differently because of the presence of the camera? Would the journalists take photos that I would find agreeable and accurate descriptors of any series of events that might unfold in their presence? I also had my suspicions of their view of the war, and how they would allow that to affect their photos.

We all seemed to be preparing for the battle we assumed was about to take place in Baquba. The journalists arrived from Baghdad around June 23. The brigade leadership pushed more mechanized infantry into our sector. The brigade planners at Camp Warhorse redrew the Task Force 1-6 sector, establishing Buhriz temporarily as a brigade area of operations, not just the responsibility of C Company. Combat was clearly in the air, and even the locals seemed to feel it.

On the morning of June 24, elements of A Company, 120th Infantry Battalion, were patrolling in western Baquba. This National Guard company of Bradley Fighting Vehicles was temporarily attached to Task Force 1-6. At approximately 5:30 in the morning, as they passed through northern Mufrek, they came under heavy fire from every direction. They returned fire and maneuvered well, reports stated, but not before their company commander and his Bradley gunner were hit with a rocket-propelled grenade (RPG), killing both soldiers.

About thirty minutes later I woke up to someone annoyingly tapping me on the forehead. The messenger, Pvt. First Class Michael Lanners, told me I was to get my platoon ready to roll into sector. I had no idea what to expect, but listening to the situation report I received from the battalion operations officer told me enough: the attack we all had been expecting had begun. The mission of my platoon was to secure and reinforce the Iraqi National Guard (ING) checkpoint just outside the gate of Camp Gabe.

It struck me as a particularly lame mission, given what was developing in the city. I was not particularly excited about working with the ING either, mainly because I had not been impressed by their performance in the past. There was some perfunctory interaction between U.S. and Iraqi security forces up to that point, but it was too seldom and too frustrating to count as positive. The Iraqi security forces seemed to understand that the U.S. forces could effectively handle any unrest. They felt little to no responsibility for the local security situation, but I could hardly blame them for that. In turn, we saw the ING as ineffective, a bit lazy, and primarily concerned with collecting a paycheck. Fortunately, leading up to the June 30 deadline for the Transfer of Sovereignty, I was beginning to be routinely surprised by the ING's abilities and their tenacity in fighting the growing insurgency.

My platoon mounted our humvees and took the short ride to the ING checkpoint. As we maneuvered between the roadblocks, the calm of Camp Gabe was replaced by a violence we had not anticipated so close to our headquarters. Smoke and automatic fire was already filling the air. We could not decide who was shooting or if we were their target. Reaching our destination along Highway 5, the four humvees in my platoon blocked all through traffic in both the east and west directions. Soldiers assigned as observers climbed atop the tallest structure nearby, and we prepared to stay for a long while. Within a few minutes of our arrival, the traffic cleared and the ominous shooting stopped.

I was immediately approached by the ING squad leader, Sergeant Ali. His English was excellent, but it was his spirit that I found to be truly remarkable. He said, pointing to his squad, "I have twenty soldiers with Kalashnikovs, and we are ready to fight." I nodded and smiled before he added, "Thank you for coming." As my platoon sergeant, Sgt. First Class Cameron Gaines, arranged the security, I gathered what relevant information I could from Sergeant Ali. He said that his squad seemed to be taking sporadic fire from the soccer stadium about 800 meters to our west, confirming for me the intelligence that the stadium was an insurgent staging area earlier in the morning. When I went back to update the platoon, Sergeant Ali started barking orders to his men, and they took their places. I was beginning to reconsider my position regarding the usefulness of the ING.

It seemed apparent that Sergeant Ali and his men would be given an opportunity to test their zeal. Over the course of the next few hours that we sat at the checkpoint, our position was mortared several times, errant AK-47 fire snapped over our heads, and random explosions could be heard throughout the city. The city was under heavy assault, but we assumed that it was probably little more than un-aimed, harassing shots by either the insurgents or the ING deeper in the city. We were too far removed from the fight to understand what was really occurring, and turned our attention to the heat. It was 136 degrees Fahrenheit and still relatively early in the morning.

While I was cursing the heat with my driver, the task force headquarters informed me that Air Force jets would be strafing the city in thirty minutes. They would drop 500-pound bombs on three targets in the vicinity of the stadium—a civics center (housing the only indoor pool in the city) and two buildings belonging to the Baquba Trade School—that had been overrun that morning by insurgents. I passed the word to my platoon that they should expect several loud explosions close to our location and then told Sergeant Ali to pass the same information to his soldiers. The Iraqis seemed to understand his instructions and took cover behind the vehicles and barriers.

Fifteen minutes passed and I was told over the radio that the bombs would drop in another fifteen. As Sergeant Ali told his soldiers what was said, they began to grow visibly excited. Sergeant Ali rejoined my group at the front of the checkpoint. His soldiers told me through him that earlier they had seen numerous insurgents operating in the area by the stadium who had been clearing out the local populace all morning long. They had even kidnapped one ING soldier, dragged him into a mosque, and tortured him for three hours. I found the story hard to believe, but later the abducted soldier showed up to work at the checkpoint and revealed the fresh knife cuts on his chest to me. The ING were eager for the bombs to drop.

I was on the radio receiving word that the bombs would hit their targets shortly, when an enormous explosion came from the direction of the stadium. I reported to higher command that the first bomb had landed early and appeared to have hit its target, our dialogue straddling the explosion perfectly. The ING standing nearest to my vehicle erupted into cheers. They started giving me high-fives and various accolades in Arabic. An excited Sergeant Ali clapped my hand and exclaimed, "They want you to do it again!" I could not help but smile at the thought that I was personally coordinating the air strike. Two minutes later, the second bomb was dropped in the same area, followed by another to the south, with both shattering explosions receiving a similar reaction from our Iraqi counterparts.

A few minutes later, the U.S. ground offensive began. The B Company commander led an assault force comprised of Lt. T. J. Grider's Bradley platoon and the Ice Platoon of Abrams tanks and Bradleys. The convoy of tracked vehicles moved through our checkpoint, some soldiers nodding greetings as they passed, and they proceeded to the area near the stadium. Sgt. Jesse Huber, one of T. J.'s Bradley commanders that day, was standing halfway out of the hatch of the enormous machine, giving me passive but confident Satan horns in response to my wave as they passed by. A few hundred meters down the road from us, we could see them stop to

Third Platoon soldiers stand by the ruins of the Baquba Civic Center after an Air Force fighter launched a laser guided missile against the insurgents hiding inside on June 24, 2004. The platoon provided security while an explosives ordnance disposal team destroyed a vehicle-borne improvised explosive devise (VBIED) abandoned by insurgents in an adjacent school. (Gregory Tomlin Collection)

orient their turrets towards various targets. Between the thunder of their direct-fire cannons and their radio traffic, we had a decent idea of what was going on down there.

Spaced ten minutes behind the armor element, two wheeled platoons moved through our checkpoint to reinforce the provincial capitol building and the Civil Military Operations Center. Lt. Paul Lashley's platoon and then Greg's platoon sped past my platoon. About 150 meters beyond our checkpoint, Greg's rear vehicle was hit by an RPG in the right rear door. In yet another amazing occurrence for Greg's lucky platoon, the rocket appeared to hit a fence, exploding prior to hitting the humvee, sending only small pieces of shrapnel toward the well-armored rear door. When I saw Greg again three days later, we discussed the incident. He was surprised to hear that they had been hit. He did not even hear the explosion over the tumultuous firing of two tanks and five Bradleys.

By around 2:00 in the afternoon, the troubled area was quiet again, and the absence of stray bullets over our heads made the extreme heat more of a noted presence for my platoon. The hottest part of the day was in its final hours by now, but the prospect of members of my platoon suffering from heat injuries was growing. We had consumed nearly our entire double load of water by this point. Sergeant Gaines and I were trying to get a resupply of water, ammunition, and other necessities from our battalion, but we understood pretty clearly that we were not the main effort at that time. My guys were confident that they could do their mission and were even more convinced that the guys just up the road had it far worse. Less than a kilometer from our location, the Bradleys' dismounts were actively clearing buildings and securing the eastern portion of Baquba in the same heat under which we were sitting.

Even though we were not the main effort, I still owed it to my guys to press our headquarters for a resupply from the camp that was less than 300 meters away from our position. Two additional wheeled platoons rolled through our checkpoint, deploying downtown for various reasons. Their occupants dropped what small amounts of water and ammunition that they could carry.

Later that afternoon, I was surprised by the arrival of Capt. Travis Cox, the battalion's ammunition platoon leader and a close friend. Travis's resupply convoy quickly assuaged most of my concern for our situation as soon as it arrived. His soldiers immediately dismounted and started piling up an enormous supply of bottled water, huge bags of ice, extra ammunition, food, and IV bags used to quickly rehydrate soldiers who were in a particularly bad way. Travis brought everything that we needed, including an almost-full can of tobacco that several of my soldiers and I devoured, to keep the enemy at bay for the remainder of the day.

Just as surprising as Travis's arrival was the arrival of two extra passengers that he also dropped at our site. They were civilians dressed in blue ballistic gear and carrying rather sizeable bags and several cameras apiece. I knew that we were supposed to be receiving some journalists into our area, but I had not yet met any of them. I learned that they were Andrea Bruce Woodall and Joao Silva, both photojournalists for the *Washington Post* in various capacities.

Travis left as quickly as he came, and I took a moment to apprise the new members of our checkpoint of the situation and the events we had seen take place. They told me that all they knew was that their colleague, Scott Wilson, a print journalist, was with T. J.'s platoon when they went into the city earlier that same day. The photographers were clearly anxious to get farther into the fight, but we could not oblige them. They would have to wait to hitch a ride with the next convoy that passed through our checkpoint into the city. The situation was particularly unfortunate for them. The very next day, Wilson's story about T. J.'s platoon and the fighting in Baquba was on the front page of the *Washington Post*.

My interests were obviously consumed by our mission at hand, but the presence of our new guests was at least a little distracting. Even though I had read a little about their profession, I really did not know what to think of them in this first encounter. They were a bit alien to me after five months of deployment. They were wearing conspicuously civilian clothing and were not under my direct control, but I still felt responsible for their safety. At least in my mind, they were probably wholeheartedly against the war. They were, after all, members of the media. There was, indeed, nothing military about them at first glance, and this fact made me further suspicious of their motives. In my own mind, I reconciled their brief presence with my platoon by admitting that relations between the military and the media had changed since Vietnam and that they were not necessarily adversarial. Glad that I had reached a more mature mental stance on their presence, I organized our new rations of water and ammunition, and I made my mistake.

I approached Joao, who was standing to my rear snapping pictures of our checkpoint. I told him that if we were to take fire again at our location, it would probably be from the north or the northeast, the direction from which we received three mortars and a wildly aimed RPG that went over our heads earlier that morning. Based on this probability, the safest place for him and his colleague was behind the large barriers a few feet from our location. My intentions were pure; I was legitimately concerned for their safety. Although his voice was calm, his words were fast: "If the bullets start flying, I want to be right fucking next to you, taking pictures." My unintended insult evoked a degree of respect for the man.

Preceding their arrival to Baquba by about three weeks, I received in the mail a copy of another book on the subject of war photography called *The Bang-Bang Club: Images of a Hidden War*. I ordered it after reading Lloyd's book. The online reviews claimed that *The Bang-Bang Club* told a more honest story of the profession than Lloyd's, while still capturing the same type of amazing stories in print. Joao Silva, the man I insulted within the first ten minutes of meeting, coauthored *The Bang-Bang Club* with a colleague of his. Now he was standing at a checkpoint with me in Baquba, while a copy of his book sat unread in my room.

It turned out that the photographers arrived too late, and were too far from the action to get any worthwhile photos. We stood out in the sun listening to the rumbling sounds of combat up the street and talked about anything we could think of. By nightfall, after all other platoons had returned to the camp, we were still sitting at the checkpoint. The cool cover of night was little conciliation for the sixteen hours of heat we had already endured that day.

And it presented new problems. Our checkpoint cut off traffic on Highway 5, a main throughway. Although most of the drivers in the city knew that the road was blocked, cars still traveled toward us at normal speeds every half hour or so. This caused mildly tense situations that required us to signal for them to turn around before they crashed into our position. Finally, around 11:00 P.M., we were called off of the mission and allowed to return to camp. We were exhausted, but we fared better than those who had cleared and secured the city earlier in the day.

The next morning, June 25, Baquba remained a relative ghost town, with only platoons of Bradleys and humvees traversing the streets in search of the remnants of the insurgency. Greg's platoon linked up with Paul's platoon at the rubble of one of the school buildings destroyed by the air strike. An informant told our battalion commander, Lt. Col. Steven Bullimore, that the insurgents left a vehicle-borne improvised explosive device (VBIED) there before they could use it against Iraqi or U.S. forces. As Greg's platoon escorted the Explosive Ordinance Demolition (EOD) team from Camp Warhorse, Paul's men found a large weapons cache in what remained standing of the trade school building. The EOD team piled the newly found sixty-plus mortar rounds, dozens of RPGs, two Russian-made machine guns and thousands of 7.62-caliber rounds on top of the old Opel sedan already laden with TNT, artillery rounds, and detonation cord, then blew the munitions with a block of C4. Not only was the controlled blast the loudest they had ever heard, but it was the only explosion reported in the city that day.

On the morning of June 26 the situation in Baquba changed in ways we had never seen before. No one knew that the all-important date of June 30, the day the Coalition Provisional Authority would officially hand over control to the Iraqi Interim Government, had been secretly changed to June 28, so the activities of the 26th were even more intriguing in hindsight. The city awoke on the morning of the 26th to AK-47 fire. No one knew at whom or from where these shots were directed. They appeared to be coming from downtown Old Baquba. Slowly, reports trickled in.

The shooting from downtown was reported and confirmed to be

coming from local members of the Islamist Party, shooting at the insurgents who were roaming the streets in their telltale black outfits. No one from Task Force 1-6 would acknowledge whether this was good or bad, but we kind of liked the idea of the Iraqi people standing up for themselves. There were also reports that important mosques in the two most troubled areas, Buhriz and Mufrek, were bellowing pleas by their imams for the people to not support the insurgency. At one mosque, speakers even asked the townspeople to support the Iraqi and U.S. security forces working to end the violence. No one at Camp Gabe could believe what we were hearing.

The shooting was so near the capitol building that 2nd Platoon, the platoon stationed at the government building during that time, reported that they appeared to be receiving mild gunfire. My platoon was the most rested, so we were immediately sent back out to the same checkpoint we occupied two days prior. Along with plenty of extra water, we also brought with us three photographers who wanted to get back into the city. Joao and Andrea were there, along with David Guttenfelder from the Associated Press. When we arrived at the checkpoint we were greeted by the same ING soldiers with whom we had served two days prior. We had gained a mutual respect for each other. One of the soldiers, Sergeant Muslim (his actual name), through Sergeant Ali's interpretation, told us that he felt a bit empty after we left, even though such a comment ensured more than a fair amount of harassment from his colleagues.

Our time at the checkpoint was uneventful and considerably shorter than the sixteen-hour stint we endured two days prior, which gave us all reason to be happy. At about 10:00 in the morning, the battalion operations officer told me over the radio to push my platoon about 300–400 meters to the west, closer to the stadium, in order to block traffic to the bypass route that skirted the checkpoint to the north. I started to have the feeling that this was going to be an incredibly dull day for the anxious photographers.

As I pulled into the next position and Sergeant Gaines positioned the vehicles in security positions, the task force headquarters radioed me with further information. Apparently several insurgents were riding around Baquba in an Opel automobile. I dreaded what was next, but I knew it was coming. I was ordered to stop every Opel driving past our location on Highway 5, one of the busiest highways in Baquba. I could not wait to tell my soldiers this news, especially the more sarcastic ones. As Sgt. Jason Brownlie noted, the order to search every Opel was like an order to detain every man wearing a mustache in this city. I spent much of the next hour rubbing my eyes and temples in frustration as my platoon of twenty soldiers thoroughly searched dozens of Opels while the photographers snapped pictures.

To add to my frustration, we noticed that we had serious maintenance problems when we established our second checkpoint. My second humvee was leaking severely from the radiator, and my fourth vehicle had blown a tire, presumably while driving over the high concrete median in the road. We parked the vehicle with the leak in the shade, and started transferring the spare tire and tools from another vehicle. After searching approximately fifty Opels and assuming that our headquarters had forgotten about the tasking, I canceled the searches, and we focused our efforts more on blocking traffic and fixing our vehicles.

Sergeant Gaines was taking care of the tire situation about fifty meters away from my position. We were no longer checking vehicles and our activity began to stagnate. The photographers' boredom with our mission became quite apparent as they started taking pictures of each other as our activity slowed to a near halt. The vehicle jack Sergeant Gaines was using to fix the tire was not very useful in the soft sand, and three local children approached with bricks to support the jack, offering something mildly interesting for them to photograph. The Iraqis were about eleven years old and said through sign language they lived in the village to the east of the ING checkpoint, only a few hundred meters away from us. The village from which they came was a squatter village, made up of rubble with a few standing shacks intermingled. Partly because of this and partly because they were so helpful, we gave them some food and bottled water.

After fixing the tire, Sergeant Gaines informed me that Haider, the oldest child, told him that someone in his small village had mortars and RPGs buried on his property. Or, that is what we both agreed he meant by watching his sign language routine several times through. We had been out for a while that day already, but Haider seemed very sincere and his intelligence was actionable. We needed to search this property, located less than a kilometer from Camp Gabe's main gate. After I cleared the operation through the battalion headquarters, Sergeant Gaines and I worked up a plan from my map, and the platoon drove our vehicles slowly around to the back of the buildings. Amazingly, Haider agreed to ride in my humvee, the lead vehicle, in order to show me exactly which house had the munitions. He seemed pretty scared at this thought, but brave enough to go through with it.

He sat in the back of my vehicle, between Joao and David. As we got within one hundred meters of the group of houses, I had him point to the house we should search. It was the middle of the day and everyone in the small village certainly knew we were there. Our plan was to use the vehicles as a distraction to their south, as dismounted soldiers moved through the village from the west. The reporters went with the dismounts.

Haider sat in between the seats of my vehicle, eating the food I had given him and playing with a pair of binoculars. He was clearly scared. Every time something fell or a noise passed our way, he jumped slightly. About every ten minutes or so, while I was standing outside my vehicle waiting for word to move in with the extra firepower, Haider would explain something to me with his hands, and even more dramatically, with his eyes. He pointed to the house, eyes bulging as if asking me if I understood. He then pointed to his eyes with his fingers. Next, and with more drama, he would press his fingers into his chest several times, and follow up the routine with a long and elaborate slicing motion with his forefinger across his throat. "If they see me, they will kill me," was the only possible conclusion I could draw from this, and from seeing the seriousness in his eyes. He meant it, and it made me hope all the more that they would find something.

First Platoon did not find anything that day, unfortunately. Soldiers searched five houses, and the photographers recorded the entire event. Haider was well crunched down behind my seat as locals began to come out of their houses to see what was going on. The soldiers and journalists returned to the vehicles a little disappointed, and I was anxious to hear exactly what they observed. While Sergeant Gaines was telling me what happened, the photographers were snapping photos of Haider. We took a roundabout way to get Haider to the back of his house, and we left as discretely as five 6.5-ton military vehicles can. A few minutes later we all returned to the base, content that at least we had tried to do something productive that day while on an increasingly fruitless mission.

When we returned to the base I went to the task force operations center to debrief the mission. Nothing. Nothing happened and we found nothing. I walked back to the barracks, soaked with sweat and hoping the electricity was back on. It was not. The photographers were sitting in the dayroom, going over the photos from the events of that afternoon. Some were good, they said, and some were not. Joao had some incredibly good photos of Haider sitting behind my seat in the vehicle.

Joao showed me and explained the photos he had taken of Haider. He kept saying, "He was so brave." Going through the photos, he worked through possible captions for the images that would properly explain the context of a scared Iraqi boy sitting in an American humvee. When he decided on the ones he was going to submit, he asked my opinion. "Do you think it would be wrong for me to publish these pictures of Haider?"

His question was important, but I realized immediately that it was addressed to the wrong person. If there were insurgents living in his neighborhood and they saw the pictures of Haider on the Internet or published elsewhere, they might seek vengeance against the young collaborator. Joao pondered, "Do you think I should publish these?"

I was ashamed to tell him that I was not the deciding authority. It was a moral question, after all, and not a procedural question. I personally had no idea what the limitations were for the reporters and assumed that they could publish whatever they wished. Apparently for Joao, he did not wish to actively participate in causing harm to Haider.

chapter 10
REGIME CHANGE
Lt. Caleb Cage, 1st Platoon Leader, C Company

by June 27, the fighting had once again subsided. The Battle for Baquba, as some would eventually call it, was over. Now, the more important story was the transition of authority to the new Iraqi government that occurred on June 28, two days ahead of schedule. The journalists were off to Baghdad to take new photos and write new stories from Baghdad's enormous Green Zone. According to David Guttenfelder of the Associated Press, Anthony Lloyd would also meet them in Baghdad.

Before their departure, Andrea Woodall of the *Washington Post* showed me the photos she had taken of my platoon over the past few days. The photojournalists had spent hours with us, and her collection of photos of my platoon was fairly extensive. The other photographers joked about the insecurity of the naked and unretouched photos that she was about to reveal to me. I did not notice any defects or shortcomings, even after she warned me of their presence. I did notice, however, that my guys looked serious, as if they were not being followed by a team of journalists that day. They had done a good job and the photos showed it. Toward the end of her collection I started to see the photos from the search of the shantytown conducted with young Haider's assistance. The images depicted Sgt. First Class Cameron Gaines, my platoon sergeant, and the two dismounted fire teams he led in searching the houses.

I was a bit angry at what I saw in this last set of photos, which showed my guys in a tactical formation, preparing to enter a house. The men did not know what was inside the house, and their faces showed their intensity. The subsequent photos in the series showed the soldiers leaving the same house with the same serious faces, but clearly more relaxed than before. The contrast did not stop there. Several photos in a row, taken from slightly different angles, had a beautiful young Iraqi girl staring into space in the foreground. With my soldiers blurred and businesslike in the background, she smiled innocently while holding a baby who was presumably her little sister. This contrast was probably what made them good photos.

No matter how good the photos were, they upset me. I felt betrayed. Andrea had been out with other platoons and had seen how they reacted to the Iraqi people. She enjoyed traveling with 1st Platoon because, as she said, we treated the locals with respect and dignity. The search team asked for keys before forcefully opening locked doors; they waved and shook hands, and they were careful not to display typical American arrogance. It was these same characteristics that immediately impressed me when I took over the platoon from Lt. Jim Gifford a few months before, and one that we all worked hard to maintain. And now, contrasted against a beautiful girl holding a small child, my guys looked like villains.

Another photo showed my guys "stacked" at a corner of a house, waiting for the team leader's word to round the corner in force. The sweat on their faces was apparent and their jaws were obviously clenched in the profile shot as they prepared to see what was around the corner. But this was only the right half of the photo. The left half was what was on the other side of that wall, which in this case turned out to be small children sitting on a step. It was the same contrast as before: a team of serious-looking soldiers and a group of playful children. I was further frustrated by the tactical implications of the photo. In order to take the photos, she had to move into the open in front of my guys, compromising their position. My soldiers did not have the luxury of standing in the open and peering around the corner, and I felt that she used that against them. Giving photojournalists the freedom to roam, I felt as though we, the soldiers, were left as naked as their unretouched photographs, allowing the photographers to peer into our most vulnerable moments. It seemed so arrogant to me that she would use her role on the battlefield, her free rein, to expose such poignant and sobering moments.

The reporters arrived halfway through the fighting in June because the intensity of the killing in Baquba and Buhriz attracted international attention. When they arrived at the checkpoint on June 24, they missed the climactic explosions of the air strikes. How could they recapture the dancing Iraqi National Guardsmen (ING), who mistook my radio conversation for a forward observer's coordination efforts? How could they portray the vulnerability of soldiers lying on a roof as mortars rained in on them? How could they capture the grief of a platoon who learned of Pvt. First Class Jason Lynch's passing in the pre-dawn hours of June 19? If the journalists were not there, and because they missed the opening moments of the fighting on June 24, how did they intend to "capture" the battle for Baquba when they arrived on the scene so late? And even if they were able to capture a clear picture of these events, they would have little to no input into how the viewer would interpret these pictures.

Perhaps an added bonus to the embed program was that the soldiers and journalists got to interact and see the human side of their opposite. Spending time with the journalists before their departure, I realized that, for the most part, they were professionals who sought a moral goal. Joao Silva signed my copy of his book before he left, and indirectly embarrassed me one more time when I actually started reading it.

I read Joao's *The Bang-Bang Club: Images of a Hidden War* in the first three days of July, shortly after he departed. Not only was it an insightful glance into the past of the journalist I had taken the opportunity to get to know in the previous few days, it was also a fascinating war memoir. It was about his days as a photographer during the final bloody days of South African Apartheid, preceding the nation's first open elections. He and his colleagues, coauthors Greg Marinovich, Ken Oosterbroek, and Kevin Carter, earned the nickname "The Bang-Bang Club" because of their apparent lack of concern for their personal safety while covering the dangerous urban battles, and their amazing ability to always get the photo.

The Bang-Bang Club goes to great lengths to show the reader the moral conflict that war photographers face, not to mention the danger. Photographer Ken Oosterbroek was killed during a gun battle just days before the elections. Kevin Carter, who received a Pulitzer Prize for a photo he took of a vulture stalking an emaciated child in the Sudan, committed suicide. While Mr. Oosterbroek died because he braved the frontlines to tell a story that the world was not otherwise hearing, Carter seemed plagued by the moral dilemma they all faced: at what point do you stop taking photos, and start helping?

What distinguished Joao's book from Lloyd's *My War Gone By, I Miss it So* was that it was introspective and personal, but not self-centered. The authors openly tout their youthful machismo, ambitions, and recklessness, but they also present their principles. To the authors, getting the message out to the world was crucial, and they were not only dedicated to that principle, they were willing to die for it.

The contact with the photojournalists during this period, along with the deeply personal and autobiographical accompaniment of *The Bang-Bang Club,* forced me to have a deeper understanding of their role and ours on the battlefield. Even though they lacked the obvious trappings of the military, and they almost certainly had a different worldview than we, I slowly started to realize our commonalities. They dressed in jeans and T-shirts (though Andrea wore the traditional Muslim scarves while traveling); they were also equipped with protective vests and helmets.

Their ability to report the truth of a situation was their most powerful weapon. If at first I saw them as merely the passive to our aggressive, I eventually realized the active role they were taking. They served on the front in one of the most necessary functions of these times: the need for timely and accurate information. It was after reading his book that I realized the absurdity of my mothering approach to the journalists a few days before. Joao had seen more combat than I had by a huge margin, and he kept choosing assignments that continued to put him in imminent danger. Of course he wanted to "stand right fucking next" to me when the shooting started. Joao's book also helped me to realize the bigger picture, something that was lost on me previously when I was looking at Andrea's photos.

With the Transfer of Sovereignty complete and the journalists gone from Camp Gabe, things became routine again, at least with respect to operations. Very significant transitions were taking place within Task Force 1-6. For various reasons our battalion commander, Lt. Col. Steven Bullimore, decided to shake up the leadership structure in his battalion. Part of the decision was easily explained by normal officer timelines, but part of it was based on personality conflicts that had grown apparent.

Most important to us as platoon leaders in C Company, the decision was finally announced that we would be getting a new company commander. We were no less than thrilled. Capt. Douglas Chadwick was scheduled to take command of C Company on July 9. It was also announced that Capt. John Bushman would be taking over B Company in early August. The other platoon leaders and I could not help but appreciate this decision from higher command.

These changes were simply huge. Not only were B and C Companies not working together as a battalion team, but the individual platoon leaders within the companies were not working as a company team, either. It was not a matter of arrogance or pride among the platoon leaders, just survival. There were leadership vacuums at the head of each of the companies, and the platoons had to do whatever they could to survive, which basically meant looking inward for support instead of working as a team.

We all decided that Captain Bushman and Captain Chadwick would not be willing to continue in this way. In college, Bushman was a catcher for the Virginia Military Institute baseball team, while Chadwick was an offensive lineman for the Army football team. They were competitive, confident, and most importantly, competent. They cared about soldiers and proved it by getting to know their men on a personal level. They thought tactically, considered the big picture, and grasped better than most the nuances of the fight we were in. The lieutenants saw this, prior to either captain taking command. Although Captain Chadwick would not assume command until July 12, our excitement was palpable.

The situation in southern Baquba that Captain Chadwick inherited was back to what we had grown to appreciate as normal. Patrols left Camp Gabe several times per day, spoke with the local populace, looked for enemy contact, and generally assessed the mood of the city. We were all relieved that the Transfer of Sovereignty was complete, and we were coming to terms with what it meant for us. Multinational Forces began to execute Operation New Dawn, which stated that now that the Iraqis were nominally in control of both governance and security, we were to take more of an advisory role. We were to allow the recruited Iraqi Army to take more of the lead in fighting the insurgency, and push the Iraqi police to fight urban crime. Of course, the operation order did not go into great detail of how this was supposed to be accomplished; we were just expected to make it happen.

After hastily acquainting himself with his new sector, getting to know the important leaders of each city district, and getting to know his soldiers, Captain Chadwick started planning his first mission. Through intelligence received in one of his many initial meetings, he felt confident that he knew where some weapons caches were being stored. We could not believe it when he called us, his platoon leaders, into his office to discuss the plan, and were further overwhelmed by the fact that he was actually preparing a written order for us to disseminate to our platoons. Although these are basic procedures, none of them had been followed under the previous regime. After several days of planning, we were ready to execute Operation Southern Justice in southern Buhriz.

The operation plan called for a fairly routine search mission involving 1st, 2nd, and 4th Platoons of C Company. As per Operation New Dawn, a platoon of recently recruited Iraqi National Guard (ING) soldiers, who were actually from the town of Buhriz, would assist in the mission. The first part of the operation entailed Lt. T. J. Grider's Infantry platoon searching a six-house compound while 2nd Platoon and my platoon secured the two roads to the south of the compound. The ING soldiers would secure the main road leading north into Buhriz. The second phase of the operation, after T. J.'s platoon searched the compound, called for his and my platoons to search more than a square kilometer of palm groves for reported weapons caches. So long as we were not engaged by enemy fire, the palm grove clearance would end the operation. Aviation assets were allocated by the brigade headquarters to screen the dense palm groves around the objective to ensure local fighters were not trying to maneuver around us during the operation.

At 3:00 in the morning on July 25, C Company left Camp Gabe and began the operation. T. J.'s search of the homes in the compound yielded nothing, and we started sweeping the groves at approximately 5:30 in the morning. While some of my soldiers provided security, others used metal detectors to search for any of the deadly contraband. About an hour after we started the search, Pvt. Ismael Quiroz, in my platoon, found something underground. He found four 60-millimeter mortar tubes and related equipment buried nearly eight inches under the earth. Five minutes after our find, T. J.'s platoon reported finding various artillery and mortar rounds in their grove to the north. Over the course of the next hour, we found dozens of rocket-propelled grenade (RPG) warheads, mortar rounds, munitions fuses, and rocket propellants. It certainly was not an enormous amount of ammunition, but it did make the day's mission seem worthwhile.

My platoon continued searching the open grove while T. J.'s men cleared several vineyards to the south. Finding nothing of significance, I called off the sweep in my section of the grove and we started moving back north toward the vehicle staging area. Over the radio I heard that T. J.'s platoon was moving back towards their Bradley Fighting Vehicles. The operation seemed to be wrapping up, and we were surprised that several hours on the ground in Buhriz had not resulted in fighting. Perhaps the fighting during June had changed Buhriz for the better.

We were about 150 meters south of our vehicles when the metallic automatic fire of AK-47s started. Immediately, two Kiowa helicopters flew north into airspace over Buhriz in an attempt to locate targets for us. The small arms fire was not hitting anywhere near the squad with which I traveled, but we moved back to our vehicles as quickly as possible, expecting the situation would worsen.

By the time we linked up with our humvees on the road just south of Buhriz, I saw two of T. J.'s Bradleys speeding around the corner and heading directly for the town of Buhriz. Dr. Dre lyrics regarding "hitting the three-wheel motion" played through my head as the massive tracked vehicles straightened out and headed north. Over the radio I heard that they stopped near the Market Street bridge, probably the most wide open and vulnerable part of the urban battlefield of Buhriz, where T. J. and Greg had been attacked at the end of May. A minute after T. J.'s report, I received orders to bring two of my four humvees forward into southern Buhriz to provide security for the east and southeastern flanks of 4th Platoon, while the Bradleys engaged insurgents to the north and northwest.

Pulling behind T. J.'s position, I understood why we were asked to pull forward. With two Bradleys, T. J. could not cover anything behind his position; his rear area was wide open. I walked over to T. J.'s Bradley to see what was going on, which was common practice for us in these situations, but our conversation was cut short by the 25-millimeter cannon on his second Bradley. I returned to my vehicle and reported that T. J.'s two Bradleys were receiving fairly regular fire, but my squad, which was fifty meters south, had not yet been engaged. Captain Chadwick's assessment was that my other two vehicles should move into position behind me, just in case anyone decided to flank us.

The main guns of the pair of Bradleys pounded away at the structures from which the greatest enemy fire originated. The enemy did not stand a chance—they were shooting AK-47s out of windows at Bradleys. The brick and mortar cover meant very little once the infantrymen made visual contact with the enemy. Explosions of the rounds leaving their 25-millimeter tubes were deafening and often alarming, but more than a little gratifying for the Americans and ING. In my platoon's position fifty meters south of the Bradleys, we received several bursts of sporadic AK-47 fire, but it was otherwise quiet for us for the moment. The enemy fire was originating from the north, but T. J.'s Bradleys were blocking my platoon's fields of fire to directly engage the enemy ourselves.

Suddenly, I received a report on the radio that we were taking fire on our wide open eastern flank. It appeared that another group of insurgents were moving to join the other attackers to the north. The enemy utilized the alleyways perpendicular to Canal Street to shoot at us, a big, wide open target in the middle of the road. While I was still receiving the report from Sgt. Jason Brownlie, one of my team leaders, I heard our machine guns rocking and squad leaders barking. Wildly aimed RPG warheads flew over our heads, and each in turn received a violent response from 1st Platoon.

T. J. had already figured out that the fight was changing, and had oriented the turret of his own Bradley toward an alley and waited for the insurgents to cross on their way north. In a chain reaction, my platoon's machine guns fired every fifteen seconds or so as we received fire, and seconds later, T. J.'s 25-millimeter cannons fired down the alley. Every few minutes the commander would call in and ask for an update and TJ would report how many bodies he could see stacked up in the alley on the other end of his barrel. After the shooting stopped and the final report of thirteen enemy dead came over the radio, the situation calmed. Immediately after his final report, T. J.'s other Bradley commander followed up in agreement, "Thirteen enemy KIA . . . and one donkey."

For the next fifteen minutes or so, we anticipated more contact. None was to come. I rehashed with my driver how unbelievably disgusting is the sound of incoming RPG fire. Not only did our open position leave us vulnerable to all seven RPGs fired in our direction that day, but we also had plenty of time to see and hear them coming. It was a momentarily low and helpless feeling that was overcome only by how pathetically inaccurate the shooters often were. We sat in the middle of Buhriz waiting for more contact for the remainder of the morning, laughing about most of the morning's events. Two-and-a-half hours passed without event before we started to hear what we were to do next.

We learned that the battalion commander decided that we were to wait to be relieved by Iraqi police. Because stability in Buhriz was eventually going to be the problem of the local security forces, C Company should not leave Buhriz without handing the situation over to the Iraqi Police, allowing the budding law enforcement agency to present a show of force. However, we only had the power to request their presence in Buhriz, and they did not seem to want to participate. It took about ninety minutes for several pickup trucks loaded with policemen to trek the five kilometers between their station in Baquba and the market area in Buhriz where C Company soldiers were hunkered down and growing more frustrated with each minute. Grateful to finally complete our relief-in-place, we took our convoy home.

Returning to Camp Gabe, we discussed the morning's success and were pleased with the outcome of the mission. We had taken no casualties, had removed ammunition from the enemy's inventory—counting the ammunition we found and what they wasted trying to hit us—and raised the bar for future operations in Buhriz by incorporating both the ING and police assets. Maybe more important was that the soldiers got to see how their new commander reacted in combat. Captain Chadwick did not disappoint them under fire, and he positively gained their respect.

After the company debriefing, I went back to my room and checked my email. It was no more than three hours after the firefight ended, and I already received three alert messages from various news sources about the fight we had just experienced. I could not believe that the Buhriz story was running that quickly, but my surprise in the speed of the Internet seemed rather pedestrian when I saw some of the photos accompanying the stories.

Several photos from the articles could have been taken on any given day in Buhriz, but one in particular stood out as unique. The photo depicted two men dressed in black with black ski masks, standing on a street corner. One stood behind the other, who was kneeling. The one standing held an AK-47 across his chest, while the other man was poised to fire an RPG down the alley to their front. One of my soldiers remarked with expletives that those photographed were obviously posing for the camera, but I was not so sure. I could not tell from the photo which street corner they were on or who their target was, even after I expended considerable energy trying to figure it out. Some of my soldiers said they had seen the insurgents from the photo, but I had not seen anyone fitting the description that afternoon, though I did feel their effects. It was an eerie feeling to be so close to these guys, and to be behind them, an opportunity I would have cherished if it had been a couple hours earlier and a bit more tangible.

The strangeness of the moment turned to pure frustration as the surprising humanity of the photo wore off. Instead of focusing my attention on the RPG team, I became frustrated at the photographer who was standing there, photographing as my enemy took aim with a rocket at what was either my soldiers or T. J.'s. If they were any better at firing their RPGs, that photo could have been taken moments before someone I knew and worked with got killed.

Of course, two realizations gave me understanding and solace, respectively, shortly after my frustration eased. First, the reporter was affiliated with Al Jazeera, a Qatar-based news agency that demonstrated little or no support for the Multinational Forces' side of Operation Iraqi Freedom. Second, the two insurgents fit the description of thirteen other guys T. J. saw that afternoon.

As was always the case after a significant firefight, the city returned to normal, and we returned to our operational routine. In the beginning of August, Steve Mumford arrived at Camp Gabe for his second visit to Baquba. On June 24, he had been embedded with 2-63 Armor, one of our neighbor battalions in the area. Unlike Andrea and Joao, he spent most of that day sitting in the back of an armored vehicle being engaged by machine gun and RPG fire. He was also not a photographer like the other two, but still dealt with pictures. He was an artist and writer. He explained to me that his favorite artist was Winslow Homer, who was famous for painting scenes during and after the American Civil War, and it was Homer who had given him the idea to do the same in Iraq. Steve also wrote essays that accompanied his works, providing the necessary context to his interestingly subjective presentation of our reality, all of which would be published later in his book *Baghdad Journal.*

He gained remarkable access in Iraq. Apparently, as one of the few Americans who could legitimately deny association with the press, government contractors, or military, he was able to travel where others had burned their bridges. During the fighting of June 24, for instance, he was sitting in a tracked vehicle, handing up ammunition to a gunner at one moment, and trying to figure out if friendly or enemy firepower had destroyed a civilian vehicle that apparently refused to stop while approaching the unit's tanks in the next. His pictures captured with incredible accuracy scenes like this one and others far less intense. Some of the pictures were full of people, life, and landscape. Others, like the black ink drawing of the backs of three soldiers who were listening as another of their friends, Jason Lynch, was being memorialized, were minimalistic but still quite realistic.

Steve had a remarkable ability to represent reality on the page, although he admitted that he, as an artist, had a much greater capacity to "lie," given the obvious personal interpretation that went into his paintings. In a conversation with me, he noted that Goya's *The Disasters of War,* about the French invasion, was surrounded in a controversy regarding how much of the war Goya really saw. And Picasso's *Guernica* was painted from newspaper clippings. Obviously, Steve had a bit more license than even Andrea enjoyed.

Steve spent a fair amount of time with my platoon during training and one patrol, and he spent a lot of time talking with my soldiers. He gathered the context of the environment in order to better gauge the responses of the soldiers. His pictures told the stories of the soldiers, the local populace and of Iraq. His essays told the stories of the pictures. One of his essays, "The Trouble with Buritz," together with his drawings, told the story of what our company had faced in Buhriz, what the local populace saw of us, and how they reacted. That is, he was able to capture the confusion and frustration felt on both sides. He noted the quiet streets of the early morning patrol, and the way an Iraqi man flung himself into an alleyway as soon as he saw us coming. He told of the sarcastic harassment the soldiers gave me when I got lost on a dirt road a few hundred meters from our last firefight only a few weeks prior.

A few days later, Steve set out on another patrol with me, this time to the district of Tahrir. No one told us before we left that the Iraqi Soccer team was playing Morocco in the Olympics during our patrol. As we left the gate, I monitored radio traffic from the capitol building, noting a higher volume of "celebratory fire" than usual, but no one could define the reason. "It's probably a wedding party," one response suggested, parroting the normal justification for civilians shooting AK-47s into the air. I saw tracer fire streaking the sky as we turned south into Tahrir, but it was pointed directly up—celebratory fire. Steve, sitting behind me in the lead humvee noted that there were a lot of people on the streets, too. As we rounded a corner leading to a wide-open field, Tahir erupted with tracer fire. The red bullets streaked up in every direction so much that it almost felt like we were in a bowl in the middle of the city.

Steve and I got out of my vehicle to talk to a small group of the thousands of Iraqis who were out on the street that night. The oldest male of the group spoke fair English and told us that Iraq had just tied with Morocco. "Sounds like reason enough to shoot your AK to me," I said to Steve, and we walked back toward the vehicles in my convoy. Positioned in the small open field in the middle of the suburb, it seemed like we were in the eye of the storm. It was calm and quiet immediately around us, but explosive and violent just outside our reach. Sergeant Gaines laughed when I approached him. "I can't wait to hear this," he said before I explained the reason for fire. He laughed and said, "Well, those bullets have to come down, and if they spook one of our gunners, there might be a lot of dead Iraqis." I knew he was right.

The humvee rooftop gunners were used to taking fire by this point, and used to responding by shooting people who were carrying AK-47s. If an errant bullet fell out of the sky and hit or impacted near one of my guys, it would have been a revolting mess. The probability of finding insurgents among the good-natured crowds milling around Tahrir seemed miniscule. I canceled the remainder of the patrol and took the platoon and Steve back to our camp. I wondered what he would write about us. Were we too scared to finish a patrol? Is that why we quit? Or were we wise in his mind for rescuing ourselves from a lose/lose situation? In all actuality, he never wrote or drew about the event.

By the end of August, the city had calmed, and we seemed to be alone again. I was able to keep in touch with Steve and Andrea for several months following their departure. I was surprised at how openly we could discuss our opinions and views, and regretted not discussing these matters more openly when they were in Baquba.

I posed my discomfort with her pictures to Andrea in an email. I wondered if she thought that the pictures that had angered me so much in late June were accurate depictions of what she had seen. She assured me, almost apologetically, that the pictures that frustrated me were not sent into the *Washington Post* because they did not represent the reality of the scene. She noted that she was lucky to have this leeway with her paper, and it was not a luxury that all photojournalists enjoyed.

Although she stood behind her decision not to submit the pictures based on their actual context, she did ask me to consider the pictures from an Iraqi's perspective. "Even when polite," she wrote, "you are strangers entering homes uninvited and invading the private space of mostly innocent people . . . could you imagine what our family members would do, how they would react, if it happened to them here in the U.S.? I have been on probably about 100 raids, with all different forms of U.S. military, and I stand by my decision not to send that photo because I think it exaggerates the situation. But, to many, the photo still shows reality." Of course, she was right. The photos did show a reality, even if it was not one that I was willing to agree was definitive.

On November 14, 2004, a piece by Andrea ran in the *Washington Post* under the title "Boots on the Ground." The preface to the article read, "For some Americans, the violence and chaos in Iraq has receded to a kind of grim background noise, distant and impersonal. Woodall set out to dispel that creeping indifference by getting up-close and specific. Here, through her camera lens and her personal journal, is Iraq as it's seen from the bulletproof window of a Humvee." Part of her journal entry covered her time spent with Task Force 1-6 in Baquba, while other sections focused on her time in Baghdad with the 1st Cavalry Division.

The photos and journal entries included in the text paint a relevant picture for the reader. In fact, she writes almost exclusively about what she sees and seldom about what she feels. She notes the confusion of soldiers who are not quite sure which house to raid, and the confusion of the homeowner whose house is being raided. She describes the scene of the aftermath of a car bomb in Baghdad, and a police officer who insists on picking up the scattered pieces of human flesh and putting them into a

Third Platoon escorts Iraq's Deputy Prime Minister, the Minister of Interior and several journalists to the site of a VBIED explosion at Baquba's most congested intersection. On July 28, 2004, sixty-eight Iraqis lost their lives in the single attack, including more than two dozen men standing in line to apply for their city's police force. (Gregory Tomlin Collection)

bag. She reflects personally on the scene of an improvised explosive device hitting a B Company convoy. And she covers the pain, frustration, and the camaraderie of the soldiers in C Company as we paid our final respects to Pvt. First Class Jason Lynch. Although nearly stream-of-consciousness at times, it offered excellent context for the photos she took in Baquba, even the ones she never submitted to her editor.

chapter 11
REVISIONISTAS: AN INTERLUDE
Lt. Greg Tomlin, 3rd Platoon Leader, C Company

During our time in Iraq, there were occasions when what people might have remembered individually, based on their own perspectives, did not reflect the decided reality of the consensus. Most of these personal historical inaccuracies were honest, brought on by the confusion of the fight or the time passed between the actual events and the rehashing. On other occasions, they were obviously an attempt to rewrite history in a more glamorous light, including details so far-fetched that they had to have been added by the unchecked imagination.

For instance, after the June 12 palm grove search near Buhriz involving 2nd and 4th Platoons of C Company, one particular leader seemed to have a considerably different account of the chain of events from the other participants. Within the first hour of returning to Camp Gabe from the mission, this leader touted to everyone within earshot his own heroic perspective of how the mission unfolded. His remarks suggested that he had safely led a company in and out of a firefight while destroying numerous weapons caches and orchestrating a counterattack that resulted in numerous enemy deaths. His unscrupulously self-serving account probably would have gone further if he truly believed he could have gotten away with it.

Those on the ground that morning remember it all a little differently. This leader left behind his personal radio, which would have allowed him to both command and control the fight from nearly anywhere on the battlefield. Those who were there remember him sprinting up the hill at the sound of the first gunshot to seek the protection of his humvee. Despite this behavior, Lt. T. J. Grider disregarded an order to break contact with the enemy and flee the palm grove. Instead, T. J. organized a base of fire, and the infantrymen of 4th Platoon courageously destroyed a sizable enemy cache and at least ten enemy personnel.

The disparity between the reality of the event and what this leader imagined was quite incredible, but understandable. His version of reality, one that most officers later agreed that he no doubt fully believed, was probably merely a defensive mechanism. It had become a pattern of his to detrimentally botch complicated situations. In retrospect, he sought to convince others how he had actually been the lynchpin that held the mission together. This approach was quite common and pathetic, but it afforded those who listened to his tales an incredible pleasure in comparing his reality to what they all knew really happened on the ground.

Sometimes the way in which the local populace perceived our operations in their community suggested that we were indeed an invincible force. In April, after 4th Platoon performed incredible feats in Buhriz, C Battery learned of developing local rumors. Some townspeople believed that the Americans fighting during that week, a platoon of infantrymen, were actually a highly trained counterterrorism unit that was a part of the U.S. Army Special Forces.

We heard rumors that the number in our task force was well over 5,000 soldiers, even though the actual number made such a figure absolutely laughable. Lt. Chris Lacour, the 2nd Platoon leader, learned from a shopkeeper that he and his soldiers were members of a specially trained, "anti-Muslim" Israeli sniper unit attached to the Baquba task force. Still others reported that the famous 1st Infantry Division "Big Red One" patch worn by all men of Task Force 1-6 on their shoulders was remarkably similar to the unit patch worn by an elite Israeli Regiment, thus closing the conspiratorial loop.

While humorous, several rumors exacerbated the disdain some locals already harbored for U.S. troops occupying their city and fueled the insurgents' propaganda. For the last two weeks of April, my platoon provided force protection at the Blue Dome, the provincial capitol building. During our stay, a local resident visited the receptionist's desk, asking to speak with an American officer. As the only commissioned officer living in the compound, I met with this gentleman.

The visitor explained that on April 9, a sniper on the roof of the Blue Dome shot his brother to death while he stood on the roof of his home in Tahrir (about 600 meters south of the capitol building). I explained that during the fighting in mid-April, anyone observed behaving suspiciously on a rooftop was a legitimate military target, because many of the rocket-propelled grenades (RPG) launched towards the government buildings and down at American patrols originated from rooftops in Tahrir. The man sadly described that his brother was mentally retarded and suffered from chronic muscle spasms. To protect both his brother and the inside of his house, the family took the man to the roof where he could freely jump, flail, and shout.

While the scene of a grown man acting wildly on a rooftop obviously attracted a sniper to shoot him, I knew that this explanation would not comfort the victim's living brother. The man did not insist on speaking with an American to seek reparations for the death. Rather, he asked that the United States Army remove the Kurdish snipers from the roof of the Blue Dome. I knew that neither my unit nor the Iraqi National Guard (ING) employed Kurdish snipers. However, the visitor insisted that we did, and he explained how everyone in Tahrir knew that the Kurdish snipers manning the capitol competed with one another to kill as many Shi'ia and Sunnis as possible during April's fighting. For a city comprised largely of Shi'ias, with a sizable Sunni minority, such a rumor could hinder the governor's efforts to build a multicultural society. Further, it hindered the endeavors of the ING to recruit a multiethnic force.

Rumors, particularly those surrounding the underhanded workings of Jews, resonated throughout Iraq. Nir Rosen, a freelance journalist writing for *Reason* magazine in March, 2004, described the reaction to the rumored Judeo-Christian conspiracy in Baghdad as a frothing, frenzied paranoia fueled by baseless lies about massive land purchases by the Jews. In turn, this would lead to Jewish custodianship of the Muslim country, an onslaught of factory purchases by Jews, and even the surreptitious sale of Jewish home appliances disguised as appliances made in China.[1]

As fundamentalism often goes, the ultra-conservatives in Iraq believed these rumors without question, as they were supported by seemingly anti-Semitic verses from the Qu'ran. But the fact remained that the masses were willing to believe even the strangest theories set out by the civil and spiritual authorities in their country: a problem, Rosan points out, that will definitely inhibit the progress of democracy in the country.

Along with this anti-Semitism, a persistent nationalism also influenced the rumors we gathered from the locals. Every time we talked to local citizens regarding violence in their community, their responses would always be the same. It was such a common response that it became a joke between all of us: The people of Buhriz are very peaceful. The insurgents are obviously not people of Buhriz. The terrorists came from outside of Iraq. The foreigners were the ones who buried the RPGs in the yards of the locals and planted the nightly artillery-round surprises on roadsides for U.S. convoys and hapless locals. No Iraqi could ever do anything like this, especially if it meant killing their fellow Muslims. At best it was absurd.

The Americans deployed to Baquba knew that the insurgency stemmed from outside the city, sometimes from Saudi Arabia, Jordan, Syria, or Iran, and sometimes from other Iraqi hotspots such as Falluja or Baghdad. But it was not an organized insurgency that was hitting each U.S. patrol in the city. Insurgents tended to organize a coordinated and massive assault about once a month or so from April through November.

On a more regular basis, however, it was definitely a local organization that was planting the daily improvised explosive devices (IED) all over town. And Buhriz was so corrupt from top to bottom that even the non-insurgents were likely to be criminals. On the day prior to major attacks in Baquba on June 24, reliable informants purported that, incredibly, Mayor Auf of Buhriz publicly prayed with insurgents in a Buhriz mosque. But the locals crowed their innocence. For the entire year that Task Force 1-6 was there, soldiers cracked a smile every time they heard that all of the bad guys were obviously foreigners, as Iraqis are so obviously incapable of cruelty to their own people or anyone else.

The lack of substantial filters that can verify information before it is produced for a wider audience will inevitably dull the edge of reality as it springs from so many disparate sources. Often, such individual accounts of reality were frustrating, but had no real lasting effect on the mission. Other times, when we heard accounts of the rumors the locals were inclined to believe, they actually did present a considerable hindrance on our ability to complete our mission of improving the security and quality of life for the people of Iraq. It became clear to both sides of the battle, the U.S. soldiers and the insurgency, that the side that maintained the power of information would achieve their successes in a timelier manner.

In a place where reality slapped you in the face at least once a day, the challenge became being the first to perceive a reality that worked for you. For the U.S. Army, Information Operations (IO) serves as the primary method for shaping verbal and symbolic messages used to influence the enemy and host-nation populations. Having served as the IO officer for Task Force 2-63 Armor during a nine-month deployment with the Kosovo Force (KFOR) between 2002 and 2003, I considered no other facet of military operations more crucial than IO for our success in Iraq.

In *Information Operations*, a post-September 11 textbook intended to illuminate the importance of incorporating information as a critical instrument in waging a new kind of war, the editor articulates that, "The most important concept to remember about information is that it is not a weapon per se; it is a process, a way of thinking about relationships. *It is about perception,* because information is an enabler" (italics added).[2]

For two months prior to deploying to the Vitina Municipality of Kosovo, I searched for IO material and studied to absorb what sparse doctrine I could find. Nowhere in my basic officer schooling did I gain an introduction into IO. Even during my stint as a faculty assistant at the Army War College, I had never heard of IO. Deciding to visit the IO directorate at the U.S. Army European headquarters in Heidelberg, Germany, I received a collection of manuals related to the subject. The IO officers were surprised that a lieutenant would visit their office, because few people outside of division and corps planning cells knew what IO was, let alone seriously talked about it.

According to *Field Manual 3-0,* the Army defines IO as "actions taken to affect adversaries' and influence others' decision making processes, information, and information systems, while protecting one's own information and information systems."[3] A dozen elements contribute to creating IO, but the most pertinent to battalion-level operations are Civil Affairs, Psychological Operations, Public Affairs, Military Deception, Operations Security, and at times, Physical Destruction.

Most of the elements of IO are not new to the Army, but it was only in the late nineties that the Army combined them under the all-encompassing title of IO in an effort to make Army planners examine the unique value of the unfamiliar assets. For combat arms officers (infantrymen, artillerymen, and tankers), IO elements can easily seem intimidating; many of the components do not fit within the conventional selection of weaponry utilized to destroy, neutralize, and suppress enemy forces.

Even more daunting for combat arms officers is how to design an effective IO campaign persuading a foreign populace to accept certain, occasionally revolutionary, beliefs. Defining, for example, a task and purpose for a Civil Affairs team to placate Kosovar-Albanians opposed to the return of Kosovar-Serb refugees is not as simple as requesting an artillery smoke mission to screen friendly troop movement. To be successful in IO, staff officers have to grasp a new assortment of tasks: deceive, influence, inform, and preserve are just a few. Based on available writings in the fall of 2002, the Army had done a good job of creating doctrine useful for division and corps planners where IO incorporated highly advanced computer and satellite technology. Where the doctrine fell short, however, was in providing detailed manuals tailored for battalions and brigades, that is, to the units and soldiers responsible for intimately interacting with a local populace on a daily basis.

Despite the earnest efforts of many doctrine writers and thoughtful officers penning articles from the Balkans and Afghanistan, few sources existed in 2002 that provided coherent instruction on the application of IO for the units that carry out the most fundamental and immediately influential forms of IO. If a battalion does not have an innovative IO officer, the commander might discount utilizing IO if he was unaware of its value. The commander might also misuse an asset, such as a Psychological Operations team, because of a lack of understanding that element's ability to serve as a combat (or peacekeeping) multiplier.

Ignorance, however, in a stability or support operation such as the NATO mission in Kosovo does not serve the mission or the people of a war-torn region justice. Such a tendency in commanders to rely on combat power, a doctrinal tool that they no doubt understand better than the amorphous and immature doctrine of IO, is understandable in an environment where the military battle is ongoing. Yet not understanding the importance of complementing combat power with relevant information will only make the war harder to decisively win. This remains especially true in Iraq today.

The more I worked to decipher the material I received in Heidelberg, the more determined I became to sell IO to the members of Task Force 2-63 during our deployment in Kosovo. Working closely with the operational planners and intelligence officers in the battalion, we developed a methodology for incorporating IO with maneuver missions and intelligence collection efforts in Kosovo. This required maintaining a constant dialogue with my fellow staff officers as well as with the leadership in each of the companies. Messages, or talking points, needed to be scripted for targeting specific audiences. A generic message parroted to everyone — Albanians and Serbs, farmers and lawyers — would not be as persuasive as separate ones designed to directly appeal to personal interests.

The weekly information papers insured that each patrol leader, prior to departing the base camp gate for any mission, was armed with talking points to deliver and questions to ask. For example, a common theme spoken throughout the KFOR deployment encouraged citizens to respect the rule of law, which many ignored during and just after the war in Kosovo, when towns were rife with looting, arson, and ethnic intimidation. While on patrol, a squad leader telling a mother of seven to respect the rule of law would most likely receive a blank stare. If the squad leader encouraged the same woman to ensure that her children did not skip school, so they would gain the education affording them the opportunity to enjoy a brighter future, the mother might be more inclined to care about whether her children attended classes and how they spent their time after school.

Task force officers involved in other local activities also received messages about the rule of law, which they could use to frame their discussions. Between country and pop songs, a company commander attending an Albanian-language radio show would explain that international businesses have little desire to invest or build factories in Kosovo until the security situation improves, which requires the youth to take responsibility for their actions. During his attendance in the municipality's Minority Leaders Meeting (comprised of Kosovar-Serb, Croatian, and Roma leaders), the battalion executive officer would remind participants that certain minority members of the community were no less guilty than the Kosovar-Albanian majority in exacerbating tension between the two ethnicities. After all, peace and stability required a good-faith effort on the part of all parties.

During my weekly IO meeting at the headquarters of Multinational Brigade (East), I reviewed the general response from locals to the messages produced by KFOR. Together with colleagues from four other task forces and the brigade staff, we discussed how best to refine messages for the following week. In the unique setting of the headquarters conference room, I spent two to three hours each week discussing IO with officers from a U.S. infantry task force, as well as men from Greek, Polish, Ukranian, and Russian units. I noticed that the majority of the task forces did not work as deliberately to incorporate IO into maneuver and intelligence efforts as Task Force 2-63. This meant that their IO campaign was designed more or less in a vacuum, with little involvement from commanders or other staff sections. IO for these units became one of a campaign of platitudes, where soldiers recited messages to Albanians and Serbs without asking follow-up questions or attempting to qualify the effectiveness of the messages.

Constructing a well-synchronized IO plan requires constant assessments, refining and rewriting messages to provide soldiers with a realistic approach for engaging the local populace on a daily basis. The Civil Affairs and Psychological Operations teams operating within the Task Force 2-63 sector had the ability to share a common message, but only if they were directly involved in the task force IO meetings. These unique teams offered special talents and assets to the armor task force. As a reservist unit, the members of the Civil Affairs team arrived in the Balkans from professions in civilian business, teaching, and city planning. The Psychological Operations team had the ability to mass produce handbills and fliers, and one of their humvees carried a large speaker with the ability to broadcast voice messages farther than a kilometer.

Technically, these teams worked directly for the brigade headquarters. However, through an open dialogue and willingness to understand each other's missions, it became possible for the special teams to act as enablers of the task force IO campaign. The two Civil Affairs teams that operated in Kosovo with our task force truly understood the importance of synchronizing efforts in the small Kosovar municipality. Civil Affairs Maj. Michael Mosquera and Maj. Michael Hoss spoke with local businessmen and government employees weekly about developing projects, and task force messages were often incorporated into their dialogues. The Psychological Operations team regularly visited the markets in two of the most populated towns in the municipality, disseminating colorful newsletters to shoppers that also related to the task force focus of the month or week. In the Vitina Municipality, the success of the Americans' ability to speak with a single coherent voice led the UN administrator and his staff to ask me if I could articulate messages for the UN as well.

Observing firsthand that shaping public opinion and morale were vital to the peacekeeping efforts in Kosovo, I was convinced that IO would need to play a similar role in Operation Iraqi Freedom (OIF) II. I shared many of my thoughts with Caleb shortly after arriving in Bamberg, Germany. During the month-long training exercise in Hohenfels, Germany, I touched on the application of IO during nearly every event. From using interpreters and talking to the press, to respecting women and waving to children, IO fit into each tactical scenario that the platoon role-played.

While no longer responsible for formulating the messages for an entire task force, I realized that a single platoon, even a single soldier, could potentially sway public opinion in a foreign land. Local inhabitants and observers, some ambivalent and others cunning, very carefully watch the actions and listen to the words of men donning khaki uniforms with the U.S. flag. With the tremendous firepower carried by soldiers in Iraq, and the likelihood of discharging those weapons while patrolling, symbolic IO often rivals verbal messages as the most persuasive method for influencing the populace concerning the intentions of the Multinational Forces.

IO does not only affect the citizens of a modest village in the developing world, but potentially, people around the world, thanks to modern media. In an age where technological advances allowed a digital photographer to capture the image of an RPG team preparing to strike T. J.'s soldiers in Buhriz and to send the photo across the world via the Internet minutes later, international perceptions about the war in Iraq can be quickly swayed by anonymous observers. The actions and words of a common soldier may rival the delicately scripted press statement of a head of state in shaping public opinion about a war.

While the training that the 3rd Brigade Combat Team underwent prior to its arrival in the Diyala Province introduced soldiers to the necessity of engaging an Arab populace differently than a Western one, more study and practical application would be required by the staffs and companies of the task forces if a robust IO campaign were to come to fruition in OIF II. If commanders did not make IO a priority, then IO would not be a priority for their subordinates either. By establishing IO as a key task for mission success, the commander ensures that IO becomes an *integrated* factor during all steps of the planning process and mission execution. Further, company commanders understand that face-to-face engagements and talking points cannot be summarily ignored. Company commanders who express an interest in using IO products ensure that the soldiers responsible for conducting the daily patrols deliver a common message.

Unfortunately, the brigade and its task forces did not invest as heavily in their IO analysis or planning during OIF II as they did in Kosovo. In part, this must have been attributed to the urban combat, which distracted the commanders' focus away from facets on the periphery of gaining sound intelligence, monitoring patrols, and leading tactical operations. During Operation Joint Guardian in Kosovo, many of the same officers responsible for planning in western Diyala formerly worked to incorporate Civil Affairs, Psychological Operations, and Public Affairs assets into task force operations.

Just as important, most junior Army leaders could recite talking points through interpreters to common Kosovars. Such was not the case in Iraq. As platoon leaders, neither Caleb nor I ever received a single battalion-level information paper or list of talking points. Always on edge during patrols where an IED or RPG might explode at any moment, few platoon leaders even cared if they contributed to the IO campaign by influencing or informing the populace with a common message.

What made IO successful in Kosovo was a deliberate effort made to adapt Army doctrine into a fashion that did not seem to intimidate leaders, from the squad to task force level. IO, like a new car or home, had to appear accessible to potential buyers. By constantly seeking the opinions of leaders at the company level, and from frequent discussions with Civil Affairs and Psychological Operations soldiers, I continuously updated and revised products. By tailoring talking points for each sphere of locals engaged by military leaders at different levels, by adjusting font and document sizes to fit papers nonchalantly inside officers' notebooks, leaders utilized the words written uniquely for them to influence a factional Albanian and Serbian populace.

As a platoon leader, I noticed as early as during the Hohenfels training exercise in November, 2003 that 3rd Brigade seemed to have forgotten the valuable IO education gained from our time in the Balkans. Perhaps because commanders emphasized the importance of combat readiness against hostile threats in Iraq, the staffs marginalized the value of good IO planning and products for Task Force 1-6. Civil Affairs and Psychological Operations teams often conducted missions that neither complemented the efforts of the task forces nor maximized their special talents. IO did not have to play a role as prominent as it did in Kosovo, but in Iraq it still needed to remain an important function in military operations.

One morning in Baquba, my platoon escorted the Psychological Operations team attached to Task Force 1-6 to the Diyala Ministry of Education offices downtown. One of our humvees towed a trailer teeming with soccer balls and jerseys. While 3rd Platoon provided perimeter security, the Psychological Operations sergeant met with the director of athletics to donate the hundreds of shirts and balls that would allow dozens of youth soccer teams to begin playing in a matter of months. As soccer is an extremely popular sport in Iraq, the goodwill gesture was quite appropriate.

The next step in advancing the IO campaign should have been for every platoon leader to tout his excitement about upcoming soccer games while conversing with local parents on patrols. Questions about whether a son plans to play on a school soccer team begs questions regarding whether parents know what their children—including older children—are doing in the afternoons and at night. Are they practicing soccer, pouting about the inability to find permanent jobs, or attending mujahadeen meetings? Without talking points from the IO officer and linked questions from the task force intelligence officer, few lieutenants took the initiative to share similar good news stories that would make it more natural to elicit information that might identify the whereabouts of insurgent cells.

An even more lucrative opportunity not capitalized in the IO realm occurred in mid-May, 2004. My platoon received the task to establish security for a ground breaking ceremony in Tahrir. Participants in the ceremony included the Diyala governor, the Coalition Provisional Authority representative for the province, the 3rd Brigade commander, and the mayor of Baquba. Various news agencies and tribes were also represented at the ground breaking.

While I knew that the event marked the beginning of the resurfacing of a major road network in the lower Baquba district, I learned nothing else about the activity when receiving the orders a couple days prior to the event. On the day of the ceremony, 3rd Platoon closed three roads to vehicular traffic, rerouted traffic at a bridge crossing a canal, and established a rooftop observation post on an apartment building. Shortly thereafter, the personal security teams for the four notable participants arrived to provide security around the immediate vicinity of the ceremony.

Following the ground breaking, Col. Dana Pittard, the brigade commander, shared with me that the Coalition Provisional Authority recently presented half a billion dollars to the Diyala province for infrastructure improvements. The Tahrir road project marked the first of many more endeavors, which the provincial government would autonomously identify, prioritize, and initiate. Prior to returning to his humvee, Colonel Pittard told me, "If Kosovo was college for you, this [Iraq] is your graduate work."

By delivering these words of encouragement, the commander implied that it was my responsibility as a platoon leader to continue to inform and influence the people of Baquba. However, there was also a deeper meaning to what he meant. The situation in Iraq, particularly accentuated in the spring of 2004, often flipped between combat operations and stability operations. An officer could not allow his men to take a myopic view of their mission, seeing patrols as entirely combat patrols or presence patrols. Members of a platoon needed to quickly make the transition between being warriors and peacemakers, even though most were more comfortable being warriors all the time.

Again, this valuable nugget of information about the project funding was gleaned only because of my attendance at the Tahrir groundbreaking ceremony. For more than a month following the ceremony, I continued to discuss the available funds while talking to locals during dismounted patrols through southern Baquba.

Invariably, shopkeepers and homeowners complained about unreliable electricity, impure water, and nonexistent sewage systems. I explained that their provincial government maintained a $500 million engineering budget. I encouraged people to speak with their muqtars (informal mayors of small villages or city districts) and mayors about petitioning the Provincial Council for a portion of the funds for their dilapidated community. After all, a representative government requires a citizenry willing to publicly advocate their convictions.

I also encouraged the locals whom I encountered to report all suspicious activity to visiting American and Iraqi security patrols, or to make an anonymous call to the police station. If the people wanted to continue to believe that everyone who shot at Americans were not locals, then the residents needed to at least notify Coalition Forces or the local police of any stranger who entered their community. Any town or district that refused to tolerate insurgent and criminal activity deserved infrastructure improvements ahead of those communities that harbored terrorists and pretended that their districts were entirely peaceful. The Diyala government would delineate between violent areas and those with a populace supporting the rule of law.

Many Baquba residents assured me through my interpreter that they would do their best to keep their communities safe for civilians and security officials, especially if that meant that their district would become a priority for roads, water, and sewage improvements. I honestly thanked them for their bravery in seeking to improve the future of Iraq by routing out insurgents and criminals. I also sternly warned them that 3rd Platoon would not hesitate to cause significant damage to their homes, shops and public buildings if insurgents were allowed to take refuge inside these buildings. However, because that was not what the Coalition Forces came to Iraq to do, the cooperation of the people would be essential for building a safer and more stable Iraq.

Upon leaving my platoon in October to work at the Diyala Provincial Police Headquarters, I sought to improve the public voice of the provincial government and Iraqi security forces. Preparing talking points for police patrols would be too advanced at that time. However, immediate press releases following insurgent attacks against civilians, public servants, and U.S. soldiers could possibly send a persuasive message to the people of Diyala about the cause of thunderous explosions before the enemy could generate rumors placing blame on callous U.S. forces. While the governor's office had a public relations directorate, official press statements to

provincial radio and television stations and to newspaper publishers normally arrived well after the fact. This proved especially true when the
enemy acted over a weekend or public holiday.

On November 30, three errant mortar rounds detonated in the Mufrek suburb, killing two children and severely wounding five. With a bit of
prodding from U.S. officers, the provincial police chief decided it would
be best to make an immediate press statement. I prepared the text for the
message. Because the mortars originated in a densely populated neighborhood of Mufrek, I capitalized on the fact that at least a handful of residents
must have observed the group of insurgents responsible for setting up the
mortar tube and launching three mortars prior to fleeing the scene. Without leaving the security of his or her own home, and while assuring his or
her anonymity, any one of the witnesses could have reported the enemy
activity by phoning the police headquarters. Because the people of Mufrek
turned a blind eye to the scene, two children died and five others received
traumatic injuries. The benign ignorance of the witnesses prevented the
murderers from being brought to justice.

By immediately working to set the story straight, the police chief
snubbed the enemy's opportunity to misinform the media that Americans
shot artillery into Mufrek with total disregard for pious Muslim civilians.
While no one called into the police headquarters to provide details about
those responsible for the attack, the retelling of the tragic story on the
radio could influence some Iraqis to report suspicious activity quickly to
security forces in the future. Upon reading the statement, the police chief
liked the idea of making press statements expediently after incidents occurred.

Capitalizing on tragedies involving civilians was not a necessarily
sinister ploy threaded into a diabolical IO campaign. It was just good public
relations to show how the insurgency was targeting the innocent, and to
accurately depict the efforts of U.S. and Iraqi Security Forces in frustrating
the terrorists' plans. These messages, along with civil projects designed to
bolster the lacking infrastructure, helped to persuade the locals that Americans were there to provide a safer and more secure environment. That is,
to win their hearts and minds, as the Vietnam-era slogan goes.

Without using its doctrinal definitions, the insurgency developed an
IO campaign of their own, which, unfortunately for Coalition Forces and
the new Iraqi government, proved highly effective. And of course it was:
They knew their own culture better; they could more easily place their

operatives undetected in key locations; and they had an overall mistrust for all things Western on their side. They were sometimes able to use these advantages to rewrite history.

Informants shared with platoon leaders and commanders in Task Force 1-6 that the locals in Baquba were being told by enemy propagandists — and some even believed — that the daily and nightly routine of roadside bomb explosions was actually artillery fire from the howitzers in the U.S. base camp just outside of the city. They were told that the Coalition Forces controlled the power supply for the city, and were regularly turning off the power in order to harass the locals. (The truth of the matter was that the Coalition could direct the Ministry of Electricity to turn off the power, but only during a handful of night counterinsurgency operations did the military direct a power outage for entire neighborhoods.) Residents were even told that the invading U.S. forces at the beginning of the war purposely left enormous caches of weapons unsecured on the former regime's military bases in order to ensure that the Americans would later be attacked, thus justifying the violent response by U.S. soldiers.

In early August 2004, C Company fell victim to a more personal example of the enemy ability to manipulate the truth. After a successful mission and subsequent firefight in Buhriz on July 25, Capt. Douglas Chadwick, C Company's brand new commander, went back into the village with a patrol of Iraqi police. While conducting a dismounted patrol of the market area in the village, the police tore down a handbill that had been pasted to a light post, presumably by the insurgency.

The note, a photocopied half sheet, claimed yet another great military victory for the people of Buhriz. It listed the U.S. losses from the 25th as two humvees, one armored fighting vehicle, one personnel carrier, eight U.S. soldiers, and several wounded. All of this was reportedly accomplished by two courageous local civilians, and not members of a foreign insurgency. In reality, C Company did not sustain a single casualty or even a marginally damaged piece of equipment. This flier, and the stories found on many just like it, could often have a lasting effect on the hearts and minds of the locals, and sometimes proved difficult to counter.

Similarly absurd stories started trickling back to Baquba from the United States, again showing the speed at which information can travel, and even more importantly, the speed at which the facts changed from one person to the next. The stories frequently involved T. J., as he and his platoon had reached considerable notoriety, especially during the months of June and July, for being the most lethal platoon in the 1st Infantry Division.

Stories ran in major newspapers and on National Public Radio that were later carried again in smaller and more local newspapers. People in T. J.'s hometown outside of Chicago read numerous tales of the all-state high school wrestler who went on to West Point, and later led troops in combat in Iraq. His former high school dedicated a baseball game to the Punishers of 4th Platoon, while one principal from his district photocopied a newspaper story about T. J. and his platoon and mailed it to every other principal in the district. More than a legend, he was becoming a bit of a local celebrity, which in a suburb of a city like Chicago is no easy task. His celebrity status was understandable, given the truly heroic accomplishments of his platoon, but after one heard some of the stories that had been cooked up, it became inevitable.

T. J.'s dad, a respected high school football coach at a school near his hometown, was the source for T. J. to learn about most of the incredible stories that started filtering in as his father overheard people talk in amazement about his son. By the time T. J. heard them, the stories had already been passed through several people and had mutated considerably. Interestingly, the stories sustained an incredible degree of accuracy at some points. The names of the locations were often correct, and the dates of the large stories also tended to coincide with periods when T. J. had been involved in actual firefights.

But other than dates and places, reality tended to be poorly represented in these stories. One example was set during the time T. J. and his platoon were in Buhriz during a firefight. Supposedly, a man approached from a distance yelling in English, an amazing detail, and held his hands in the air. As the man approached, T. J. ordered his men not to fire on the civilian, as he was not displaying the necessary hostile intent. As the man got closer and closer to the line of soldiers, T. J. continued to escalate his tone and level of seriousness in his voice in an attempt to get the man to stop where he was. T. J. fired a warning shot into the air, but the man kept walking toward him and his troops. Not knowing what to do, but certain that he could not let the man get any closer, T. J. shot the man in the chest, exploding the hidden vest of a suicide bomber at just the right distance from his soldiers to prevent any friendly injuries. It appears that his instincts were razor sharp that day.

In another story from Buhriz, possibly even during the same day,

T. J. apparently further exhibited his heroic instincts, but this time with a little panache. The scene was similar to the previous story. A man was said to be approaching T. J.'s position from a distance, but this time he was carrying an AK-47 over his head. Again he was speaking English. This time, he was yelling out praises for the Jihad, and as he got closer, T. J. and his men could hear his professions of faith more clearly. As he got even closer, his chant changed, and apparently the Muslim man "wanted to be a martyr" for Allah. Because he was carrying an AK-47 and not heeding the demands for him to stop, T. J. in his typical sardonic tone, turned to his men and smirked, "All right, let's make him a martyr." The platoon opened fire with every weapon available, sustaining their fire until the man's soul was probably safe at home with Allah.

Of course, these stories are more than mere distortions of the truth; they do not even approximate actual events during any firefight that developed. In fact, they are so similar in detail that it is possible that they actually started as the same story, generating fresh and unique details as they made their way through different circles, and wound up getting back to T. J.'s father as two distinct stories.

The media, the only real non-military record of the war that future historians might use to reconstruct its actual events, also played several interesting roles in reporting events in various forms of factuality. News stories never seemed to demonstrate a malicious disregard for the truth, and quite often, stories provided very factual accounts. But there were countless times when the print or televised media simply got the story wrong.

The stories were at their best when they were covering a "human interest" piece, like so many of the ones that had been written about T. J. The reporters writing these stories were blessed with the luxury of not covering an actual event that was restricted by complex activities and contradicting accounts. They could weave detailed stories together based on true accounts because they were in direct control of the presentation of the truth.

A factual, as-it-happens news report covering an attack of any kind presented a much larger burden on the shoulders of the media. It was not that the stories covering the actual battles or occurrences in the city were incredibly flawed throughout. It was far more often the case that they would miss the mark on certain facts. The number of casualties would be too high or low. Cardinal directions of attacks from the city's center would be wrong. Sometimes they did misrepresent the facts, though probably unintentionally, and the story read by those who experienced the event firsthand was nothing like what was experienced.

A fairly remarkable change occurred in reporting after the Transfer of Sovereignty on June 28, when the United States returned governmental control of Iraq to Iraqi interim leaders. Internet search engines and email news alerts allowed easy access to every story about Baquba as soon as they started running. Sometimes the Internet would be carrying a story before the platoons operating in the area had returned to the base camp. After the 28th, the emailed news stories changed in tone quite a bit.

Where before Task Force 1-6 received full credit for successes in Baquba, stories reported after the 28th often gave credit to the Iraqi Police and the ING. It did not bother soldiers tremendously and made many laugh more than anything. The only reasonable explanation for this change in reporting was that the news sources often received their information directly from the U.S. Army. And the U.S. Army deferred substantial credit for successful missions to the local security forces in order to bolster their esteem within Iraq and around the world. It was surprising to see how easily the news agencies of the world accepted the approved release of the U.S. Army public affairs teams. Even more surprising, Al Jazeera, the leading Arab-language media, was often as willing to reproduce the same information as some of the more mainstream American news sources.

The first significant example in Baquba where the Iraqi security forces received undue credit occurred on July 25, following C Company's firefight in Buhriz. The 1st and 4th Platoons engaged the enemy for more than two hours along the alleyways of southern Buhriz. T. J. reported that his platoon saw the fallen bodies of thirteen enemy personnel lying in the dust near their vehicles. Lt. Col. Steven Bullimore, the battalion commander, ordered C Company to maintain contact until the Iraqi police could link up with the soldiers. The colonel wanted to conduct a "battle handover," leaving the police on the ground to preserve the peace. However, the police hesitated to enter Buhriz.

During the firefight, I sat on the roof of the capitol building on Highway 5, listening to company radio traffic on an Army radio while hearing the shots and booms echo from five kilometers to the south. I also observed the Diyala Provincial Police Headquarters and the Baquba city police station, which shared a busy intersection with the capitol. More than an hour went by following Lieutenant Colonel Bullimore's request for Iraqi police support before a single police truck left either station to drive south into Buhriz. When several trucks finally departed the two stations adjacent to the capitol building, a Kiowa helicopter pilot, who tracked the police's movement from the air, reported on the radio that the vehicles stopped at the Buhriz police station, located nearly two kilometers north of where fighting ensued. Thirty minutes later, the police finally drove south to linkup with the Americans by the market street bridge that had long since gone quiet.

Prior to the company's return to Camp Gabe at 1:00 in the afternoon of July 25, Internet news sites had already posted a story detailing the involvement of local police and ING in Buhriz. According to the press report, the guardsmen cleared a palm grove, uncovering a sizable weapons cache, and responded to an attack by killing at least thirteen insurgents. While the numbers matched those reported by C Company leadership, the description of the participants was inaccurate.

T. J.'s men did most of the shooting, and Caleb's men located the camouflaged cache with metal detectors. Aside from the timidity of the police, the guardsmen who assisted in screening the southern road into Buhriz during the operation shrank behind their trucks after the first bullets zipped by. However, compared to the actions of the same indigenous forces during the attacks in April, when policemen tore the rank from their epaulettes and disappeared from the streets for a week, Iraqi security forces demonstrated greater courage on July 25. Perhaps the skewed news story reported by both Western and Arab medias, including Al Jazeera, helped to harden the resolve of Diyala security forces to become more vigilant in protecting the populace, while also causing trepidation for those contemplating future attacks.

Caleb and I spent many hours discussing the sometimes humorous and sometimes frustrating way in which perceptions were shaped in Iraq. While still skeptical of certain official reports and media stories, we still found measurable progress through our endeavors. However, not all Americans in Iraq agreed with our assessment. In fact, in searching for one of the most vocal critics who received momentary national attention, we did not even have to look beyond the gates of Camp Gabe.

On June 6, 2004, an op-ed piece appeared on the cover of the Sunday Outlook section of the *Washington Post* titled, "The Military: Losing Hearts and Minds?" It was written by Capt. Oscar Estrada, the Civil Affairs team chief for the 82nd Engineer Battalion sharing Camp Gabe with Task Force 1-6. In his article, the reservist struggled to answer whether protecting oneself as a vulnerable soldier in Iraq retarded one's ability to gain the trust and support of the Iraqi populace. As a Civil Affairs officer, he was responsible for identifying and prioritizing local problems that either the Army could assist in alleviating through the funding of public projects, or that the Army could bring to the attention of the local government with logical recommendations for how the public servants could tackle the issues.

In his article, Captain Estrada explained that he worked earnestly to meet with village leaders and outline public works deficiencies such as the construction of a water treatment plant for Buhriz. However, he saw other efforts made by the Army, such as a project where soldiers gave a dollar to every child who collected a bag of trash from the cluttered roads and vacant lots, as pithy and demeaning. He also questioned whether the Army's methods for protecting soldiers from the real dangers of living in Iraq as a foreign military were causing the Iraqis more grief about the occupation than the Civil Affairs and medical programs could ever hope to counter.

He recounted participating in a patrol traveling along "Blue Babe Highway" north of Baquba where, upon linking up with the Brigade Reconnaissance Troop under attack from unknown forces in a palm grove, everybody at the scene "was shooting all over the place." Soldiers killed a peasant's cow simply because it grazed in the general locale of the enemy. The author selectively quoted radio traffic between a dismounted leader clearing the palm grove and his troop commander to make the commander appear callous. He also described a visit to Buhriz where a child spat on a humvee, and the caretaker of the water treatment facility displayed personal scars incurred during a detainment by Coalition Forces. Pointing around his home, the facility custodian explained that the existing damage was cause by a nearby firefight.[4]

In the July 26, 2004 edition of the *Army Times,* Captain Estrada's face appeared on the cover with a three-page investigative story inside titled, "Speaking Up, Beaten Down." Due to what the brigade commander, Colonel Pittard, deemed as an outwardly pessimistic op-ed piece that "failed to recognize successes and focused exclusively on problems — without offering any solutions," the Civil Affairs officer lost his position to be reassigned to another Civil Affairs team in a more obscure portion of the 1st Infantry Division's area of operations.

Commanders in the brigade, including the reconnaissance troop commander involved in the Blue Babe Highway attack whose radio call sign appeared in Captain Estrada's editorial, felt that Captain Estrada failed to elaborate on all the facts surrounding the specific attack on the highway, notorious for its IEDs and ambushes against U.S. convoys. What was the size of the enemy force found on the highway? Did not the brigade commander personally compensate the farmer who lost his cow? The Civil Affairs officer acknowledged in an *Army Times* interview that he could have included greater details about the incident; however, "in the end, the piece was my sharing a question, a doubt, that has developed in me and others based on what we see and hear on a daily basis."[5]

Captain Estrada recounted in his June 6 editorial that, "we rolled in[to Buhriz] with two Bradleys and several humvees packed with heavily armed troops," and then noted that the local populace displayed visible disgust at the U.S. presence.[6] He ignored the fact that the two Bradleys stopped in a wide area nearly a kilometer north of where the humvees parked on the lively market street. During that mission the purpose of the Bradleys, with T. J. in the gunner's hatch of one of them, was to reinforce my platoon, which was responsible for escorting the reservists. Only if a serious attack ensued would the Bradleys enter the heart of Buhriz.

I personally question the completeness of the truth concerning Captain Estrada's encounter with the water treatment plant caretaker who asked the Civil Affairs officer about U.S.-caused damages to his home. This visit occurred on the same patrol in which I escorted Captain Estrada's team to Buhriz. During our stop at the treatment facility, located in Tahrir on the east side of Canal Street, I watched the Civil Affairs personnel enter the building and return directly to their humvees without stopping at any other structures.

Colonel Pittard directed Lieutenant Colonel Bullimore to interview the water facility caretaker, and according to what was explained to the *Army Times,* "the man denied being hit, and instead told the commander the U.S. soldiers were 'very polite.'"[7] The Iraqi may have changed his story, or perhaps Captain Estrada chose to selectively interpret the gestures that the custodian made, because an interpreter was not present for the Civil Affairs officer's entire interaction with the man.

Captain Estrada was clearly frustrated with what he observed as an unsuccessful mission in Iraq, and this prompted him to write his letter to the *Washington Post.* I believe that the Civil Affairs officer spoke from the heart. What he described, however misperceived, was his perceived reality at that point in time. After several months of earnest efforts to meet with sheiks and provincial administrators, he probably got to the point where he thought the labors of his team were made entirely in vain. Perhaps his visit to Buhriz and the attack on Blue Babe Highway proved compelling enough to cause his disenchantment.

I, too, nearly became as disillusioned with our mission as Captain Estrada did, after one particular experience. However, my disillusionment did not take place in Iraq, but rather, a year earlier in June 2003, while deployed to Kosovo. During a weekly municipal Minority Leaders Meeting, the Kosovar-Serbian leader of the town of Vitina informed the assembled representatives of the UN, KFOR and local police that Kosovar-Albanian teenagers had desecrated tombstones in the Orthodox cemetery in Vitina. A woman who buried her husband the week prior emerged from the cemetery earlier that morning in tears and shrieked to anyone who would listen that the temporary wooden cross marking her late husband's grave had been shattered. The traditional gifts of candies and liquor that previously rested by the burial mound had been opened and their tattered wrappings discarded near other tombstones.

With more than eight months in country, we knew to question the allegations claimed by both Kosovar-Albanians and Serbs. Lt. Col. Jeffrey Kulp, the commander of Task Force 2-63, sent me to the cemetery to investigate. Not only did I find the widow's allegations to be true, but as I wandered through the overgrown cemetery, I found a dozen granite tombstones broken from their concrete foundations, apparently by sledgehammers.

As I reported my findings to Maj. Fred Nutter, the battalion executive officer, who co-chaired the Minority Leaders Meeting with a Russian UN official, I found tears welling up in my eyes. After eight months of devoting ourselves to providing a safe and secure environment, and coaxing the segregated populace to obey the rule of law, I felt at that moment that Operation Joint Guardian and KFOR were superfluous. I thought that the people of Kosovo were so unscrupulous that they could not even respect their dead. For the remainder of the week I questioned whether the UN and NATO would ever make a difference in the Balkans.

Eventually I overcame this demoralizing experience. I was able to put the incident into perspective with everything else that I had observed in Kosovo. For months I had attended every minorities meeting, negotiation, and medical outreach program that the task force facilitated in the Vitina Municipality. Having spent hours speaking with locals near their homes, inside radio stations, and over Turkish coffee at café tables, I knew that generally the people of Kosovo had the potential to improve their future.

Plenty of people did care about making a difference in their communities and improving the future of their children. Progress, although not optimal for all parties involved, occurred in measurable ways throughout Kosovo. The grave desecration was the single catalyst to cause me to question the optimism I maintained for the past eight months, probably because of the utter senselessness of the act. However, I eventually regained my faith in the operation and departed from the nine-month deployment with a deep sense of satisfaction from what I perceived to be the reality of our mission.

Pessimism is often one of the easiest of emotions to have, especially in a place like Iraq, where so many are calling into question your motives and actions in countless media and forums. Likewise, if one is able to step back from the deluge of inaccurate and sensational information and truly examine the daily changes that are taking place, optimism is often easily achieved. Such optimism is necessary when you are trying to convince twenty-year-old soldiers or the local Iraqi population of the real benefits of your task at hand.

If you accepted the adage that "perception is reality," then you would undoubtedly also accept a rather pessimistic view of the mission in Iraq. But if you took a hard look at the reality of the situation, such an existential quagmire was quickly and easily dashed by the reality of the efforts to improve the country. Varied perceptions—genuine or the delusional result of selfish service—could be funny after the fact. However, if unquestioned, the perceptions could later augment a skewed version of the truth, either in ourselves or in the media. But in the big picture, the possibilities for skewed truths seemed only to be available for those that really did not matter, and not for the ones whose only lasting characteristic was their finality.

It did not really matter if the leader described above in the Buhriz palm grove firefight actively falsified history by placing himself at the heroic fore. Those who participated in the mission knew the truth, expected such pathetic behavior, and easily laughed off the man's pretensions. It certainly did not matter that T. J. was being touted as the next General Patton in his home town, a fact that caused him more harassment than pride. It only mattered marginally that some Iraqis embraced the absurd anti-Semitic conspiracy theories or the conjectures that claimed U.S. soldiers could be so cruel as to emplace the IEDs that killed innocent Iraqis.

The real truths, the only truths that mattered, could not be damaged by the false light that ego or memory sometimes shed. They were too undeniable and unforgettable, and they were reinforced more every day that Task Force 1-6 remained in Iraq: An artillery round planted under the side of the road would kill you or damage your vehicle when it exploded. A Bradley Fighting Vehicle 25-millimeter main gun would do the same to the other side, but more surgically. The most important resource in the U.S. Army is the people, because they will watch your back, they will get you through the deployment, and they will get the job done. And, a bad leader will more often than not take himself out of the equation through his own actions, rendering himself more of a nuisance than a real danger.

NOTES TO CHAPTER 11

1. Nir Rosen, "Babylonian Hostility," *Reason Magazine*, March, 2004, Internet, March 15, 2004.

2. *Information Operations: Warfare and the Hard Reality of Soft Power*, ed. Leigh Armistead (Dulles: Brassey, Inc., 2004), 1.

3. U.S. Government, *Field Manual 3–0*, (Washington, D.C.: 2001), 11–16.

4. Oscar Estrada, "The Military: Losing Hearts and Minds?" *Washington Post*, June 6, 2004, Internet, August 10, 2004.

5. Joseph R. Chenelly, "Speaking Up, Beaten Down," *Army Times*, July 26, 2004, 15.

6. *Washington Post*, Internet, August 10, 2004.

7. *Army Times*, 15.

PART 5
holidays:
orient and occident

chapter 12
RAMADAN IN AMERICA
Lt. Caleb Cage, 1st Platoon Leader, C Company

id-October to mid-November proved to be a period of many questions and many omens. The previous year, November (which contains most of the celebrations of any gravity for Muslims during a calendar year) had been the bloodiest month across Iraq for coalition forces. Would it be the same in 2004, even after we enjoyed nearly three months of relative peace and quiet since June's crescendo of insurgency operations? We, as the occupying culture, knew that the significant differences between Ramadan and Lent (or any other vaguely approximating Western substitute) would require some explanation for ourselves as well as for the soldiers.

For instance, while operating within our sector, we were to demonstrate respect for the self-denial of Muslims, which was most poignant in the unwritten prohibition of indulgence in tobacco while outside the gates of the camp. This rule was generally overruled by the first soldier who could spot a local Iraqi smoking a cigarette on the street, at which point the American would point the incident out to his cohort and several small clouds would begin to form. During Ramadan, more than at any other time deployed, we felt the pressures of our divergent cultures commingling together on their soil.

The omens surrounding Ramadan came quickly and, not surprisingly, eerily. As we began to receive our briefings on the holiday in early October, no one could tell us exactly which specific calendar days started and ended the month-long period of Ramadan. This, of course, reminded all of us of similar time troubles in April, when the brigade continually changed its mind about when its battalions were to begin observing Daylight Savings Time. Nearly seven months had passed and we were still struggling with local applications of time? They have this holiday every year, right? Should we not be able to hammer this out, many asked with little result. Finally, our task force intelligence officer began producing successive and contradictory answers to this question.

It transpired that the exact dates of Ramadan had something to do with a "new moon," the one element that seemed redundant in the successive intelligence reports. Specifically, we were told that we would know Ramadan began when we were able to distinguish between a piece of black thread and white thread when we held them up to the moon. This set of instructions evoked bursts of uncontrollable laughter within the confines of our company-level meetings with our commander, Capt. Douglas Chadwick. I still do not know what this means. I do not think it is necessary to recount here that this seemed a bit too talismanic a procedure for us to even consider using it as a method for any operational planning, even at the platoon level. We received the same frustrating answers regarding the end of the holiday, the time that most of us agreed would be the bloodiest for the battalion. These explanations amounted to, "We don't know, but sometime in mid-November."

At the company level we pieced together whatever information we could, and usually laughed at what we were being passed from our superiors. Greg, having served within the Muslim communities in Kosovo before Iraq, answered many of our questions regarding the cultural aspects of the holiday as well as their apparent disregard for a proper calendar. Obviously there were cultural differences between the European Muslims and those of the Middle East, but we were beginning to develop our schema. Slowly, as October approached and commenced, we developed the necessary information to prepare ourselves for Ramadan.

On October 15, while the others were foregoing rest in order to delve knee-deep into their preparation for the Islamic holiday season, I left my platoon for two weeks of Rest and Relaxation (R and R) in Reno, Nevada. I did not quite know what to expect in heading home, but I knew I could handle two weeks off. In June, my best friend, Rob McDonald, sent me a photocopy of a chapter from *All is Quiet on the Western Front,* where the author, Erich Remarque, deals with his protagonist's brief furlough from the front lines. On a later occasion, Captain Chadwick showed us, his lieutenants, a short film written and produced by a classmate of his from West Point who was at that time a film student at Columbia University; the film dealt with the existential frustrations of contrasting life on the front lines (in Baghdad this time) with a brief and tormented life in the peaceful U.S.

Determined to enjoy my leave thoroughly and not fall prey to a reflective process that seemed clichéd, I chose to actively ignore the geographical, social, cultural, and climate contrasts that separate combat life in the Sunni Triangle with a social life in Reno by discontinuing my journal and only reading the news of Baquba when I could not resist temptation anymore. Luckily, in the two letters that I received upon my return to Iraq from Reno, my friend Rob had chronicled the time, urging comment in response.

Leaving Baquba left me with many fears. Could something happen to someone in my platoon while I was gone? The other leaders in my platoon were excellent, to say nothing of the hardening the soldiers themselves had developed, but the thought of enjoying a vacation while they were stuck in the combat zone left me uneasy, not to mention feeling a bit guilty. Upon returning to the States, would my family be the same way I left them eleven months ago, during my Christmas vacation? Would this experience have changed me in ways that were imperceptible to me but would appear clear and obvious to others? Would my body be pierced with the surging pangs of anticipation at the first sudden sound, leaving me embarrassed and my mother most likely in uncontrollable tears? These questions plagued me as I said goodbye to my platoon at the airstrip, but the excitement of finally going home was simply too overwhelming to process any of these fears.

My leave began with an ungodly long and tedious four-day journey from the low desert of Iraq to the high desert of Nevada, which transitioned nicely en route. I was traveling with four other lieutenants from our brigade. I knew Lt. Dave Meyer vaguely from school and slightly from our time together in different units in Bamberg, Germany. Lt. Sean Gniazdowski and I also went to school together but I did not know him. Lt. Peter Guellnitz was a long established good friend of mine, as we had served together in the same battalion for over a year. Last was Lt. Neil Prakash, a tank platoon leader who earned the Silver Star for his participation in the Baquba fighting of June.

We started out from Camp Gabe, a place well known for its austere level of comfort and service, and moved up to the Balad airbase about an hour away. The airbase is a logistical monstrosity and the provider of supplies, ammunition, and comfort for most operating units within northern Iraq, most especially the installation itself. Our platoons were often dispatched to the base to escort supply trucks, and the trip was often treated as a small R and R period in itself. It was nice to visit, but nicer to know that we would only be there for a day or two. Knowing we would be there for at least twenty-four hours, we indulged in a tragically awful movie theater experience that was only alleviated by our outright and open mockery of the outlandish movie plot as well as the noted hilarity of how much higher the quality of life was at this base compared to our own camp to the south. The transition to normalcy for the other lieutenants and me began upon arrival at this airbase, and the only method of dealing with our discomfort with the change was through laughing at the absurdity of it all.

From the Balad airbase, the flight to Camp Doha, Kuwait revealed the next step upward in our transition to the comforts we had known and welcomed in the United States. Doha is a massive complex that has been in use since the end of the first Gulf War, meaning that the garrison has had plenty of time for improvements. It is a strange mixture of the urban and suburban, all in the same place. At the same time, the structures and layout of the base remind one of a generic industrial neighborhood in an equally generic city in the U.S. Meanwhile, the paved roads, countless SUVs, services, and amenities all make you halfheartedly expect to see a parent with a car full of kids trying to get to soccer practice. The confusing illusion collapses, though, five times a day with a distant but recognizable call to prayer from a local mosque outside the gates. We were close, but we were not quite home.

In Doha we ditched our military accoutrements, including our helmet and thirty-five pound body armor. Turning in our gear was the final step out of the military lifestyle to which we had adjusted. Now we just had to figure out how to complete our mental assimilation stateside, a task that we all silently tried to figure out how to conquer. We could fill ourselves up with fast food, marvel at the tenacity of those willing to wait in line for thirty minutes in Kuwait for a cup of genuine Starbucks coffee, visit a library, shop in stores that rivaled those in the U.S., or do basically anything else we wanted. Gone were the gnawing thoughts that you could be called at any minute, no matter what your state of dress or consciousness, to execute a combat mission. Gone was the nagging reminder to ensure you had your weapon in sight at all times. Most importantly, gone was responsibility for an entire platoon of fellow soldiers, who, in relaxed or intense times, you were dedicated to bringing home. With the relief from pressing responsibility, the U.S. could not help but be close.

The next morning, the five of us split up for our final destinations, noting that our time together, instant friendship for those of us who had not previously known each other, was a giddy and concentrated sort of "mini R and R" in its own right. The flight from Kuwait to Dallas, Texas was desperately long, and with a plane full of excited soldiers, the vaguest references to local temperatures or arrival times from the cockpit elicited cheers and ruckus from the passengers. As we landed in the different terminals within the U.S. for brief layovers, we were awaited by hordes of well-wishers and gracious Americans willing to wake up early to a last-minute phone call to greet and welcome soldiers returning to their country. Many wanted to talk, while others wanted to give a soldier a long hug. The line in Dallas was so long and aggressive, it was not easy to discern if it was more of a receiving line or a gauntlet. More importantly, I did not care. I was back in America now, even if I was still in the same uniform I had been wearing for nearly two weeks.

Starting in Dallas, where I found my follow-on flight to Reno, the number of uniformed people around me began to slowly dissipate. By the time I landed at home, my cohort went from nearly 500 fellow soldiers to just two of us. I was so diffused among the American populace that it was easy to put that other life on the shelf and to ready my mind for a break in the truest sense.

Back in Reno, I praised the crisp, cool desert air, the presence of my family and friends, and everything else I cherished. My friend Rob arrived from New York for a week's visit a few days after I did. From the initial moment that I landed, I realized I was back in a place I knew. Ramadan was a distant worry at that point, as well as the other taxing stresses I encountered and had grown so accustomed to that they passed without question. The disparity between the two realities, cushioned only softly by four days of healthy transition, was obvious, but both seemed natural when immersed in either. America seemed natural because it was all I had known for the first twenty-two years of my life. The struggles in Baquba also seemed natural, because the consequences were too high for it to be unnatural.

The two weeks off were incredible. Whether I was indulging in a decent meal with my family, or having a good time with friends, I could not help but enjoy myself. The war was behind me, at least for a brief moment. Most of the contrast between Reno and Baquba, two obviously different ends of the spectrum, went unnoticed as I focused on enjoying myself and my family.

A poignant moment during my memorable break, as Rob reminded me in his letter, occurred on October 23. A group of my old high school friends, at one time the closest I had ever had, were throwing an early Halloween party. An hour before the party, nine of us, friends and siblings, gathered at my brother's house after a six-hour long and raucous lunch, and decided to put together our last minute costumes for the event. John, an enormous, barrel-chested man, managed to squeeze into a corset. My brothers adorned the apparel of a construction worker and a Soprano. Rob dressed in an old and ill-fitting karate uniform. Meanwhile, we watched in awe as the four ladies appeared from the back room dressed as a pimp, a schoolgirl, and two prostitutes.

Our amazement was mostly derived from the fact that the reaches of a closet in that house had the atrocious clothing assortments that they had assembled. I, never wanting to work harder than I have to, donned my desert camouflage gear that clearly reeked of my station in life. There, in the living room, we stood together, a cross-section of America: a fireman, a housewife, mortgage brokers, various tech financers, a prominent Early American historian and a soldier. All of us were slightly uncomfortable with our lack of forethought in preparing for the evening activity, but we were all free to mingle and counter-mingle for the night as ourselves or as our new personae.

At the party, it was obvious that our costumes were upstaged by those of the people who had actually decided to plan ahead, and the mood was clearly darker than we were prepared for. There were countless demons and anthropomorphisations of death, transvestites of nearly every feather, Jesus—the short order cook in a Christ robe, sandals, a hairnet and an apron—and sundry perversions of superheroes we had all known as kids. We drank a homemade concoction dubbed the "Shirley Temple of Doom," caught up on old times, and prepared ourselves for the main event of the evening.

Ryan DeRicco, my old and close friend, and his band were playing their final show together that night. The only categorical adjective they can muster for their music is "hardcore," which seems appropriate after listening to them on several different occasions. Throughout the show, as Rob would later note in one of his letters, he, Rob, became increasingly aware of the surreal nature of the context around him. "There you were, a soldier masquerading as a civilian masquerading as a soldier," he said. I was surrounded by booze and transvestites, mixing violently to loud, live music. The contrast between my life less than a week before and where I was that night was striking, he said.

The next morning, in an attempt to figure out some of the band's lyr-

ics in the liner notes, my brother found several songs to be rather unpatri-
otic, to say the least. One set of lyrics to a politically-charged song read, "If
it's worth fighting for, I would rather run." In his letter, Rob asked me what
this made me think. My honest response was "nothing." Nothing crossed
my mind that night as I paid attention to my friend's band playing. Why
should it have? I was among familiar company, who, no matter their opinion of me or my job, had their right to it, and that, even if unrecognized
at the time, was far more important than any political differences we may
have had. After all, what better testimonial for the beauty of the United
States is there than a uniformed soldier being accepted into a converted
garage while listening to indecipherable lyrics that bashed everything for
which he was currently fighting? I did not realize it at the time, but I was
back in a land where tolerance was a virtue, and where we could all heat-
edly disagree and still share in a friendly Shirley Temple of Doom.

The only real effort to keep track of activity within Baquba occurred
almost daily when I checked the news on the Internet. On October 24,
I read the news of a fight in Baquba from several different sources. Although the facts surrounding the fight were considerably different from
one source to another, it appeared that the Ramadan attack we had been
expecting had started while I was listening to my friend's band play the
night before. The first week of Ramadan was a time of continued peace in
Baquba. Sure, the daily improvised explosive devices (IED) continued, but
that was nothing new, and as long as people were not shooting directly at
you, the area was considered to be relatively contained and peaceful.

According to the news reports on the 24th, an unknown number of
people started shooting directly at a convoy from my battalion for eight
straight hours that Saturday morning. Details from the fight were always
scarce, but the scenario could be generally gleaned from the different stories I read and heard. It did not surprise me that the fighting that shook
the tenuous security situation in Baquba happened in Buhriz. Early in the
morning of the 23rd, Lt. Paul Lashley and his platoon from B Company
conducted a routine patrol that took them through the northern portion of
Buhriz. It would be Paul's last patrol as a platoon leader before taking over
as the B Company executive officer. As the platoon approached Buhriz, it
was ambushed from both sides of the road with several rocket-propelled
grenades (RPG) and AK-47 fire.

The soldiers returned fire, called in support, and continued to fight.
In time, 2nd, 3rd and 4th Platoons from C Company arrived to provide
support. The fighting continued throughout the majority of the day as the

American soldiers established stronghold positions, moved through the thick palm groves bordering Buhriz, and were hit with intermittent attacks. Remarkably, none of our soldiers suffered an injury that day. Even more remarkable was the fact that the many of the attackers that day were in their young teenage years. I received an email from Greg with some details of the fight and the reassuring news that my platoon had not been involved.

I began my return from my leave in the States on November 2. Newsworthy attacks in Baquba seemed to have ceased after the fight reported on October 24, and my mind continued to be at ease for the remainder of my time at home. Lt. Dave Meyer, my reacquainted friend from the trip out of Iraq, and I had planned to meet in Dallas, where we would both catch our military charter flight back to Camp Doha, Kuwait. My flight arrived from Reno about three hours early, but I could not find him amongst the hundreds of other soldiers. Finally, when we boarded, his name was not called. I knew that he had to be on this flight, but no one could give me any answers. It was not until I reached Kuwait and met again with Lt. Neil Prakash that I found out where Dave was. He had been called back to Iraq off of leave a few days early so that he could accompany his platoon to Falluja, where a major U.S. offensive was about to happen, Operation Phantom Fury. My thoughts were mixed between sincere appreciation for not being called to come back to Iraq early while I was on leave, and the sobering notion that my vacation was clearly behind me. The transition back was not quite as polite as the one I had experienced a few weeks before.

Often, before I left on R and R, when people referred to "the election," I had trouble discerning which one they meant, the U.S. presidential election in November, or the Iraqi election to be held in January. The U.S. election was in its final hours while I was home, and I was still reeling from the dramatic outcome when I got back to Iraq. It was an important election, one that attracted huge numbers to the polls, and one that would decide a great deal about the War on Terror and continued U.S. involvement in Iraq. The most important part of the election to me was, as I sat in a tent in Northern Iraq, watching John F. Kerry concede. He, after giving it all he had, had enough respect for democracy to accept the vote count. Aside from a few hitches with a couple hundred years between them, the U.S. election process has followed this model. I was left wondering how the losing Iraqi political parties were going to respond in January, after the election in Iraq.

Peaceful transitions of power are, after all, rather important indicators of the inherent respect for the democratic system within a country, as a peaceful transition of power is often associated with a burgeoning civil society, to put it into the terms of political science. It appeared that the insurgency realized that this gauge would be used in measuring success in Iraq. At least, they seemed to realize this as the election grew closer. Trend analysis, a constant in any conflict and maybe especially when trying to defeat an insurgency, often told us what, how, and why the enemy was thinking. That is, their actions spoke plainly about their intentions.

During the complex attacks observed in April and June, the enemy distributed fliers, and bussed in foreign fighters and weapons from other parts of Iraq. The insurgents trained their elements to move and fight in squad-sized elements, and they were more effective with their RPGs and AK-47s than any sort of local militia could rightly have been. In addition to hitting U.S. patrols, the insurgents also concentrated their assaults on soft governmental structures, such as police stations and civic centers. They were trying in Baquba what they had been fairly successful at doing in other regions of the country: forcing instability and proving the poor ability of Iraqi security forces to maintain the peace.

Between early July and the end of our tour in the city, the tactics used by insurgents against the motorized rifle platoons of Task Force 1-6 strikingly changed. Aside from some occasional potshots on U.S. patrols, there had not been a major engagement in Baquba since July 25, when Lt. T. J. Grider's and my platoons fought in Buhriz. But in Buhriz, we stood a good chance of getting shot at every time we drove through that town, because of the criminal element (to include the mayor and other pillars of the community). What we were not seeing during the fall were the large-scale attacks in our sector, such as those in April and June. We were not even seeing the indicators that such complex attacks were possible. Of course, the nearly constant IED threat continued to plague us, but we had grown used to them enough to refer to them casually. The firefight in northern Buhriz in the last week of October had been the first contact of any significance received in three months.

The reason why the insurgents changed their tactics from attacking infrastructure and the Americans, at least in Baquba, was because of the level of force we were able to use in repelling them. Baquba is not Najaf or Falluja. It is not a city of great religious importance, and although it is a city of great domestic political significance, it does not even register much with the international community. Because of this, our hands were not tied when we were attacked. We had free rein in the city; we patrolled it several times a day to ensure that our presence was known. When we were hit, we hit back deliberately. It took only a few months for the enemy to learn that it would be a difficult victory for them if they continued to engage large numbers of soldiers who had larger amounts of armor and better weapons.

The fact that we had not been attacked in three months had a lulling effect on us in a singular way. That is not to say that we were growing complacent in our jobs, though we were getting a bit bored with the routine patrols at all hours of the day. Rather, the big picture activities were lost on us. We knew that we were most likely not going to be attacked when we left the gates (there had even been a period of two days without a single IED in Baquba), and we were growing more secure in the thought that the enemy could not effectively hit us while we were in the camp itself. But we were also noticing some truly negative aspects of the peace. Before, the locals would talk fairly openly to a patrolling unit and sometimes even approach the soldiers. During the beginning of Ramadan, the reception we started receiving in the city districts was a bit colder. It was not negative, per se, but it was cynical for sure. We were also noticing a decrease in the effectiveness of the Iraqi security forces compared to their performance following the Transfer of Sovereignty at the end of June. Whatever progress we noticed with the Iraqi police and the Iraqi National Guard (ING) was quickly deteriorating due to a massive exodus within the ranks. But again, this was of little worry because we had not been aggressed in a long time.

What we at the platoon level were not recognizing was the shift in tactics by the insurgency. As mentioned, the enemy knew they could not effectively combat and destroy the U.S. forces in Baquba. Instead, they turned their focus to the local security forces and government. The intimidation and violence against the security forces was by no means rampant and constant, but it was at least partially effective in decreasing their morale and causing some of the exodus. Harassing flyers would circulate with the names and addresses of police officers or interpreters on them, announcing that the "collaborators" would be killed if they did not quit their support of the occupying force. Assassinations and many attempted murders were carried out against low-level officials and ordinary members of the security forces. And explosions at checkpoints, targeting the Iraqi soldiers posted on guard duty, became more common as well. Without facing U.S. forces head-on, the enemy had figured out a new way of exacting their desired goals without facing military defeat in Baquba.

While the attacks on Iraqi agencies and officials continued to be the method of choice for the enemy, the direction of their activities changed drastically, coinciding approximately with the beginning of Ramadan. Insurgents chose Ramadan to start their movement in an important new direction. The elections were looming, fewer than three months away, which meant that insurgents had to prove the instability of the presiding government and shake the faith of the citizens. It also meant that there was real power to be had in January, which meant that politicians seeking to gain some of that power could either use the insurgency to do their bidding or mask their actions behind the moderate chaos in their country.

Greg, who had been promoted to captain in November and was well settled into his new job as the American advisor to the Diyala Provincial Joint Coordination Center, was privy to much more of this information than the rest of us. His new job was to coordinate the movements and actions of the police and ING, whether they were moving on their own or in tandem with U.S. forces. He also analyzed a significant portion of the trend information in our brigade's sector and across Diyala. His statistics showed a sobering increase of anti-Iraqi activity coinciding with Ramadan.

For example, on October 23, in one of the most gruesome discoveries since we arrived in Iraq, the bodies of forty-nine Iraqi Army soldiers were found on a highway in the vast wasteland of eastern Diyala. On October 27, hooded men stopped a car with three Iraqi police officers inside, killing two and wounding the third. On November 2, a hand grenade exploded outside of the home of the police chief in charge of the border patrol for the province, although no one was injured. On November 6, a vehicle approached and attacked the passengers of a police car with grenades and AK-47 fire, killing one and injuring four. On November 7, both an Iraq police and ING patrol were hit within hours of each other, leaving dead and wounded behind. These were the new sorts of attacks, and we knew that they would continue for as long as U.S. forces remained in Iraq.

The other attacks in this same time period were at least as alarming, if only because their focus was so much different than what we had grown to expect. Within a two week period, there had been an assassination attempt on the governor of Diyala and a senior provincial security official. Insurgents successfully assassinated a provincial council member, the assistant governor for administrative affairs, and the assistant governor for resettlement and compensations. The mayor of a community near Baquba was killed, as well as two members of the Baquba City Council. Even a former Iraqi Army colonel of no legitimate political power was murdered in the streets of New Baquba one afternoon.

With many murders and attempted murders caused by insurgents, there was almost no doubt that the local Sunni minority were also knocking off some of their stiffer Shi'ia competitors in an attempt to secure victory in the January election. If the murders were not acts of political insurance then they were fairly clearly attempts to shatter any lasting faith that the locals might have had in the possibility of building their nation in the coming election.

A flier published by the insurgents surfaced on November 15 throughout Baquba that clearly announced to the people of Iraq that the "freedom fighters" had found a new target. Silhouetted by a masked man who looked more like a comic book ninja than an aspiring martyr, the following text appeared in Arabic:

Information and Warning

To the Americans' Tails and their followers:

To the people who sell their place in Heaven for a cheap price . . .

To the people who roll their honor in the dust from the spies, police, National Guard, translators, Fire Department and Media Workers (TV, Newspaper) and everyone who helps the USA Army to build their stronghold or give them advise.

To all of you:

Be aware that your blood and your money are more palatable to us than American blood and money. You, your money and your houses are the targets and nothing will save you from this. Just quit, and come back to your mind and be Muslims. This will save you.

TANZIM QA'IDAT AL-JIHAD FI BILAD AL-RAFIDAYN

The fact that the author chose a word that could be translated as "palatable" to describe the desirability of the common Iraqi man's blood suggests that many insurgents realized they could not destroy the foreign military power in Iraq; therefore, they would focus on undermining the new Iraqi government and economy. Regardless of the fact that the United States returned political power to the Iraqi people at the end of June, and that the January 2005 elections would install a government body selected by a plurality of the Iraqi people, the "freedom fighters" could not tolerate freedom in Iraq. That is, they would not accept any version of freedom tainted by a Western ideology that potentially challenged Islamic fundamentalism. To Greg, the contradictions in the insurgents' own ideology had never become as pronounced as when he read the translation of this flier. The enemy had learned that they could not decisively engage U.S. forces to reach their goals. So, during Ramadan, they tried a different approach, an approach that proved to be somewhat successful.

In an ironic twist, we found the attacks against Iraqi civilians and those consorting with the Coalition increased during the month of Ramadan, a time when the Muslim community is supposed to be more pious. Instead of praying, meditating, and fasting, as called for in their religious doctrine, the terrorists perverted the ideology of Islam to justify more fervent attacks against their fellow Muslims. The rationale of these individuals must have been that killing Muslims and their fellow humans during the time of Ramadan actually made them more devout than choosing a peaceful recourse. A fundamentalist, by definition, seeks to return to the basics of his religion, whereas an extremist chooses obscure and radical beliefs as the foundation of his creed. Senseless acts of violence proved to us that the people we were fighting were not Muslim fundamentalists, as we were told through nearly every media outlet, but rather Islamic extremists.

I returned to this extremism in action from a two-week vacation in the United States. It could hardly be considered a situation of chaos, but our three-month streak of comparable stability had been broken, and the information about the rampant assassinations and assassination attempts from Greg was quite sobering. We all knew that the enemy had recently modified its tactics, and the change was so new and obvious that it left us wondering how else it could evolve. We were also starting to hear of intelligence suggesting another offensive, like those we had seen before within Baquba, was in the works, but this information was still too inchoate to act upon.

And then on November 9, two days after I arrived back at Camp Gabe from my vacation, T. J. and I were awakened and told to get our platoons ready immediately for a mission. The company runner said that, Maj. Arthur Weeks, who recently switched positions with Maj. William Chlebowski to become the battalion operations officer, wanted all platoons in the battalion ready to go in ten minutes. T. J. and I got up and laughed, sharing jokes about crying wolf and overreacting to situations without letting them develop. Of course, we made sure our platoons were ready to go in ten minutes as per the major's request. A few minutes later, my platoon was lined up at the gate right behind T. J.'s enormous Bradley Fighting Vehicles. Captain Chadwick was also with us, not quite sure what to think about the situation, either.

We ventured straight into the center of the city, where all hell was supposed to have broken loose. Iraqi policemen appeared on the streets in force, along with countless ING soldiers. There were hundreds of them, everywhere. Shots rang out occasionally, but no one was really reacting to them. We sat in the middle of that stalemate for a while, and finally received a report about what was going on in the city that required an entire combat task force to respond at once. We received word, via the task force radio frequency, that six or seven guys raided a police station and were now holed up in a school somewhere in the city district of Mufrek.

The police and ING were present at the school and handling the situation. Our presence in the city with them might have given them a boost in morale and spirit, but the local forces were so spread out and out of touch with leadership that if our platoons had started shooting anywhere, we would no doubt have killed several members of the Iraqi security forces. It was clear that something was going on in Baquba, but we were informed that a platoon of ING knew which school the insurgents were in, and they were making their way toward it at that time.

The leaders of C Company agreed that by sitting in the middle of the road, our soldiers were just targets, and we suggested to higher command that we begin to move. About five minutes after we drove forward by only a few hundred meters, a mortar round exploded in the very area where our vehicles had just been arranged. Anxious to do anything other than remain stationary, we finally received orders to conduct a "movement to contact," meaning that we were to move slowly and deliberately in the hopes that we would draw enemy forces out of hiding.

Once we started moving through the mass of local security forces, we received a follow-on mission. There had been reports of a car moving north on one of the city's major highways, stopping every couple of kilometers and setting something in the median. We were to simultaneously "move to contact" and clear those possible IEDs. This was no problem, and not necessarily that abstract a mission, but the combination of the two missions made it nearly impossible for us to accomplish both tasks with any real speed. It took us nearly eight hours to clear eight kilometers of road and the six IEDs that had been planted, prior to returning to

Camp Gabe. We were all frustrated that day because aside from clearing the IEDs, a truly necessary and constant job, there was really no reason for so many platoons to be out in the city that day.

T. J. and I wrestled with this same cynicism seven days later when we were again awakened by a soldier informing us that we needed to have our platoons ready to roll in ten minutes. We asked and the soldier replied that yes, all of the rifle platoons in the battalion had been directed to do the same thing. It turned out that there had been some real contact that day. An unknown enemy force engaged 3rd Platoon of B Company (3/B) while they conducted a patrol in a western part of Baquba that morning. They returned fire and killed a few insurgents found with RPGs and IEDs in their car. My platoon was sent west of the Twin Bridges to link up with 3/B and Capt. John Bushman, the B Company Commander. Without drawing any additional enemy fire, we began to move back to Camp Gabe almost immediately after my platoon linked up with 3/B. En route to the base, we were redirected into the Tahrir district of Baquba, where we met up briefly with T. J.'s platoon, apparently also searching for enemy activity.

A few minutes later my platoon heard gunfire to our north in Old Baquba. Captain Bushman sent 3/B into Old Baquba to investigate and placed my platoon's vehicles in the southern portion of the district to provide southern security. No sooner did we get into our security position than 3/B received RPG and small arms fire a few blocks to their north. My platoon pushed closer to 3/B to provide support. After briefly coordinating with the 3/B platoon leader to designate where each of us would maneuver our men, my platoon moved toward the shooting emanating from behind a 6-foot tall, 8-inch thick wall.

Sgt. First Class Cameron Gaines, my platoon sergeant, dismounted from his humvee to walk over to the wall. Putting his back against the brick wall and then pivoting around to see what stood on the other side, Sergeant Gaines observed a man holding an armor-piercing RPG, poised to fire, twenty meters away on the opposite side. As quickly as the platoon sergeant pivoted around the wall, he pivoted back. He made it behind the wall at exactly the same time as a massive explosion came from just behind him. Not only did he get out of the way in time, but the RPG round hit the thickest part on the entire wall, and the grenade did not penetrate through to the other side.

After the few moments it took for Sergeant Gaines to realize that he was still alive, he grabbed the brush guard on the lead vehicle and told the driver to pull up to the corner. He put the vehicle between him and the nearby enemy, hunched over the hood, and told the .50-caliber machine gunner to shoot where he was shooting as the vehicle pulled forward and the enemy came into sight. Spc. Thomas Zaragoza drove the vehicle slowly forward while Sergeant Gaines started shooting when he saw the enemy who had fired a rocket at him moments before. Pvt. First Class Clinton Mayo, the machine gunner, observed where Sergeant Gaines' rounds were going and started lighting up the nearby corner with his .50-caliber machine gun. Together, the two Americans killed two masked men standing with rockets, hand grenades, and rifles.

At Captain Bushman's order, I sent the soldiers from two of my platoon's humvees to join 3/B in clearing houses south of our position. While we were establishing our security position for the 3/B soldiers searching houses in the area, we had to make sure that cars parked along the shoddy road were not wired with explosives. Our primary means of opening the locked vehicles was with an axe that we always had with us. During our vehicle searches, a team of soldiers discovered an assortment of RPGs, AK-47s, and ammunition inside the back of a gray van. Two other cars near the van contained caches and contributed a generous portion of the seventy RPGs, twelve machine guns, and various other munitions collected that day.

The most intriguing items we found within the cars were not the stocks of ammunition or even the insurgents' medical supplies. More intriguing was the food the insurgents had apparently carried with them in the expectation that they would be out on their excursion for awhile and would require sustenance. Because it was the last day of Ramadan, a period when Muslims fast from dawn to dusk, I found it surprising that these devout Muslims would be carrying food with them at all. When I brought out the food, consisting of several bags of local dates and bottles of water, my interpreter, Omar, told me that this was typical for pious Muslims. When the prophet Mohammed first fasted during the period that was later to be termed Ramadan, he broke his fast with only water and figs. The interpreter laughed at this, recognizing the same irony Greg and I had discovered before. "I guess it is okay to shoot grenades at people during Ramadan, but not to eat," Omar chuckled, lighting a cigarette.

Although we busied ourselves searching the vehicles and maintaining the security of our perimeter, there had not been any real fighting in an hour or so. I finally took note of the three dead bodies that were sitting near my vehicle. I noted how little it bothered me to see violent deaths up close for the first time in my life. Throughout all of our firefights in the city to date, we had never been so close and personal with the enemy dead as we were that day. Before, we had engaged enemy forces from a distance of at least 150 meters, and fellow insurgents quickly collected the bodies before we could ever move in close enough to confirm our marksmanship. On this day, though, 1st Platoon had moved into the enemy's lair and held the positions that they once occupied when they were still alive. We had caught them unprepared, off guard, and spread out when we moved into their neighborhood that morning.

While we were cataloguing our supply of enemy weapons and equipment, 3/B continued clearing houses to our south. Once they completed their searches, several of my soldiers received permission to search one final house from which we believed the insurgents were also operating. A small group of us entered the front gate of the yard outside the house. Immediately, we found a heavy machine gun sitting on the tile in front of the house and blood smeared toward a palm tree in the corner of the yard about ten feet away.

Sergeant Gaines and Staff Sgt. Ottress Thomas, a squad leader, went over to the tree and found a young man dressed all in black and bleeding profusely from a huge injury in his groin. Spc. Garret "Doc" Larsen, our platoon medic, stripped him down and immediately provided first aid. The wound was a gash in his crotch, stretching from top to bottom. His testicles were protruding from his scrotum and his thigh muscle was hanging out of the inside of his leg. Our interpreter questioned him while he was being treated and the translator told us that the young man spoke with a dialect from Falluja. The insurgent also answered the questions differently each time he was asked.

It appeared that the wounded insurgent, along with another, we would later learn, were standing just inside the wall, right next to the first two men that Private Mayo shot and killed a few hours earlier. Several rounds penetrated the wall, hitting this particular insurgent before he dropped his machine gun and sought refuge behind the palm tree. While Doc Larson took care of him and reported that the man would likely survive the wound, we had to finish searching the house. First, we had to complete searching the yard, which aside from the small front lawn consisted only of a slightly larger backyard. To get to the backyard the team had to move through a narrow walkway that lay between the exterior wall of the house on one side and a brick wall on the other.

It was so narrow that the soldiers could not hold their weapons in a proper aiming position as they moved into the back. Spc. Michael Griffin was the team's point man, followed by his fire team leader and two others. They moved quickly over the fifteen or twenty feet to the corner of the house where Specialist Griffin stopped and prepared to take a look around the corner. He peered around the corner and saw another person slouched in the far corner of the yard, also apparently injured by Private Mayo's initial shooting.

Specialist Griffin only had time to bring his weapon up in front of him and squeeze off a couple rounds before he hit the ground with a scream. As he fell towards the ground, additional enemy shots continued in his direction, hitting the wall that was right behind him. Before being carried to a humvee, Griffin managed to tell his team leader that the insurgent shooting at them was injured and located in the back right corner of the yard with a pistol.

Doc Larsen immediately applied first aid to Griffin's wounded leg and we loaded him in the backseat of a truck. While he was being loaded, I reported the casualty to Captain Bushman on the radio. He informed me that Lt. Jason Harmon's 2nd Platoon from C Company would be standing by one block to my platoon's south to take Specialist Griffin back to Camp Gabe. Only fifteen minutes passed from the time he was shot until he was back at the aid station on our base for treatment.

Specialist Griffin received three pistol shots, two more than we saw in the few moments it took to load him into the truck and get him to 2nd Platoon's position. One of the bullets hit him in the body armor, shattering a magazine full of M-16 rounds and not penetrating. The bullet we noticed hit him in the left thigh, breaking his femur, but not hitting his femoral artery or causing much other internal damage. The third bullet hit him in the stomach, directly below his body armor, and fractured his pelvis. Once stabilized at Camp Gabe, he was flown to the Balad airbase and eventually to Walter Reed Army Hospital for surgeries and recuperation.

After 2nd Platoon evacuated Specialist Griffin to the base, we refocused our efforts on killing the last insurgent on that particular piece of property. The house was cleared by a fire team, but it was quickly filling with smoke. The wounded insurgent in the backyard, in an attempt to blow up the house, threw a piece of burning cloth into a bucket of gasoline, which in turn caught the back of the house on fire. Sgt. Jason Brownlie climbed onto the roof of the house to see if he could see the determined insurgent crouched in the corner, but he could not. We could not see him from the neighbor's roof, either, but he continued to shoot whenever we started to get close to him. Realizing our limited options, Sergeant Gaines threw a fragmentary grenade into the corner of the backyard. With the enemy finally silenced, we were able to move freely around the entire grounds.

Now that the house was finally cleared, we decided to clear the school that was directly across the street. The open front door to the simple structure led into a few small rooms. I led a small team into the building to see if it posed a threat to our position, as the house across the street obviously had. Through the front windows on the door, we saw that the foyer to the building was empty, and then we moved in. I stumbled over a foot that was protruding from behind the door as we made our entrance. After the team was inside, we pushed the door closed and saw a dead body lying there. His hands and ankles were bound and a bullet hole marked the middle of his forehead. We later found out that he was a major in the ING who had most likely been murdered earlier that morning while the insurgents began staging their attack on the city.

My platoon had been in the city for about three hours, and it was time to consolidate everything we intended to confiscate. We carried the weapons and ammunition we found to a collection point within 3/B's position. We then moved to T. J.'s position on another city block, where half of his platoon was still clearing a couple of buildings. From T. J.'s initial arrival, the locals in that area were receptive to the presence of the infantry platoon. A young woman approached him on the street with her children, pointed to a nearby school, and told him that ten to fifteen men with masks and RPGs were holed up inside the school. She had children, she said, and she did not want them to get hurt. The woman did not seem particularly angry, but frustrated at what was going on in her city.

The fact that she was willing to point out the location of the insurgents and not aid the enemy in fighting the Americans who were standing in the wide open streets could have very well meant that her frustration was aimed at the insurgents. Greg experienced several similar incidents at the provincial police headquarters that same day. Citizens from all over the city were calling in on the 1-2-3 telephone hotline, a hotline that had achieved low success in the past, to report sightings of insurgents and suspicious vehicles around the city. Part of it was, no doubt, that the citizens of Baquba were growing weary of the destruction to their city, but the tone and persistence of the phone calls also led us to believe that there were other issues at stake. Most surprisingly at the time, we found that the locals were tired of having their lives and religion marred by self-proclaimed fundamentalists responsible for the attacks throughout their community.

My platoon pulled our humvees up behind T. J.'s Bradleys to secure the rear of his position. T. J. shared his concern with me that our task force simply did not have enough forces on the ground to fully secure the area and continue to push to the west in order to search all of Old Baquba. He hardly got the sentiments out of his mouth before we began hearing AK-47 fire to our rear, the area my platoon had just vacated. Our soldiers continued to clear building after building, but T. J. and I wondered when we would receive orders to terminate our search operations.

After about an hour of supporting T. J.'s position, my platoon received permission to return to base. We folded our security position and started the short drive back to Camp Gabe. As we drove back we saw many enemy bodies along the ground. There were probably about ten that could be seen from the street. As we rounded one particular corner, I saw Specialist Griffin's nametag sticking up on his desert-colored uniform shirt on the side of the road. Apparently, the medic who was attending to him on the drive back to the base had thrown it out of the vehicle to get it out of the way.

We returned to Camp Gabe, and my platoon, weary from the day's fighting but fairly certain that we would get called back out, refueled the vehicles and completed an ammunition resupply. We were all tired, sweatier than we had been since the summer ended, and the thought of Specialist Griffin's situation was in the forefront of all of our minds. We were all burnt out but, indeed, there was an operation already planned for us when we pulled back onto the base. While Task Force 1-6 concentrated efforts in Old Baquba throughout the day, a group of insurgents overran the police station in Buhriz. Greg worked to send Baquba police to reinforce the station prior to its collapse, but a series of visible IEDs and enemy fire originating from northern Buhriz choked the emergency forces on Canal Street by the old governor's mansion. Now, 1st, 2nd and 4th Platoons from C Company would conduct a movement to contact to Buhriz, clear the station of insurgents, and ensure that a fresh group of local police reestablished their presence in Buhriz.

An hour after our return to Camp Gabe, we returned to the streets of Baquba. The enemy had well prepared Canal Street for our visit to Buhriz. Stretching for three kilometers parallel to a canal, it was the only road to provide northern entry into Buhriz. If you wanted to visit the Buhriz police station, which sat a kilometer into the northern portion of the vertically elongated town, you had three options. You could use the direct, northern road along the canal from Tahrir. You could utilize a circuitous, unimproved road from the east, which would not provide a platoon of humvees, let alone Bradleys, with stealth or speed. Finally, you could enter from the south, and run the three-kilometer gauntlet of the entire town and its narrow market area that the soldiers of C Company knew only too well for its enemy attacks. Clearly, the enemy knew that we would enter from the north, and they took advantage of the late afternoon to seed the way with IEDs.

Staff Sgt. Trent Merit sat in the turret of the lead Bradley heading our task force convoy, and he shrewdly identified a massive IED on the side of Canal Street while heading south towards Buhriz. Our convoy paused while one of T. J.'s Bradleys poised to fire a 25-millimeter round at the device to cause its detonation. Before the gunner could fire a round, but after the convoy had backed away from the bomb, the IED blew up, pretty well announcing that insurgents were watching our movement. A few minutes later we continued our trek into Buhriz. As soon as we entered the housing area of northern Buhriz, we received AK-47 fire from some nearby buildings. Private Ismael Quiroz, a humvee gunner in my platoon, was hit in the wrist, quickly evacuated, and would recover in due course.

T. J. and I received orders to encircle the police station with our platoons as a security force. Once in position, we received sporadic small arms fire from the palm groves and fields behind the station. This, in turn, received an answer from the 25-millimeter main gun on T. J.'s Bradleys. After some time, the sporadic fire became progressively less erratic and more constant. T. J. received a report that Sergeant Merit had been shot in the throat. A frenzied evacuation occurred, and the wounded infantryman returned to Camp Gabe for further examination. None of us, based on the report we had just heard, wanted to consider the probability of him surviving a throat wound.

When the operation ended we learned that what transpired was a bit more fortuitous. As a Bradley commander, Sergeant Merit constantly exposed his head and upper torso in the vehicle turret. While positioned adjacent to the Buhriz police station, he held his carbine rifle in front of him in order to respond quickly and surgically to targets of opportunity. During the initial spray of enemy bullets, an AK-47 round hit the very front of his rifle barrel, shattered the muzzle, and sent shrapnel into his face, followed by the deflected and slowed round, which hit his chin and exited behind his jaw bone. It looked like a throat shot, and no doubt it was still serious, but we shared much more hope upon receiving this update.

After Sergeant Merit was evacuated, the 25-millimeter seemed to suppress or kill the attackers enough for some relative quiet. At this point, we were only waiting for the police to arrive and take back their building. We waited for another half hour until a group of forty policemen finally showed up. After an urban assault like none other that I had ever seen or heard, the police finally pronounced the building cleared. Fifteen minutes later the police reported that they had their positions set for the night, and the Task Force 1-6 elements received our orders to return to Camp Gabe.

No more than fifteen minutes after we left, the police vacated their station in Buhriz, returning to their homes. All had been for naught. As far as the police were concerned, success in Buhriz meant ensuring the enemy no longer inhabited their police station. Success did not require the police to remain in the station themselves, especially after considering just how dangerous Buhriz had become. We returned to Camp Gabe that night after a long day of fighting and contemplated the changes we had experienced that day. This long day of fighting also marked the end of the Ramadan period.

By the end of the so-called Ramadan Uprising, we had learned a great deal about the disposition of the insurgency in Iraq. Our enemy was clearly no longer willing to confront U.S. forces head on, and instead, turned attention toward the less organized and less mature Iraqi security forces. We also verified a contention we had debated all along, that Islam is not a religion of hatred, fear, and violence, but one that often embodies respect and generosity. The insurgents' blatant disregard for the most basic of Islamic principles during the revered holiday stood in stark contrast to the piety of sincere Muslims residing throughout Baquba.

The reaction of the local populace during the Ramadan attacks who reported suspicious activities in their neighborhoods to U.S. soldiers and to the police also gave us a great deal of pride in what we were doing for the future of Iraq. If the locals, devout Muslims or not, could shrug off and fight through the nonsensical dictums of the terrorist elite, they too could live in a land full of tolerance and hope. This realization left us with optimism about the locals' future involvement in the January 2005 elections. However, we all remained convinced that in their last-ditch effort to prevent Iraq's first exercise in democracy, the insurgents would wreak much violence and catastrophe throughout the country.

chapter 13
CHRISTMAS IN IRAQ
Lt. Caleb Cage, 1st Platoon Leader, C Company

"Zeus" was how we often referred to him in the meetings where we were inevitably discussing his capture. Zeus was not his real name, but it was the widely accepted pronunciation of Abu Zuis, the name that would appear in countless Task Force 1-6 mission orders and meetings throughout the year. At first, having not seen the name spelled, I assumed it was a nickname given to him by his minions, a reference to the power he wielded in the town of Buhriz. Or maybe, even worse, it was a nickname he had given himself, originating from pathetic arrogance. Because we heard so much about this villain, I was anxious to figure out the origin of his name in order to better profile him in my own mind. I was disappointed to later realize that his mythological name was probably unknown to him and had been derived from an American bastardization of the Arabic "Zuis." Unfortunately, the members of my task force did not even purposefully call him Zeus with any intention of pigeonholing him into some heroic category or to mock his slight stature. It was all just a matter of pronouncing a translation.

Zuis wore many hats in Buhriz, nearly all of which made him a very wanted man. There was little doubt that he was extorting money and privilege from the government petroleum distribution center, as well as taking percentages of the contracts the U.S. government was pushing into the town to revive its economy. For several months this was our perception of him, although we also knew that he was a former Iraqi Special Forces officer and ardent Ba'athist. Over time, we would gain a much better picture of who he was and what he did.

Aside from running the mafia in Buhriz, Zuis was also the leader of a Sunni insurgent organization with the menacing title "the Black Flag." It was not the only anti-American organization in the town, but it was probably the most active. This was indicated most boldly in the fact that sometimes, immediately before and during firefights, men could be seen standing on rooftops waving large black flags while their peers were trying to outmaneuver us in a less symbolic way. Zuis's paramilitary and criminal organizations often fused to accomplish tasks that either mutually benefited from illegal activities, such as moving and staging weapons within the profitable arms circles in order to have them ready for an attack at a later date. On a larger scale, Zuis was also one of Baquba's primary connections to the higher echelons of terrorist organizations, and he served as the intermediary and facilitator when Al Qaeda wanted to bus insurgents and weapons in for an attack in our city.

You could not have found a more perfect man to hate in our city. He was not just financing the insurgency, nor was he even a common fighter in the attacks. Zuis led complex attacks, facilitated future attacks, and personally profited from the process in every way he could. Given his intriguing name and his background in the Iraqi Special Forces, there was no doubt that he would be our most sought-after target. Our battalion became absolutely preoccupied with capturing Zuis, as it certainly should have. His capture seemed to become at least a small part of every operation we conducted in Buhriz.

We began trying to capture Zuis and his lieutenants as soon as Task Force 1-6 inherited the sector, and we increased the pressure on their organization over time. The 3rd Brigade Combat Team also shared an interest in him. During a rehearsal for the mission where Greg's and Lt. T. J. Grider's platoons would raid the home of Ali Septi on June 17, Col. Dana Pittard, the brigade commander, told the group of assembled officers that he would not be satisfied until both Ali Septi and Abu Zuis were captured or killed. Ali Septi turned out to be the easiest to find and kill, but Zuis proved to be more elusive.

Zuis would go from being one of a list of several insurgents we wished to capture to being the sole target for battalion-sized operations. Obvious in the number of operations that would happen before he was finally detained, Zuis always seemed to escape in some fashion before our arrival. We always assumed that he narrowly escaped, and of course also generally thought that certain policemen had assisted by forewarning him about our planned missions. The mythology that made up Zuis's persona within the task force was only enhanced by his ability to evade capture, and even more so by the uncorroborated reports that he had been shot and wounded during several of the major city-wide attacks but continued to lead the Black Flag. Our preoccupation eventually turned into a form

Soldiers from 1st and 3rd Platoons participate in an early morning raid on May 24, 2004 in Buhriz during the search for insurgency coordinator and financier Abu Zuis. (Gregory Tomlin Collection)

of fascination as we desired more and more to remove him from his position of power within Buhriz.

Capturing Zuis coincided with our battalion commander's more immediate focus by the middle of November. At the end of Ramadan, Multinational Forces throughout Iraq turned their attention toward ensuring a secure environment for the upcoming elections scheduled at the end of January 2005. As soon as our world calmed back down following the fighting of November 15, the plans were set into motion to destroy the capabilities of the insurgency to disrupt the elections. Detaining Zuis was a very big part of thwarting any possible attacks against Americans, Iraqis, and the future polling sites. We knew that there was an insurgency plan in place for attacks during the national elections two months away, and information slowly trickled in about what types of attacks they could be. Zuis was reportedly bragging to the people of Buhriz that the streets of Iraq would be flooded with blood on the day of the election, and he was purportedly meeting with a Syrian Al Qaeda liaison to ensure this would happen. With the threat building, our battalion realized that offensive efforts were the only way to maintain the fruits of the successes we had already achieved to date.

Operation Backbreaker went into effect the day after Thanksgiving, with the intention of destroying the enemy's ability to negatively affect the election in any way. No small part of this was capturing Zuis. It was well known that the elections in Iraq had to be incredibly successful for our presence in Iraq to appear to be legitimate, but they just had to *appear* to be unsuccessful for the insurgency to gain legitimacy. With this in mind, the thought process behind the U.S. military operation was that since the insurgency had a full month of offensive operations during the Ramadan holiday, and while they almost certainly did not achieve the momentum they expected they would, we did not want them to be able to parlay any of their small successes into any substantial foundations during the elections. That is, while the insurgents had a month of offense during the Muslim holiday season, we too would have a month of offense spanning from Thanksgiving to Christmas morning to ensure that the balance was once again unquestionably tipped in our favor.

There was another reason for a month-long, five-phase offensive operation. Immediately following Ramadan, Operation Phantom Fury commenced in Falluja, a troubled city on the other side of the Sunni Triangle. The mission in Falluja was to take the insurgent stronghold back, and forces from nearly every combat unit in Iraq would play at least a minor role. The phenomenal successes of the Coalition during the intense fighting in Falluja almost assured that there would not be any negative consequences, but we expected them all the same. Over the course of the last nine months that we had been in Iraq, a very clear pattern had been established: whenever a major U.S. offensive commenced to establish order in another city like Najaf, Samara, or Falluja, the fleeing insurgents would often scatter to places like Baquba and begin to cause problems there, too. We had seen this pattern repeatedly, and our expectations greatly colored the battalion analysis for the execution of our own offensive operations in Baquba. The American attack in Falluja and the impending national elections both meant that the Judeo-Christian holiday season would be quite eventful.

Operation Backbreaker intended to resolve the nuances and intricacies of both threats. There were a total of five phases in the operation, and all would focus on increasing security for the elections. The first phase required a complex raid intended to capture Abu Zuis and some of his lieutenants. He and his lieutenants were expected to be at a local fueling station in southern Buhriz, controlling prices and extorting money from the citizens of their town, who depended on fuel to get to work, plow their fields, and heat their homes. Phases two and three were meant to remove any stockpiled weapons that might have been staged in suspected locations throughout the city from the enemy inventory. Phase four was a raid on a local coffee shop where local insurgents were known to hang out, and where, we began to suspect, they were planning their strikes against the polling sites on their election day. Phase five was scheduled to end on Christmas Eve with the construction of a brand new Iraqi police station, intended to replace the bullet-riddled structure that had been fought over several times in the last year. Additionally, a new Iraqi Army checkpoint would be built in the dilapidated governor's mansion on Canal Street in southern Tahrir, to complement a recently constructed check point at the southern entrance of Buhriz.

On the day following Thanksgiving, phase one commenced and resulted in considerably overwhelming returns. Although Zuis was not captured, more than fifty people were detained that day from the gas station, several of whom were clearly on our wanted lists, but most of whom were released the very same day. The captures of the known terrorists or terrorist associates would certainly lead to more intelligence, which would lead to future successes. The gas station raid, as it came to be called, went very well. Even though we were not able to capture our main target, we sent a message that we were willing to move in force and detain large numbers of people, if only to question them for a single night.

Phases two and three, the palm grove sweeps to capture the enemy arms stockpile, were also hugely successful operations. The suspected locations of the weapons were inside the dense, kilometer-deep palm groves on the banks of the Diyala River. The palm groves all over the city were regularly used to conceal munitions and enemy movements before, during, and after attacks, but these groves in particular were especially suspicious because they were in Buhriz. Our clearing operations in July inside the palm groves to the immediate south of Buhriz had been relatively fruitful, and continual reports and tips were pushing us to go back. For phases two and three of Operation Backbreaker, nearly the entire task force, plus the Brigade Reconnaissance Troop, would cordon the area and clear it with metal detectors. Because the palm groves were several square kilometers large, this would require two long days and plenty of soldiers to complete the mission.

Luckily, the intelligence was better than could be expected. The members of the reconnaissance troop began finding bunkers throughout their segment of the palm groves, many of which were full of military equipment and munitions. Other units searching the groves did not have as much success on the first morning of the search, but everyone seemed to find at least a small cache in their area. All told, in phases two and three of Operation Backbreaker, six transportation trucks of equipment and ammunition were recovered and later destroyed. As the battalion moved past Chanukah and toward Christmas with great successes in the first three phases of the planned operation, phase four, the coffee shop raid, was postponed indefinitely due to intelligence that got more and more questionable as the scheduled day approached.

The postponement of phase four was frustrating for the members of the task force. First, it was going to be a direct and targeted raid in the center of Buhriz, something that we had not done to this level to date. Second, it was going to involve the three available platoons from C Company, and a platoon of specially trained Iraqi soldiers operating under the supervision of a team of U.S. Special Forces—an enormous force that would both immediately give us the upper hand in the fight as well as tax our every ability to maintain order. Tactically, we also needed to raid the coffee shop. It was known to be the command and control node for insurgent leaders in the area, and was also where Zuis was reportedly meeting his Syrian comrade. We had videos of insurgent leaders blatantly cursing the new Iraqi government and U.S. forces with the coffee shop in the background, and anti-Iraqi forces speeches that had been made from the steps of the shop. Lastly, the coffee shop was a very public spot, used by the enemy who were unthreatened and undaunted by any recourse from the Iraqi security and American forces, so such a raid would prove to be hugely symbolic. Canceling the raid seemed to take all of this off of the table for the time, while we proceeded with phase five.

Before the elections, I believed that the fifth phase of Operation Backbreaker would have been the single most frustrating experience of my entire tour in Iraq. The mission, as stated previously, was to improve security within Buhriz by building an Iraqi Army checkpoint and a police station to replace the older building in Buhriz. B Company, led by Capt. John Bushman, was tasked with building the checkpoint in the former governor's residence, and C Company was tasked with building the police station, which was only about 500 meters south of the new checkpoint, both in the northern portion of the troubled district of Buhriz.

The plan to build the station was a logistical nightmare. Capt. Daniel Edwan, the newly appointed Diyala Provincial Police Coordinator, was given the enormous task of administrating this mission. The physical structure that would become the police station was only recently completed when he inherited the problem, and there was a lot to do to turn it into a functioning, secure, and accessible police precinct in Baquba's toughest neighborhood. Because of this fact, the police station needed to be built in Buhriz prior to the elections. If there was a single place from where we could guess trouble would begin during the elections, it was almost certainly going to be Buhriz. Because we expected there to be trouble in nearly every district in the city during the elections, we were almost certain it was going to be worst in Buhriz. An established police station in the area would at least give us a few more options when trouble did arise, and perhaps deter a little aggression in the meantime.

The building itself needed limited improvements, thanks to Capt. Jim Gifford's use of civilian contracting as the Civil-Military Operations officer, the position he assumed upon relinquishing 1st Platoon to my leadership. Brick observation points still needed to be built on the rooftop to protect the police who would assume guard duty upon our departure. Enormous reinforcing baskets needed to be filled with dirt and arranged so as to line the inside of the perimeter wall as extra protection from potential suicide bombers and other of the basic types of explosions possible in Buhriz. The landscaped yard surrounding the building also needed to be gutted in order to provide for a protected parking lot for police vehicles.

By far the most time-consuming aspect of the entire mission was the completion of the area just outside of the compound. Two football field-sized swaths of dense palm groves sat exactly to the north and exactly to the south of the new compound. Because of the density of the groves, an insurgent could easily move close to the police station and then attack it undetected and undeterred. Therefore, it was decided, both groves needed to be bulldozed in order to provide open fields of fire and more security for the new Iraqi police fortress we were constructing. After that enormous task was completed, we needed to string barbed wire around the perimeter of the compound to further secure it. While Iraqi contractors, police, and U.S. engineers completed these requirements, the platoons from C Company would be responsible for providing the necessary security from the roof of the building and on the ground.

The security plan was much more complex than the simple remodeling described above. Because of the numerous variables, completion of the police station was scheduled to take from four to ten days. This fact alone amused none of us, as four days would have taken us to Christmas Eve, and ten days would mean that we would spend Christmas in Buhriz. Three platoons from C Company would move in prior to any new construction efforts to secure the area. 3rd Platoon, Greg's old platoon, was tasked with clearing several houses to the north of the building and providing a northern road block, while T. J.'s platoon was tasked to do the same thing to the south. Intelligence suggested that some of Zuis's colleagues lived in the houses the infantrymen searched, and battalion wanted to use the occupation of the new police station as an opportunity to grab them. My platoon was tasked to clear and secure the two buildings that would become the new police station.

Once we had the entire area secured, the plan became a bit more complicated. 3rd Platoon and half of T. J.'s men would be sent back to Camp Gabe to rest for twenty-four hours. The other half of his platoon and my full platoon would provide security for the building and the workers. Every twelve hours, half of T. J.'s platoon would return from Camp Gabe to relieve the other half, and every twenty-four hours, my platoon would rotate with 3rd Platoon. Aside from the security plan, Captain Edwan contracted Iraqi workers to provide the labor for the structural improvements, and U.S. soldiers skilled in using heavy excavation equipment would clear the palm groves, fill the reinforcing baskets, and provide all other forms of the necessary skills required. Such a large-scale operation required large amounts of food and water for the soldiers who would be living there until it was complete. During the late afternoon on the first day, according to the operation plan, Capt. Travis Cox's support platoon needed to arrive with several large containers full of supplies. Heaters would be unloaded first, to keep the sleeping rooms more comfortable — optimistically assuming that the electricity worked — followed by any number of other amenities.

After nearly a month of planning, phase five of Operation Backbreaker finally kicked off on December 21, making it almost certain to all of us in C Company that we would be spending Christmas in Buhriz. Within an hour of leaving Camp Gabe to execute the mission, the site was secured, dawn began to illuminate our efforts, and the enormous supply trains and equipment started rolling into Buhriz. Anticipating our extended interval in Buhriz, Captain Cox's soldiers did indeed provide a generous amount of supplies to us. Most notable was the stack from floor to ceiling of cans of tomato juice and the worst orange soda that has ever been made. There were literally thousands of cans inside the large con-

A member of 1st Platoon provides security alongside Iraqi policemen on the roof of the Buhriz Police Station during its construction in December 2004. (Provided with permission by Douglas Chadwick)

tainer dropped off in the parking lot of the compound. All of this was unloaded and stored in the main living area of one of the future police buildings. Clearing the palm groves, which everyone expected to take several days, actually moved at an incredible speed and was complete during the daylight hours of the first day. The finer details of the operation would continue to last for several more days while our platoons rotated in and out every twenty-four hours.

On the night of December 21, our first night at the site, excavation and construction in general had halted. Most of the people left at the site were the security elements from C Company. The town of Buhriz was very quiet around us, which might have been attributed to the nation-wide curfew imposed by the Iraqi government until completion of the elections, just over one month away. The largest threat for my soldiers on the roof was, as far as we could tell, an attack from the opposite side of the Diyala River, which flanked us directly to the West. With the police station positioned nearly at the edge of the river, overlooking it by a hundred meters or so, it could have been attacked relatively easily from the other side of the river. While the river was wide enough to make a targeted attack from the other side more difficult, it would have also provided a natural obstacle between us and the aggressing force. Because of this threat area, a preplanned artillery target was established in the palm groves on the other side of the river, which was fine as far as the soldiers of C Company were concerned, albeit a little close for us to feel completely at ease.

Throughout the construction operation, the most frustrating annoyance to my soldiers on the roof was trying to get the police working with us to do their jobs. When they were not pulling security with my soldiers, the police were supposed to be carrying bricks and sandbags to the roof of their new station. This seldom happened without the verbal insistence of Captain Edwan or Sgt. First Class Cameron Gaines, my incredibly persuasive platoon sergeant. Although they kept a few policemen on the roof with AK-47s, the Iraqis were written out of the security plan fairly early on the first day due to what could be categorized as a general malaise.

By nightfall, my squad leaders, Staff Sgt. Thomas Bramer and Staff Sgt. Ottress Thomas, divided the duty shifts between themselves and rotated their soldiers throughout the night, while my platoon sergeant and I also chose our alternating shifts. It remained incredibly quiet for the first few hours of the night, but at approximately 10:00 in the evening during the first night we were there, we heard the distinct sound of a rocket-propelled grenade (RPG) being launched and its subsequent explosion very near or perhaps on the southern wall of the compound. While I was receiving reports regarding damage and casualties, one of T. J.'s Bradleys returned fire with its 25-millimeter main gun toward the enemy forces. Within a few minutes, all was quiet again, and no casualties or damage had been received from our position. The attack, I later learned, originated from the corner of a house about 250 meters to our southwest, where the attackers could easily maneuver and hide, given the density of the urban build-up and population around them.

The next night, at nearly the same time, almost the exact same sequence of events occurred. Because 3rd Platoon had replaced my platoon, I was listening to the events over the radio from Camp Gabe, much like I had done so helplessly and so many times before while the company executive officer. This time, though, I was not as helpless. I had a platoon that I could muster, so I began warning my platoon sergeant and squad leaders that we might be going back out to support the other platoon earlier than anticipated. On that night, I heard over the radio, the Bradleys pursuing the RPG team to the same corner from where they had shot the night before, and down a dark street. Although they shot several times at the RPG team, all the occupants of the Bradley could find when they rounded the corner was a pool of blood and some remnants from an RPG launcher. We did not know whether the high explosive, 25-milimeter rounds had essentially vaporized the insurgent or if he had been dragged off by comrades, but the Bradley returned to its roadblock position and waited through another very quiet night.

On December 23, the morning my platoon and I were to return to the police headquarters, I had been given some bad information from the battalion operations center. The battle captain told me that when I went out to replace 3rd Platoon that morning, we were only going to be out there until 12:00 in the afternoon. This seemed plausible to me because the progress on the building was moving ahead of schedule. If the work crews had accomplished so much on my first day out there, I could imagine them nearly completing the construction on my day back at the camp. Because this information came from the battalion operations center, I took it to be true and unfortunately failed to prepare for the worst-case scenario: that we would be there for another twenty-four hours.

Upon returning to the building without most of our sleeping equipment, Captain Chadwick disabused me of the notion that we would be heading home at noon and wondered incredulously why I would fail to prepare in such a way. Instead, he would be going back to Camp Gabe for a meeting, and my platoon would remain on site for another twenty-four hour period, even after the construction was complete. This was to allow the Iraqi police a transition period, as they would be populating the building once C Company left. Because police stations in Buhriz tended not to last very long, the policemen were terrified of what would happen to the place once the Americans left. If nothing else, we could give them a little peace of mind and confidence that if we would stay there and defend the place, they could, too.

The most important thing we could do, Captain Chadwick told me, was to slowly move out of our role as the primary line of security and force the police to understand that role and assume it. He did not want us packing up our gear and taking our weapons off of the rooftop at 6:00 in the morning and then leaving at 6:15. He wanted us to take the weapons down from the rooftops before dawn, emplace a greater number of Iraqi police than U.S. soldiers on the roof, and then we could leave. The Bradleys that had been blocking the road directly in front of the building would also be moving out. I suggested to the commander that this was a particularly dumb way of doing things in that it would leave us unneces-sarily, in my summation, vulnerable to attack without proper recourse. He noted my apprehension about residing in Buhriz overnight with only my platoon and removing our main and secondary offenses, but I was ordered to follow through with the plan. As frustrating as it was to tell my soldiers of this plan, the commander was right: we would have to assume some risk in this process in order to force the Iraqis to take charge of their own security. That night no RPGs came from the far corner that served as the source of attacks during the previous two nights. The situation was strangely quiet and uncomfortably cold.

At 4:30 in the morning, my fire team leaders were instructed to start taking down all of our heavy machine guns from the roof, an order that did not seem to get any more popular the further down the chain it went. While we would leave two 240B machine guns on the roof until the very last moment, soldiers were not excited about sitting in the new sta-tion after loading their .50-caliber machine guns and MK-19 automatic 40-millimeter grenade launchers onto their humvees, out of reach in case of an attack. Everyone knew that we were supposed to start leaving at 6:00 in the morning, though, so they realized the futility in arguing.

At almost exactly 6:00 in the morning, at first light as we had seen so many times before, Spc. Dustin Wenzel saw a man pop around the same corner from where we had taken fire before: the corner to the south, about 250 meters from the building. It was the sudden movement that caught his eyes, but he quickly noticed the RPG he was carrying. A second later, both were shooting at each other. Specialist Wenzel's suppressive fire with the machine gun forced the RPG gunner to shoot wildly before jumping back behind the wall, resulting in no injuries at the police station. Almost simultaneously, at least in our collective memory, we started taking fire from the west bank of the river. The B Company element 500 meters to our north that was building the new Iraqi Army checkpoint had received no real contact during their construction phase so far, but began taking the brunt of the insurgents' cross-river attack shortly after we were attacked from the south. Both our position and theirs were punishing the attackers in response.

Sgt. Jason Brownlie controlled fire from the roof of our building over the course of the next forty-five minutes to an hour. It seemed as though there was constant shooting the entire time. Of course, because we did not have any of our heavier machine guns on the roof, the soldiers were shoot-ing anything they had, from their M-16s and M203 grenade launchers to their AT-4 anti-tank rocket launchers. Because most of the security work had been done on the building, and because the attackers were shooting from out-in-the-open positions, there was a fair amount of glee and some rather hilarious cocksure remarks from the soldiers as they countered the insurgents' attack.

The attacks continued to come from the far side of the river, though, and my soldiers continued to scan and provide security on the rooftop for several hours to come. The most jarring sound during the fight came when the preplanned artillery target on the western shore of the Diyala River was fired upon from Camp Gabe. Every time artillery lands within 250 meters of you, it is going to make you shudder. These 155-millimeter rounds raining down from Capt. Peter Guellnitz's cannons at Camp Gabe shook the entire police station and rattled the teeth of everyone at our position.

Once the firing stopped, I sent in my last report to the battalion operations center and returned to the roof to check out the situation. No wounded soldiers, no damage to the property, and, I noticed, no policemen on the roof, either. I looked around the entire rooftop several times and noted that nearly half of my platoon could be found presently defending the building, while the other half was anxiously waiting to be told to replace them. The Iraqis were supposed to be standing right next to my soldiers, protecting the building of which they would soon assume custodianship, but they were not there. They had run inside when the shooting started because we were there to protect them. Why should they risk their lives when we would do it for them?

Hours later, when everything calmed down, we began to consolidate our equipment again, in order to take it back to our base camp. I went into the main room where I slept that also doubled as our dining room, and noticed that the room was absolutely empty. My sleeping bag, which actually belonged to my commander because I had left mine at Camp Gabe, was missing, along with my shirt and several other personal items. Most amazingly, the thousands of cans of the disgusting orange soda and every bit of food we had packed in the room were also gone. I then realized what our Iraqi colleagues had been doing while we were shooting and being shot at on the roof of their police station an hour earlier.

Around noon on December 24, after several threats from various members of my platoon, I finally retrieved my lost clothing and equipment from our Iraqi colleagues, and 1st Platoon left, tired and frustrated. Operation Backbreaker was officially over when my platoon returned to Camp Gabe on Christmas Eve. All in all, the month-long operation was an enormous success. Its few shortcomings were critical, though. We still had not caught Abu Zuis, and the failure to gather enough intelligence to execute the coffee shop raid during phase four weighed heavily on all of our minds. Zuis absolutely needed to be captured before the elections, and whether this was at the coffee shop or at his home, it mattered little.

As soon as my platoon returned to Camp Gabe after our thirty-hour stint at the new Buhriz police station, we started learning about and preparing for Operation Trebuchet. As soon as we heard the name of our next mission, we started mocking those who create such titles. It was early in the afternoon on Christmas Eve when we returned, and we learned we would be leaving for the next operation in Buhriz at around midnight on Christmas morning. The operation would involve three platoons from C Company, the reconnaissance troop from the brigade, and a U.S. Special Forces team. The target site was broken into two different locations, both given to us by detainees from the gas station raid who suggested Zuis could be found in that general location. There were two target areas because we were not sure exactly which house would provide access to Zuis or those who knew his whereabouts. The reconnaissance troop would be assigned to accompany the Special Forces team in the westernmost complex and the C Company platoons would be assigned to raid an eight home, walled-in complex about 500 meters directly to the east of the former location.

The platoons left at exactly midnight on Christmas morning to hit the two complexes simultaneously. All eight homes in the C Company complex were cleared quickly by two platoons, and it was determined that we were in the wrong set of homes. Conversely, the reconnaissance troop soldiers with the Special Forces team had more luck. The four houses they searched all contained members of Zuis's immediate family. We did not hold any detainees that morning, but we were for once relieved that our intelligence was quite strong and that we had probably only missed Zuis because of the late hour. After all, insurgents tend to practice their craft after nightfall, or sleep in the palm groves when it is most likely that Americans will come knocking in the hours of darkness.

A week later, the New Year arrived without event and scheduled operations continued. Surprisingly, the surfacing of actionable intelligence regarding the coffee shop from phase four of Operation Backbreaker set the planning back into motion, which was very welcomed by those tired of holding the hands of Iraqi police and conducting mundane, low-yield raids again and again. Everyone knew that plans were being made by

1st Lt. Caleb Cage, Platoon Leader, 1st Platoon, C Company, assists in searching for the Task Force's primary target, Abu Zuis, in January 2005. (Caleb Cage Collection)

insurgents to disrupt the elections, and our best intelligence led us to believe that the coffee shop would have the highest payoff if we decided to raid it. The plan that was established required our battalion, and especially C Company, to prepare for the boldest operation we had ever done: a daylight raid in downtown Buhriz during the peak hours of commerce and traffic. According to the reports of a handful of informants, Zuis had apparently been informed of our plan and had introduced a new tactic into his inventory. If U.S. or Iraqi forces got too close to capturing him, he would remotely detonate a car bomb that was parked within his vicinity, to create chaos and allow him to escape. We never found out if such tactics were developed, but we knew that he was capable of such deviousness.

Finally, a few days into January, the plan to raid the coffee shop had been completed. We would conduct the raid on January 10. We began rehearsing for the raid on January 4 when we were given an enormous surprise: Zuis had turned himself in, to our brigade commander. Our surprise in this fact was relatively calm, as Zuis had promised to turn himself in for immunity numerous times throughout our time in Baquba. The fact that he had turned himself in this time was the only real difference. The real surprise came a few hours later, when we learned that he had been set free following the meeting with the commander.

Questions loomed. Why had we risked our lives for so many nights to capture this criminal if he was only going to be released in order to pursue a diplomatic solution? What would have happened if we had captured him? Would he have been set free? Spc. Aaron Vandayberg and Pvt. First Class Jason Lynch gave their lives in earlier battles in Buhriz, where Zuis might have coordinated the fire of those responsible for ending their lives. How could this menace be set free? The only consolation to our disappointment was the knowledge that perhaps we did not understand the big picture well enough to truly grasp what was going on.

On January 7, while the battalion was still halfheartedly preparing for the coffee shop raid, we received interesting news once again. Zuis was to arrive at the brigade headquarters yet again, and this time, if deemed appropriate, he would be detained for good. My platoon was called to wait outside of the headquarters building at Camp Warhorse, across town in Baquba, and escort him to the detainment facility if such a decision was made. On the morning of the 7th, we arrived and waited outside for several hours. Talk of how anticlimactic it would be if we actually "captured" him in this fashion was used defensively to cover up the fact that we were all giddy to be a part of the capture of a man who had caused us much frustration and heartache over the past ten months. For reasons unknown to me, Zuis and his previously unknown cousin were escorted out to my platoon's humvees at approximately 10:00 in the morning, and we took them back to the jail facilities at Camp Gabe.

Prior to escorting them to our vehicles, we had to first search and restrain them. Soldiers from my platoon provided security while other soldiers did the mandatory searching. We placed flex cuffs on their wrists, and we started moving them towards the vehicles. The two men were absolutely surprised; no one had told them they were to be detained that day. Sergeant Gaines took a degree of pride in explaining their situation to them. While they were being escorted to the vehicles, Sergeant Brownlie approached me and showed me the tag of Zuis's black leather jacket. I noted that the jacket had been made by "Zeus Manufacturing Company," and I believed for the first time that his name might not have been lost on him.

It was a huge relief for my platoon and for the battalion to have him in our custody. Less than three weeks away from the upcoming elections, for which we were planning and facilitating feverishly, we now had in our custody the man who could very well be the mastermind behind the impending attacks. January 7 was almost the last major and necessary victory for the battalion in setting the stage for successful elections in the province that our own presidential administration had dubbed to be one of four trouble zones in Iraq.

Even with Zuis out of the picture before the elections, we knew that he still wielded considerable power in Buhriz. There was no doubt that the porous prison facilities would allow him to communicate relatively freely with his underlings who would no doubt continue to plan their attacks more zealously now that their leader was captured. We also knew that the meeting scheduled to take place at the coffee shop would go on with or without Zuis, and the raid planned for January 10 still needed to be executed. All kinds of rumors flurried regarding whom Zuis and the leaders of the Black Flag were supposed to be meeting. At first it was believed to be someone very high up the chain in the Al Qaeda organization, but it was later determined to be a Syrian intermediary. Whatever the case, on the afternoon of 10th, just as we were finishing our final preparations for the raid, we were told that the meeting was cancelled, and subsequently, so was the raid. However, a week later, on January 17, we finally received the green light to move toward the coffee shop in force.

The raid was everything we hoped it would be once it finally took place. My platoon was the raiding element, in conjunction with members of the Iraqi Army and the U.S. Special Forces. Lt. Jason Harmon's 2nd Platoon of C Company, along with T. J.'s Bradley platoon, fended off probing attacks to our perimeter. There we were in the middle of the day, during the height of their business hours, and we planned on staying in the market area until the raid was through. This was risky because, as we had learned numerous times in the past, it was almost guaranteed that you would be shot at with some type of enemy weapon if you remained in the same place in Buhriz for more than an hour. After my platoon encircled the exterior of the the coffee shop on foot and T. J.'s men mounted rooftops in the vicinity, several enemy personnel shot RPGs and small arms fire in our direction.

After receiving the RPG fire, T. J.'s platoon closed with and destroyed attackers from several directions, surprisingly quickly. With a secure area to work within, my platoon completed the mission within two and a half hours. The raid yielded seventy-seven detainees, many of whom were released the same day, but a sizeable number of whom were detained and sent through the Iraqi court system. Even though we did not capture the Syrian terrorist we had hoped to capture, the people of Buhriz would later tell us that breaking up the business at the café was a good step toward preventing future criminal activity in the area. If nothing else, we had a few more people who were suspected of planning attacks against the polling sites that would open in fewer than two weeks' time, and had sent a message to the members of the insurgency in Buhriz who had so daringly used the coffee shop as a headquarters and meeting place for the months up to our raid.

Following the mission on January 17 would be a two week period in Baquba that would make the stress of building a police station in Buhriz seem like nothing at all. The elections in Iraq would be on one hand the most rewarding experience for many service members in Iraq, and on the other, the most incredibly frustrating experience. Since approximately a week before the coffee shop raid, the platoons had been tasked on subsequent missions to scout out the polling sites, all of which were public schools scattered throughout the province, locate their entrances, determine their security weaknesses, and, finally, strengthen those weaknesses by blocking roads with concrete barriers and setting up wire blockades. It was a tremendously tedious logistical challenge. Meanwhile, during nighttime patrols, the platoons were collecting information regarding the elections from the locals to see if they had registered and to see if they intended to vote. During the two weeks before the January 30 elections, the workload would only increase and become more frustrating. But at least Zuis had been captured, and the battalion had set the conditions as much as possible for successful elections in Baquba, a place where successful elections seemed impossible to many skeptical locals and outside observers.

chapter 14

THE EVE OF A NATION

Lt. Caleb Cage, 1st Platoon Leader, C Company

for months during the deployment, Lt. T. J. Grider and I sat in our room discussing its end. Earlier in the deployment, we both viewed the duration with respect to our mid-tour leave. The leave was a break from the reality we were experiencing and three fewer weeks (including travel) that we would have to spend in Iraq that year. Upon our return to Baquba after the respite, we would have a new perspective: four months left for him, and three months left for me until we both reached the scheduled end of our tour in February 2005. After much strategizing about the perspective of the time remaining, we eventually agreed on one point: all we had to do was make it until December, when we would begin to see the light, and through the end of January, and we were essentially done with our tour.

T. J. coined this perspective, and he was right. Trudging through November was more bearable, at least in terms of our private discussions, because we knew that January would be a month of much culmination. The coffee shop raid in Buhriz on January 17 was decidedly, although only anecdotally, our tactical culmination, a capstone requiring us to call on everything we had learned throughout our year. The Buhriz raid would not be the last one that we would conduct, but it was certainly the last of its magnitude and scope. More selfishly, we also knew that as soon as January 30 ended, it would be only a matter of days before soldiers wearing the 3rd Infantry Division patch would join us in Baquba, replace us after only a year off, and quickly begin taking over our area of operations.

The elections were as much a fresh start for the people of Iraq, the intended audience in this instance, as they were for the soldiers deployed and deploying to the region. It was a goal, and with so much at stake, it shaped our combat operations leading up to the elections and provided us with an honorable rationale for accepting the risks we assumed, sometimes daily. Even outrageous decisions by politically minded leadership echelons above us mattered less when we couched the mission in terms of the elections. Although my platoon would be tasked with providing security at the Diyala capitol building for the elections while everyone else was facilitating more directly, January 30 still served as a fixed rallying point for the calendar-driven morale of the soldiers at the end of a long deployment.

Perhaps due to the end nearing, January also seemed to be sort of an intellectual or reflective culmination for those of us who sought to understand the cultural intricacies involved in this war. In the days prior to my platoon's departure for its two-week rotation to the capitol building, T. J. and I had yet another of our conversations that attempted to make sense of an intricate world using homely or grotesque analogies. He was particularly good at this.

We were discussing the upcoming elections and how successful they would be at democratizing the country. I embarked upon a rather inconclusive set of statements, not even an argument, that I had been trying to work through since before the war began. It appeared to me that the elections, representing liberty, were absolutely the first and necessary step toward pacifying the region. I rejected the assertion that modern democracy was a Western construct and that the people of the Middle East were simply incapable or unready to accept democratization on its terms. I found that argument to be akin to arguments used by the southern slaveholders in antebellum America that slaves would not know what to do with their freedom. It was a racism, an "othering" that did not fit into my worldview. T. J. responded, after a moments' reflection, that he thought our democratization problem "was a lot like our shitters," which, after laughing, I realized was rather appropriate.

The shitters to which he referred, the camp latrines, had been a constant source of frustration throughout the deployment. The buildings we occupied—the former Iraqi Republican Guard barracks—had real toilets and showers, but figuring out how to keep them functioning was another issue. The showers were gravity-fed from tanks on the roof that constantly ran out of water. Likewise, the toilets did not flush if the rooftop tanks were empty, which was a problem because the tanks had to be filled by an outside source. Instead of establishing the more rustic, but also traditionally more common and functional outdoor latrine, complete with a detail of human "shitburners," decision makers within the battalion seemed content to continue the use of the useless toilets.

It was not as if they were not actively trying to fix them. Several sets of local Iraqi contractors were hired for exorbitant sums to fix the toilets. Each team was inevitably fired for one reason or another, and progress was always slow to undetectable. We kept hearing fantastic updates: the latrines are 45 percent complete; the latrines will be operational by July 7; then in August, the latrines are 95 percent complete. Finally, exactly six months after our arrival, a water pump was rigged to a water supply that pushed water through hot water heaters, amazingly, and flushed toilets almost on command. Modernization was no longer a pipe dream fueled by the presence of porcelain relics of better days, but a reality.

T. J. pointed out that the approach to fixing the latrines was preposterous, even if it was a rather mild inconvenience considering our lot in life at the time. "First of all," he said with conviction, "we are living like we are in America still, and not Iraq." The bathrooms were used as if we were still in a modern country, where convenient knobs and levers carry away and refill whatever we wanted. We could not do that in Iraq. And then, in order to fix the problem, we hired Iraqis? That was absurd, he concluded with appropriate disdain. "If you want to have toilets functioning like we were used to in the United States, you *do not* hire contractors who most likely live in homes where the toilets flush into the streets," he said. He went on that it was analogous to what we were trying to do in Iraq on the national level, referring to the attempt we were taking at democratization. T. J.'s analogy was dead-on accurate in its homely way, and expressed an idea that had been at the root of our frustration for almost a year: democracy is a culture, not just a system, and developing this culture of tolerance in Iraq, one that was still maturing in the West, was as difficult as getting toilets to function properly, and perhaps even more so.

As we prepared to set out for our final two-week tour at the capitol building, one of the few buildings in Baquba where the toilets and showers almost always worked, my platoon was assigned one final patrol to Buhriz. I felt a little uncomfortable when I saw the mission schedule, but I quickly got over it. It was mid-January, after all. There was not even enough time left on the calendar to sweat a little patrol, even if it was in Buhriz. The night of our patrol, I went to the platoon barracks to check on our preparations for the evening, and saw the soldiers faithfully preparing as they always had. When I joked with one of my fire team leaders, a young non-commissioned officer, about the attention to every detail they were paying to the mission preparation, he caught me off guard with his answer: "None of us wants to be the last guy to die in Iraq." Sgt. Jason Brownlie, another extremely capable team leader, was in charge of the pre-mission routine. I told him that we were to leave a soldier behind for the night's mission, and to make room for what would turn out to be our last embedded reporter.

Michael Yon, I was told, would be joining us for the final patrol in Buhriz. We had run the gamut with embeds so far, including relatively famous CNN personalities, a wartime artist, a reporter for *Rolling Stone,* famous photojournalists, and various others in between. The most memorable journalists were the most interested in finding the ground truth and would stay for a few days or weeks to genuinely get to know the soldiers who were executing the ground mission. Other times, we would barely notice their presence on an objective during an operation or mission as they clicked away with their camera or took notes. Often, we would never know who they were, who they were with, or care that they left. We would only see their version of our story a few days or weeks later. Michael Yon was one of the more interesting examples of the former type: the type dedicated to the story, the reality, and not necessarily the telling of the story that editors and a polarized nation would appreciate on its merits.

When I found out that we would have Mike along with us for the platoon's final patrol of Buhriz, I asked around about his background. I was intrigued to hear that he was formerly in the U.S. Special Forces and had written several books about his experiences. News like that traveled fast and was generally accompanied with theories and grand conjecture, like those that had encouraged us to believe that Camp Gabe had been demolished by air strikes upon our arrival a year before. I learned more after talking to him, and with a little help from the Internet. He had entered the Army Special Forces straight out of high school under a new and brief provision that allowed for direct enlistment into unconventional forces in 1983. In other words, before I was in grade school, Mike was being schooled in the arts and sciences of guerilla warfare with the Green Berets. As a function of the time, 1984, Mike referenced both the Soviet threat and the Islamist threat, passively acknowledging the transitioning times, in his memoirs entitled *Danger Close.*

A few hours later the platoon gathered at the vehicles, as we had before every mission to date, and we went over the mission plan, the contingency plans, and other movement instructions. It was our standard routine, and so standard that I tried to read my troops' non-verbal communications a little more closely than usual. I expected to see the fire team leader's assertion that no one wanted to be the last to die in Iraq on the faces of the soldiers, but it appeared that that feeling had been replaced by something far more normal: this was just another mission, it just happened to be one of our last. I introduced Mike to the platoon, explained what he did, and we boarded the vehicles. Walking towards my humvee, I let him know what our past experiences were in Buhriz and asked him if he had any questions. His response was flat: "Do you have an extra weapon?" Special Forces qualified or not, I regretted to inform him that such a thing was against the rules. I enjoyed being a platoon leader too much to accommodate him, I added.

Buhriz was more quiet than usual that night, as were the portions of Baquba we drove through. Returning to Camp Gabe from the unremarkable mission, neither Mike nor I were ready to sleep, so we joined T. J. in our dingy, notoriously ill-kept room for coffee and more discussion. For the next couple of hours we discussed Mike's past projects and what trajectory had brought him to Baquba. But mostly, we discussed his latest research topic extensively: cannibalism. The more he talked, the more questions we asked. To our amazement, he shared that most of the cannibalism he had witnessed had taken place in remote areas of India, along the Baranas River. He became interested in the subject when he heard that Americans were participating in the flesh eating, and that a small cult of cannibals had formed in California. He was as wide-eyed as we were about the subject as he discussed going undercover to film the rituals. Although he adamantly and openly admitted to being more of a gatherer of interesting data than a scholar, and especially not a theologian, he described the cannibals as adherents to an ancient form of Buddhism grounded by moral relativism versus nihilism. He remarked that this was a "very dangerous way of thinking," and provided plenty of examples to emphasize his point.

While the three of us talked—he talked, we asked dumbfounded questions—I spent considerable energy trying to associate his study of cannibalism with his presence in my room in Baquba, Iraq. I was truly puzzled and reached into the depths of my own mind about what the connection could be. While he was telling stories about people pulling dead bodies out of the river to consume them, making percussion instruments out of the skulls of babies, and promising video footage of it all, I simply failed to make the connection. Was there a sect of cannibals in Iraq that I had not heard of? Was this group eating out of some sort of religious adherence or out of some physical necessity? My mind wandered, trying to find the definitive connection.

One possibility finally occurred to me. A few weeks before Mike's arrival to Camp Gabe, a captain from the battalion headquarters gave me a copy of a *USA Today* column by Ralph Peters, a staunch supporter of the invasion and the author of *Beyond Baghdad: Postmodern War and Peace.* In the article, entitled "The Return of the Aztecs," Peters attempted to address by metaphor the surrealism, from the U.S. perspective, of the terrorists' use of video beheadings of Westerners and sympathizers, a trend that was on the rise at the time. His analogy attempted to compare the extremists' actions with those of the "blood cults" of Aztec origin. I regularly discounted Peters as too one-sided to be taken seriously, but I was willing to accept some credibility here in this, the vaguest of connections but the best I could think of.

Mike told more and more details about watching humans eat the flesh of their own on the riverbanks of India. Maybe, I continued to consider, he learned of a deeper connection between the blood cults and cannibals and was in Iraq to ferret out the unspeakable truths of such a group. After I finally broke down and asked him what the connection was, he said that he had simply taken a break from the gruesome study of cannibals and wanted to write about the positive aspects of troop involvement in Iraq. It had never occurred to us that a visit to Iraq could have been a break for anyone, but we had not focused the better part of the last two years watching humans eat their own, either.

While our conversation remained on the subject of cannibalism, as it did throughout the night, I realized that I might own a book that could be useful to Mike. I grabbed a copy of Colin Turnbull's *The Human Cycle* from my shelf and asked if he had heard of it. In the 1940s and 50s, Turnbull lived in India and Africa with various tribes and detailed his experiences in several important books including *The Human Cycle, The Mountain People,* and *The Forest People.* When I cracked the book, the dust jacket of the book revealed that Turnbull had, in fact, visited and written about the people of Baranas, India, the area in which Mike had recently encountered primitive cannibalism practiced in our time.

My reason for purchasing the three books was innocent enough and had been a few years prior to the deployment. However, my reason for packing them along with me to Iraq was embarrassingly naïve. During my junior year of college, I studied political philosophy under Dr. Louis Pojman at West Point. In one of our many memorable and lively discussions about state planning, coercion and the human responses to mandated civilization, Dr. Pojman recommended Turnbull's two most indispensable works, *The Mountain People* and *The Forest People,* as contrasting examples of how societies react to forced assimilation. These works, at least in part, laid the foundation for the theory of cultural relativism that would eventually grab hold of anthropology departments across America, and also take various other analogous forms and disciplinary titles in humanities departments. I had owned the books for several years intending to read them, but only got to them during the deployment.

I brought the books with me because I thought they would be helpful in understanding the culture and people of Iraq, which, before the deployment, I believed to be primitive. This belief was based on several works that I read during our preparation for the deployment, especially Bernard Lewis's vaunted *What Went Wrong?* Lewis's book has been criticized in the past for trying to understand Middle Eastern culture through the use of modern Western constructs. It seemed to me that some of the criticisms were well founded when I read the book, but his thesis rang true to me in the months before the deployment. After the fall of the Ottoman Empire, Middle Eastern culture turned back to its historic roots, while the West became fascinated with the new. This disparity seemed to be at the heart of our troubled attempt at democratization in Iraq and clearly and broadly informed my opinion while in Germany, waiting to deploy to Iraq.

In time I learned that while there was enough primitive thinking and activity in Iraq, or more accurately for my own experiences, in Baquba, Turnbull's books did not provide an overtly useful model for better understanding what I would experience. My ill-conceived notions were not categorically useless, but they were, at the very least, overstated and clearly seen through the Western lens.

The majority of the people I encountered while on patrol or at the capitol building, the two missions that consumed most of my platoon's time during our stay, were not traveling Bedouins of the open desert; they were static city dwellers. I knew that Iraq had several substantial cities, and others had even compared pre-war Baghdad to some of the Eastern European cities I visited shortly after the Berlin Wall came down, but my pre-deployment notions regarding Iraq were mainly based on dramatizations in the rolling fields of Germany and the open desert of Kuwait. That is not to say that no one exhibited behaviors, customs, or tendencies that we would call primitive, using the Western paradigm. It was, in fact, a strange mix of old and new.

Common mud huts had satellite television dishes and mediocre electricity supplies. Houses a kilometer away from our camp had toilets and running water, but the refuse was often carried away only as far as the open sewage trenches in front of the homes, as T. J. had pointed out in his democratization metaphor. These countless slit trenches were everywhere in the dirt roads of the city, and often made travel unpleasant, if not difficult and downright unhealthy. The most remarkable image manifesting the unequal mixture of old and new was the daily passage of a donkey cart carrying a several-hundred-gallon tank of fuel, mixing awkwardly with the ferocious city traffic. These images, and many more, were routine and normal, but still never failed to elicit stupefied remarks about the obvious incongruity by anyone who noticed them.

The local human culture itself also exhibited this same mixture of old and new. Although several hundred thousand people lived within the limits of Baquba, tribal tradition still flourished. You could see it in their names as al Jabouri or al Tikriti denoted their stock and their deference to a specific sheik and familial honor code. More than once I heard the phrase "me and my brother against my cousin; me and my cousin against my tribe," and so on, detailing the chain of loyalty for which a young Muslim man is responsible, no matter the costs. This element of the Arab culture, at least as I found it, is so pervasive and different from the west, and so important to the culture, that it made progress very slow.

The books we discussed that night in the room were helpful to me, but in a different way than I imagined. They wound up telling me more about the way we thought than helping me to understand the unsophisticated Iraqis I encountered every day in Baquba. After a few solid hours of discussions about cannibalism and war, we parted ways. However, Mike and I had several more opportunities to speak during our remaining weeks in the city. He also became one of the more famous wartime bloggers, a term I had not heard of when I met him in Iraq.

On January 18, my platoon finished loading the humvees with the necessary supplies for our two-week stay at the capitol building, as we had done countless times before in the year prior. The short trip from Camp Gabe to the capitol building would be the last time that I had to worry about anything related to patrolling until after the elections. While living at the capitol building, 1st Platoon was clearly more focused on going home than on the upcoming elections. We would be there for two weeks and then depart the facility two days after the elections. We had no part in their execution of the elections whatsoever and could only facilitate in the case of a real emergency downtown. While there was a quiet sense of being left out, we all knew that the headaches experienced by those just outside our government building would be extraordinary. Manning the

An Iraqi soldier stands guard on the roof of the Blue Dome. A squad of Iraqis was attached to the U.S. platoon that rotated through the two-week security stint at the capitol, and it provided the Americans with an opportunity to grow better acquainted with their host-nation comrades. (Gregory Tomlin Collection)

government building was an easy and mostly welcomed duty: alternating with 2nd and 3rd Platoons, my platoon assumed sentry duty at the governor's office for two out of every six weeks. We had established a good relationship with many of the Iraqi Army soldiers, Iraqi policemen, interpreters, and various others with whom we guarded the facility. We anticipated the two weeks to be as uneventful as our many other rotations through the facility.

The capitol building, popularly referred to by Americans as the Blue Dome, was a domed centerpiece to the city located inside a walled compound and situated directly adjacent to the most important intersection in the city on Highway 5. The Ba'ath Party originally constructed the relatively ornate building as its provincial political headquarters. The three-story roof provided good visibility in all directions, and the fortification proved able to endure attacks of every kind throughout the year. The static security mission was only disrupted during a city-wide attack or an occasional car-bomb just outside the gate. Another platoon in the company trucked in meals and generator fuel nightly.

T. J.'s platoon was the only platoon in C Company that was not a part of the regular six-week cycle at the capitol building, and they had been left out all year. What they brought to the fight—trained infantrymen, Bradley Fighting Vehicles, and double the personnel of the other three platoons in C Company—were simply too vital to the battalion, and putting them at a fixed site seemed irresponsible to the decision makers. This fact was a point of contention among the soldiers, especially his infantrymen, who could have used the break. No matter how I tried to sell it to T. J., there was no denying that the guard duty was indeed a break from the rigors endured during the normal patrolling regimen.

The soldiers pulled long hours in the hot sun on the rooftop observation posts, or at the gates, where people seeking to do business with the provincial government entered and exited. While they worked longer hours over the two weeks at the capitol building, they at least had a schedule, some predictability in their lives. They knew that during the day they might have to pull four, four-hour shifts under layers of Kevlar and cloth, but at least no one was going to wake them up thirty minutes after they laid down to tell them they had to go assist in a dangerous combat mission or a boring, last-minute logistical mission. As we had done so many times before, we established ourselves and our routines within moments of our arrival. The various personalities at the capitol building, including those of my own soldiers, always made for intriguing situations and discussions in the relaxed, almost detached atmosphere of the compound.

Walking through the single room barracks a few days after our arrival, I watched as one of my more reflective soldiers had a discussion with an Iraqi Army soldier who was Shi'ia, and who had been an English teacher before the invasion. The Iraqi Army quarters had a small television in it, and they were watching an Egyptian soap opera. The Iraqi soldier asked my soldier what would happen in America if the members of a community found out that one of their neighbors was a homosexual. The Iraqi soldier was taken aback by the soldier's answer that, except in certain parts of the country, no one would really give it a second thought. The Iraqi soldier said that this attitude was a major source of frustration for the people of his country. They regularly saw translated television shows and advertisements that depicted equality for women and homosexuals, and that they viewed this as simply too much. He went on to say that most Iraqis believed, in his opinion, that if a man were to be discovered as being a homosexual, then he should be jailed or possibly executed. The soldier did his best to pass along the idea that individual freedoms, the kind we were trying to establish in his country, outweighed social or cultural mores, at least in theory, but a variety of barriers made this an ultimately wearisome exercise.

Every morning, after the compound officially opened, Mustafa, a 15-year old capitalist, would arrive at the gate. Every compound in Iraq probably had at least one Mustafa: a guy who could get you anything you asked for with only a moderate markup. Ours had worked with our predecessors and came highly recommended and regarded. He had learned enough English to curse you, cheat you, and ask you outrageous questions regarding your personal life, sometimes in one sentence or transaction. He was fascinated by the material wealth of Americans, and more times than I can recall asked how many houses and cars I owned in America, how much they cost, and how many wives I had. He could get annoying with his constant questions, but he was always welcome to add his unique color to the drab walls and dreary shifts of the capitol building.

The night before the elections, I stopped by observation post Delta on the roof of the large government building during my usual rounds. Spc. Jorge Pineda, also known as "Paco," was sitting at the post in his usual state, calm and generally pleased with everything around him. The night was spectacularly cool and quiet, two conditions that complemented each other so well in Iraq, as we looked out over the rooftops of the city and half expected the power to shut off at any minute. He was quick to laugh as usual, a characteristic that earned him much respect within the platoon, as I mocked him lightly for one thing or another. We talked about his plans upon leaving the Army, a valid career decision that fewer of the soldiers than I had expected were planning on exercising. This consisted of moving back to Chicago to join the police and possibly opening a restaurant in Mexico City, where he had family.

I asked Paco what he thought about the elections, if they would be violent, and if they would work. He was optimistic, a chronic condition for him, and he expressed frustration with much of the negativity that seemed to have entered the platoon's lexicon as the mission slowed down and the elections approached. On the roof he said what we all believed, or at our most cynical moments, wanted to believe. He said that there were a lot of sorry people in Iraq who insisted on controlling people. His reason for hope was with the kids, a fact that seemed clichéd to me before the deployment, but had grown in stature upon real interaction. His heart went out to the barefoot kids, sometimes playing soccer around sewage ditches and enduring their violent surroundings.

It was a mindset that I would have mocked as naïve ten months prior, but I got the impression that even then Paco would not have doubted the children's innocence and genuine enthusiasm for U.S. soldiers. Paco's optimism was grounding and stunningly pure, especially with the national elections only a couple of hours away. I realized there on the roof that we were all sort of exhaling. The year was not over, but that light we saw at the end of December was a distant memory by now, and after the elections, we could almost see ourselves back in Germany. Paco was right, I concluded on my way down from the rooftop, there was plenty left to fight for.

The bathrooms on the first floor of the capitol building were possibly its finest quality, even better than the fixed schedule and the surety with which you could plan your time. They were by no means exquisite, but they were perfectly practical. The facilities were made up of three rooms in all, two with toilets and one with a shower. They did not work all the time, and even when they were working, there was no guarantee that the hot water heater was. They were fairly rickety, too. The toilets could not handle toilet paper, which had to be deposited in a garbage bag. The small washing machine was made of cheap plastic and seldom did much in the way of washing clothes. Most of the windows were broken out and replaced with pieces of cloth or cardboard, depending on what was on hand when the previous placeholder fell victim to the elements or a practical joke of some sort.

They worked, though. The more mechanically inclined members of the platoon, especially the incredibly talented Spc. Thomas Zaragoza, could regularly be seen toying with various parts of the water heater, pipes, and tanks in order to ensure that it stayed operational, and they always seemed to, for the most part. The toilets were connected to a septic tank that, to be emptied, required that we accept the risk of a massive tanker truck into the compound several times a month. It just seemed like a necessity to us, and an unpleasant one at that, but the increased security risk never once came back to bite us. With a careful eye from watchful soldiers, cooperation with the locals, and assimilation to the existing infrastructure, we were able to enjoy hot showers, running water, and flushing toilets for the last two weeks of January as the Iraqi public awaited their first opportunity to vote. Perhaps T. J. was right after all about shitters and democracy.

PART 6
reformation

chapter 15
HOPE AND SALVATION
Capt. Greg Tomlin, Military Advisor,
Diyala Joint Coordination Center

Col. Kamal Ibrahim Ahmed met quietly with several of his closest comrades at the Iraqi Army Staff College in Baghdad in mid-March 2003. A flight instructor and career army aviator, Colonel Kamal loved flying his Hughes 530 nearly as much as he relished watching his two toddlers play at home. In hushed tones the officers contemplated a situation that looked increasingly inevitable — the U.S. military invasion of their homeland.

As senior colonels, this cadre more accurately understood the capabilities of Iraq's armed forces than any foot soldier or private citizen who was inundated with the propaganda ministry's platitudes of military infallibility. Colonel Kamal's peers had been too young to serve in the Iran-Iraq War, but they completed accelerated training programs in the mid-1980s. Combat veterans of the invasion of Kuwait, they also served in the campaign that U.S. military planners dubbed Operation Desert Storm in 1990. Throughout the previous decade they commanded and trained air squadrons over the narrow strip of Iraq straddled by internationally imposed no-fly zones.

In 2001, despite the efforts of their propaganda ministry to skew reality, the colonels learned of the *blitzkrieg*-style invasion of Afghanistan and the rapid fall of the Taliban regime to U.S. Special Forces and Afghan rebels. They knew U.S. President George W. Bush labeled Iraq as part of an "Axis of Evil," with Iran and North Korea as the other members of the triumvirate. Clearly, the reprehensible acts of felling the Twin Towers and tearing a gaping hole into the Pentagon jarred the United States into mobilizing its populace and military for a long-term and far-reaching war against its enemies.

In mid-March 2003, with 170,000 coalition troops poised on the Iraqi-Kuwaiti border, Colonel Kamal knew that the next objective of the U.S. would be Iraq. Facing this looming conflict, the colonels at the Staff College asked themselves how well their army and air force would perform against the U.S. military. Their verdict: "we will be annihilated."

They believed that when war commenced and U.S. missiles honed in on deep, strategic targets in Iraq, the Staff College would most certainly be a high payoff target. So Colonel Kamal returned to his family quarters on the grounds of the Staff College, rounded up his wife, his two-year-old son and one-year-old daughter, and drove to their family home in Muqdadiya, a Diyala town forty kilometers northeast of Baquba. Upon ensuring his family's safety, Colonel Kamal returned to the military college to see what he could do to save his Hughes 530. *Ensha Allah* — "God willing" — he would preserve his helicopter for use after the impending war ended.

When the shock of the initial air strike reverberated through Baghdad on March 20, Colonel Kamal and several of his colleagues climbed into their helicopters and flew separately to isolated locales in central Iraq. The flight instructors would not fight, nor would they encourage their former students and subordinates to challenge U.S. Apache and Kiowa attack helicopters.

He and his copilot landed in a field on the west bank of the Tigris River. Clad in their green slacks and button-down service shirts, the two men camped beside their helicopter for two days. Before dawn on the morning on March 22, Colonel Kamal awoke to the sound of a thunderous explosion. A U.S. missile made a direct hit against his Hughes 530. As he later recounted, "I knew it was 5:10 because the fire illuminated my watch so that I could see what time it was when I lost my helicopter."

With the remnants of his prized possession still smoldering, Colonel Kamal and his copilot shook hands. Then they parted company to begin their separate treks home to reunite with their families. They had hoped God would save their helicopter from destruction, but alas, such was not God's will. For Colonel Kamal, his professional military service ended with his hope of preserving his Hughes 530.

Eighteen months later Colonel Kamal sat across the table from me in the conference room of the Diyala Provincial Joint Coordination Center (JCC). After handing my platoon over to Lt. Peter Whitney on October 1, 2004, I moved to the provincial police headquarters to serve as the Multinational Forces liaison and officer in charge of the JCC.

A U.S. invention, the JCC was designed to organize and monitor the appropriate response to serious events that occurred in the province, from civil emergencies to insurgency operations. Following the overthrow of Saddam Hussein's regime, JCCs built throughout Iraq became the genesis for providing an Iraqi-first response to crises. This would preclude the necessity for Multinational Forces to snuff every criminal's and insurgent's endeavor to derail stabilization efforts throughout the country. It would also offer Iraqi security forces the critical, real-world experience they needed to gain confidence in their own abilities and earn the trust of the people they pledged to protect. The focus of our attention in the Diyala JCC rested primarily on Baquba, because the majority of significant activities in the province occurred in the densely populated capital and its surrounding villages.

Members working in the JCC fell into two groups. First were liaisons from the various security forces, hailing from the Iraqi police, border guard (Diyala shares a 197 kilometer border with Iran), Iraqi Army, fire department, and the explosive ordnance demolition (EOD) team. Second, there was the staff, which was comprised of a provincial director of security and four shifts, each consisting of a deputy director, an operations officer, an intelligence officer, and two field agents. The majority of the staff formerly served as officers in Saddam Hussein's army, and they were hired based on the rationale that as professional soldiers and graduates of the selective Baghdad Army Staff College, they were trained to manage operation centers.

The JCC sat inside the Diyala Provincial Police Headquarters. Located 300 meters south of the provincial capitol building in the center of Baquba, the sprawling two-story police station was a favored target of insurgents. Prominent scars etched into the walls of the compound from numerous rocket-propelled grenades (RPG), mortars, and machine gun bullets told the story of dozens of attempts to drive U.S. forces and police from the headquarters. Several car bombs exploded near the compound, targeting lines of unassuming citizens waiting to apply for the opportunity to fill the ranks of their police force.

I arrived at the police station feeling a bit guilty about leaving my platoon halfway through our mission in Iraq, knowing that they would continue to face the dangers of patrolling Baquba for another five months. Much like our two-week stints at the capitol building, the JCC provided me with a predictable work schedule and a significant increase in personal security. Transitioning to the police headquarters reminded me of a U.S. Army officer's tour of duty in Vietnam during that conflict. An officer spent the first half of his yearlong tour leading a platoon or company, and then spent the latter half as a staff officer or military advisor. In contrast, combat arms soldiers and non-commissioned officers rarely escaped from spending their entire year commitment patrolling the jungles of Vietnam.

However, shortly after my arrival in October, the police headquarters took two indirect fire attacks in the same number of weeks. During the first attack, a rocket launched from directly across the street in Tahrir punched through an air conditioning unit on the second story of the police station, where the U.S. contingent lived. Without exploding, the rocket next broke through a wooden door, landed in the hallway, and finally rolled to a stop near a ping-pong table. In the second attack, six 60-millimeter mortars impacted against the compound, with one of the rounds exploding on the roof just two meters from my bedroom. In sharing my early impressions of the JCC with friends, I joked that someone did not want me to get too comfortable at the police headquarters.

Initially, I was opposed to moving to the JCC. Following my time as a platoon leader, I wanted to serve in the Civil-Military Affairs staff section of the 3rd Brigade. Based on my experience in Kosovo the year prior, I knew that I was suited for and enjoyed working with host-nation officials, and I hoped to do so again in Iraq. In June I wrote a request to Maj. Fred Nutter, the brigade operations officer, with whom I had served in Kosovo. He told me that he would ask the brigade personnel officer to draft the orders necessary to bring me to the brigade headquarters.

My task force commander, Lt. Col. Steven Bullimore, on the other hand, insisted that I go to the JCC. Unbeknownst to me when I wrote to Major Nutter, Lieutenant Colonel Bullimore was not simply assigning me to the police headquarters on a whim. Rather, he took fully into account my Balkan experience in addition to the efforts I took on foot patrols in Baquba to engage the locals. During my first week at the JCC, Lieutenant Colonel Bullimore dropped by for a visit and told me, "I can't see you working anywhere else." Indeed, how could a U.S. soldier get any more directly involved with Iraqis than interacting with dozens of them on a daily basis?

When Task Force 1-6 initially arrived in Baquba, the JCC functioned as a Joint Operations Center (JOC) out of a modest room in the back of the station. There were liaisons from the various security agencies, but it did not have a staff outside of its police telephone operators and translators. As the U.S. officer in charge, Lt. Jason Harmon worked to collect intelligence reports, gain situational awareness of developing crises and arrange for an Iraqi response. These were all duties of the JCC. However, there was something missing in the JOC. The JOC did not have the manpower or proper facilities to anticipate and plan for upcoming security operations. The JOC only had time to react to crises, not to anticipate them.

In August 2004, 3rd Brigade sent Capt. Daniel Edwan to the JOC to transform it into a JCC with the capacity to synchronize efforts for current operations *and* prepare contingency plans for possible future emergencies. In its metamorphosis, the Baquba JCC also expanded its responsibilities outside the city limits to serve as the provincial coordination center. Captain Edwan arrived in Iraq as C Company commander in Task Force 2-2 Infantry, the 3rd Brigade unit responsible for the town of Muqdadiya and central Diyala. During his time with the infantry battalion, Captain Edwan worked to build a JCC in Muqdadiya. Impressed with the results, Col. Dana Pittard, the 3rd Brigade commander, sent Captain Edwan to Baquba.

Without any previous training or experience with a civilian organization such as the Federal Emergency Management Agency (FEMA), Captain Edwan designed and oversaw the construction of a modern and functional JCC in Baquba. Contractors expanded the size of the JOC room, added a conference room to the building, and built a series of offices in the wide main corridor of the police station. Captain Edwan also planned to create a separate city JCC room adjacent to the provincial one, and this separate facility was completed just two days prior to the Iraqi national elections on January 30, 2005.

In tandem with the physical construction, Captain Edwan began the hiring process to staff the maturing coordination center. He wrote a series of duty descriptions before interviewing candidates to fill the positions of four separate shifts. To locate competent officers, Captain Edwan turned to the provincial Military Advisory Council.

Established by the previous brigade deployed to Baquba, the committee consisted of former generals, colonels, and majors who lived in Diyala. The council served as a conduit for U.S. forces, the new provincial government, and the ex-Iraqi officers to foster a mutually beneficial relationship. The former officers, many having devoted their entire adult lives to their country's armed forces, found themselves without jobs, pensions, or any monetary benefits for their previous service. Such a group posed a potential threat to building a new Iraq if their government and the Multinational Forces failed to acknowledge their previous service and social standing. Unquestionably, a portion of the frustrated officers, nostalgic for the "good old days," financed and passively supported the insurgency

Members of the Diyala Provincial Joint Coordination Center (JCC) assemble around the director's desk with Brig. Adel Mullan (wearing cap), the provincial chief of police, and Capt. Gregory Tomlin. (Gregory Tomlin Collection)

to some degree. A handful actively organized and led destabilization efforts. Others, however, like Colonel Kamal, were prepared to help build a democratic Iraq. As proud men, they also hoped to regain the ability to independently support their families.

For the new government and U.S. forces in Diyala, the well-educated senior officers served as a promising pool of leaders who could influence their community, tribes, and prominent civilian friends to support a wide range of initiatives to improve the security of their country. The Military Advisory Council received its own office in Baquba, and its members participated in a weekly meeting with the governor and Colonel Pittard at the capitol building. Arguably, the only other group to seriously rival the officers' influence in Diyala was the Sheiks' Council.

Captain Edwan selected Maj. Gen. Ayad Ibrahim Baqi, formerly the last aviation Inspector General of the Iraqi Army and a helicopter pilot with more than 5,000 hours in the cockpit of a Huey, to serve as the Diyala Director of Security. His new JCC staff included former brigadiers, colonels, and majors who were either members of the Military Advisory

Council or were friends of committee leaders. Upon arriving at the police headquarters, they assumed a rank structure identical to their former military hierarchy. Eventually this would prove problematic, because Captain Edwan and I identified several junior officers, police sergeants, and civilians working in lesser positions who deserved to assume positions of greater responsibility. However, many of the former colonels argued that protocol would not allow for field grade officers to be subordinate to junior officers. We learned that military rank was an inseparable part of their personal identity.

Every morning excluding Fridays (the day of rest in Islamic countries), the JCC held a security meeting to review the significant events of the past twenty-four hours. Participants from each of the security agencies working in the province provided details about serious crimes committed against civilians, illegal aliens intercepted while attempting to cross the Iranian border into Diyala, and noteworthy discoveries made by police and Iraqi soldiers while conducting patrols or manning roadside checkpoints. As I compiled the data in English for U.S. intelligence officers and commanders, the JCC operations officer also prepared a summary in Arabic for the governor's office.

At the head of the conference table during these meetings sat the Diyala Director of Security, Major General Ayad. The security meeting had to be his meeting and not mine, even though I was often tempted to cut certain participants off in the middle of their unsolicited dissertations and steer the agenda back on course. The general facilitated the discussion and kept the agenda moving by asking each agency liaison in turn to provide a report.

I learned quickly that agency liaisons, men holding the rank of major or colonel, did not always believe it necessary for their agency to do much more than document a serious incident such as a murder or unknown explosion. In-depth investigations seemed to be reserved for a handful of cases, and most of those investigations became forgotten long before they were solved. Besides taking notes, my tasks during the security meetings included asking prodding questions after hearing daily summaries and encouraging security leaders to delve deeper into the significance of criminal and insurgent activity. The senior leaders needed to brainstorm on their own about how to anticipate future attacks and how to nab known criminals.

During one of my first attendances at a security meeting, while Colonel Kamal sat across from me as the operations officer for the day, a police brigadier complained that the general populace did not provide the police with enough information to solve crimes or capture insurgents. Around the table, graying colonels and majors nodded their heads in agreement, lamenting the fact that they received little feedback from civilians about ensuing crimes.

I mentioned that I joined them at the police headquarters after spending six months walking the streets of Baquba. I noted that while police and Iraqi Army patrols could be seen driving along the roads between the districts of the city, rarely did I observe an Iraqi security element dismount from their pickup truck to talk to the people. Perhaps, I recommended, it would be better if Iraqi security leaders required their subordinates to spend more time inside the city districts. By establishing a rapport with the citizenry in an effort to gain their trust, Iraqis might inform their police and army about suspicious activities and blatant wrongdoings in their communities. I explained, "Before they can depend on your services, the people need to believe that their security forces share a genuine interest in protecting their community."

Once again, the group of Iraqi officers nodded their heads, and this time many murmured "*Ensha Allah.*" General Ayad moved on to the next point of interest in the meeting, while I sat perplexed by their response to my recommendation. None of the officers wrote anything down in their calendar books or asked someone from another agency if his men had any more success gleaning information from the populace. My proposal, just like every significant event summarized during the meeting, was noted in the official Arabic and English minutes, and that, as far as the Iraqi participants were concerned, was sufficient to fulfill the purpose of the meeting.

The fact that many of the officers repeated *Ensha Allah* also bothered me. During patrols and while guarding the capitol with 3rd Platoon, smiling Iraqis often quipped "God willing" to me at the end of our conversations about improving the security situation or quality of life in Baquba. I wondered if the words had lost their meaning to the majority of the Islamic faithful. *Ensha Allah* was intended to be said as a blessing or a motivational adage to inspire a devout Muslim to perform well as he or she set out on a task.

In a majority of the cases where an Iraqi told me *Ensha Allah*, however, I felt that the person used the phrase as an escape clause so as not to assume blame in failing to reach an objective or goal. It was no more a blessing when spoken by most Iraqi officers than it would have been if used by an atheist. Certain lackadaisical leaders, I felt, even ended conversations with those words as a way of discretely backing out of all agreements made during specific meetings. If an expensive project failed, if a crucial deadline was not met, or if a hundred policemen failed to report for a joint operation with U.S. forces even after an Iraqi general agreed to make it so, the Iraqi public servant could not be blamed because God did not apparently intend for the mission to come to fruition.

Other influential Iraqis, however, were neither cynical nor blasphemous. People like Colonel Kamal were simply even-tempered, content with the status quo. As intelligent people, they identified problems, but for cultural reasons remained content for the problems to fester, even after identifying a solution for the problem. God willing, or with hope, the future would be brighter.

It reminded me of the Reformation debates in Europe about good acts versus good intentions, and the ability to join Christ in heaven by pious acts or merely by good intentions. Hope and salvation became a metaphor for the debate over the situation in Iraq. For our near-term goal, salvation meant orchestrating successful elections on January 30, only a few months away.

Gen. Gordon Sullivan, a former Chief of Staff of the U.S. Army, published a book shortly after retiring from active service entitled *Hope is Not a Method*. Numerous times while typing away on my laptop during the daily JCC security meeting, I considered constructing a large banner with the title of General Sullivan's book written in bold Arabic. It would have made a fine slogan for the security meeting participants and an excellent retort to any security officer who shrugged off failure with *Ensha Allah*.

I truly cared about whether the Iraqi security forces and transitional Iraqi government could function independently, free of corruption and duplicitous leadership. After all the patrols 3rd Platoon conducted in the intense summer heat, after the close combat fought against insurgents, and after losing Pvt. First Class Jason Lynch, I could not write off the importance of improving the situation in Iraq. Measurable progress would not come from Multinational Forces doing all the work. It required Iraqis to understand their duty as ordinary citizens, as public servants, and as security leaders, to create a better future for themselves.

A successful Iraq would never look like the United States; it needed to be firmly rooted in the good mores and traditions of their ancient civilization. However, a successful Iraq required citizens to not tolerate criminal activity in their communities. It required police and soldiers to dutifully complete their missions, no matter how harrowing, and it required government leaders to see themselves as public servants first and foremost. As the officer in charge of the JCC, I found my new vocation to be working to impart this philosophy on the senior Iraqi security leaders of Diyala. If the generals and colonels could understand that hope is not a method, then they could eventually impart this philosophy to their subordinate leaders until all members of their respective organizations absorbed this philosophy.

I had to be careful to not personally direct JCC operations, even when an Iraqi leader seemed hesitant to make a decision or provide an order to effectively overwhelm enemy forces. To improve the staff's readiness for future emergencies, I built thirteen reactionary drills for hypothetical civil emergencies and counterinsurgency operations. Each drill required the staff to identify which agencies needed to be contacted, what to do if the situation elevated in severity, and what reports needed to be published. Over the next couple of months I would write a situation on the dry-erase board in the evening, when activity tended to quiet down in the JCC. My translator would write in Arabic underneath my letters, and the deputy director on shift would begin to work with the staff to write out a solution for the problem.

In addition to the drills, Captain Edwan continued to invest heavily in the infrastructure of the JCC. Aside from the physical construction of a second JCC that would be completed in time for the elections in January, laptop computers and Internet service were purchased for the JCC. A college computer professor from Baghdad came for several weeks to teach the JCC staff how to use Microsoft Word, PowerPoint, and Excel. A select few began to manage the JCC e-mail account to expand communications with the five other JCCs in the province and the Interior Ministry in Baghdad. By the time of the elections, the communications officer would be interacting with other Diyala JCCs via a Yahoo! chat room.

The importance of advising versus managing the JCC became evident to me following the first significant joint operation that we conducted following my arrival at the police headquarters. I awoke to the sound of distant RPG and machine gun fire on the morning of November 9, 2004, at about 6:30. After the fire continued for several minutes, I realized that this was not an isolated hit-and-run engagement. Arriving downstairs in the JCC, my translator explained that groups of insurgents were attacking both the Mufrek and Buhriz police stations. The police inside both stations reported that groups of two to three insurgents hid atop roofs and within alleyways only a hundred meters from their locations. My mind flashed to the 3rd Platoon rooftop operations on the Buhriz agriculture building in June, a structure positioned next door to the currently besieged Buhriz police station. I could see the black-clad insurgents aiming RPGs, and I could hear the crack of bullets hitting brick walls.

Returning to the present, I knew that the priority of the JCC, after gaining situational awareness, would be to reinforce the stations with additional personnel and ammunition. Only with this reinforcement would the police gain the confidence to conduct a counterattack—assuming the insurgents did not quickly meld back into the community.

Within the hour Colonel Ali, the JCC deputy director on shift, and I coordinated with Major General Whalid, the provincial chief of police, and his colonel responsible for the Baquba city quick-reaction force, to reinforce the police stations under attack. The lieutenant colonel commanding the Iraqi Army battalion in Baquba also arrived at the JCC to provide his assistance. The police agreed to reinforce the stations, but only if the Iraqi Army secured the roads leading toward both stations. If the Iraqi Army destroyed enemy blocking positions along Canal Street toward Buhriz from Tahrir as well as an enemy machine gun team at Mufrek Traffic Circle, then the police could advance to reinforce both stations.

Meanwhile, behind the closed door that separated the U.S. radio room from the JCC, my brigade and battalion operation centers called numerous times for updates on the situation. The battle captains and operation officers at Camps Gabe and Warhorse wanted to know when to deploy U.S. platoons in humvees or sections of Abrams tanks and Bradley Fighting Vehicles to destroy the insurgents. Neither headquarters wanted the insurgents to overrun a police station because U.S. forces would then have to raid the building to retake it. I understood their concerns, but based on the response by the Iraqi security forces—albeit a leisurely response by U.S. standards—I believed that the Iraqis would successfully handle the situation on their own.

The Iraqi Army deployed twelve pickup trucks with four to six soldiers sitting in the back of each. Half went south to Buhriz, and half traveled east towards the Mufrek Traffic Circle. Despite the town's reputation for harboring fierce insurgents, the Iraqi Army found little resistance in the late morning hours as they drove into northern Buhriz. Upon engaging a handful of insurgents who either fled or were evacuated by their comrades, the soldiers reached the police station, much to the relief of the police inside. Several police quick-reaction patrols followed the Iraqi Army patrols into Buhriz to restock the policemen's spent ammunition.

Efforts to end the siege of the Mufrek police station did not work as smoothly. After crossing the bridge from Old Baquba toward Mufrek, the Iraqi Army discovered strong enemy resistance at the Mufrek Traffic Circle. Insurgents positioned in two public schools facing the traffic circle fired RPGs and machine guns at the army pickup trucks. The soldiers held their ground on the east side of the traffic circle and returned fire. Two soldiers were wounded in the firefight. Finally, the insurgents fell victim to their common blunder: running out of ammunition. Without any detailed logistical planning, the insurgents only had the ammunition for their weapons that they carried on themselves.

Leaving behind several of their RPG launchers and even a machine gun, the insurgents melted away into Mufrek. The Iraqi soldiers eventually crossed Mufrek Traffic Circle, cleared the schools, and reported to their commander that the police could pass forward to the police station. Additional police quick-reaction patrols and a special police unit maintained by General Whalid at his headquarters fought from the traffic circle to the police station, another 500 meters deep into Mufrek. By noon, the police and Iraqi Army had defeated the insurgents.

Seventeen policemen became casualties in the day's engagement. At the JCC, I contacted Camp Warhorse and requested that the most seriously injured Iraqis be taken to the brigade medical facility for treatment. As our medical facilities were more advanced than Iraqi ones—especially our trauma unit—the U.S. military often treated severely wounded Iraqi security forces after firefights, improvised explosive device (IED) detonations, or assassination attempts.

General Whalid announced that his men killed seven insurgents; however, other insurgents acted quickly to remove the bodies before the police could search the deceased. As the police patrolled the streets that afternoon, local residents in Mufrek and Buhriz reported that the insurgents wore masks, suggesting that they were nearly all local residents who did not want their identities revealed. Police also found a minibus and car left by the insurgents at the Mufrek Traffic Circle. A man discovered hiding inside the car was arrested and would spend at least two years in prison following his interrogation.

During the operation I reminded the JCC deputy director and operations officer that while our attention was focused on two districts of the city for obvious reasons, we could not forget about monitoring security throughout the rest of the city and province. The operations officer agreed and worked with our communications officer to contact the guards at the hospitals, government offices, electrical plant, and water pump. The deputy director coordinated with the JCC traffic police liaison to deploy extra traffic police patrols to key intersections throughout the city to offset the absence of police who were participating in operations in Mufrek and Buhriz.

Throughout the morning, the JCC received calls from residents of Mufrek, Khatoon, and Mualimeen, reporting that insurgents were planting IEDs along Highway 2, south of the Mufrek Traffic Circle. The security guard at a pediatric hospital described several occupants of a gray van digging a hole directly in front of the hospital and then placing artillery shells into the hole before driving south. These reports proved valuable for Caleb and Lt. T. J. Grider, who would lead their platoons on missions to clear the IEDs with the U.S. EOD that afternoon. Upon arriving on Highway 2, the U.S. soldiers were able to focus their search for devices based on the locations provided by civilians to the JCC. By dusk, the U.S. EOD destroyed six IEDs.

For the first time since the beginning of Operation Iraqi Freedom (OIF) II, U.S. forces in Baquba did not have to respond to a complicated attack synchronized by insurgents in two separate locations. Both the police and Iraqi Army suffered casualties, but the lieutenants and sergeants leading the patrols in Mufrek and Buhriz held their ground until completing their mission. Inside the JCC, the situation map was regularly updated during the fight, and the principal police and army leadership utilized the JCC as a personal war room.

On the JCC television screen, which remained on either the Al Jazeera or Arabia news networks, the Baquba attacks made a headline story in the afternoon. According to the Al Jazeera anchorman, insurgents killed over a dozen police and overran a police station. We all chuckled at the absurdity of the story and wondered whether the press received the story from the insurgents before or after the actual attack.

Only one event marred the day's achievement. At 6:50 that same morning, an IED detonated beneath the Diyala River bridge on "Blue Babe Highway," three kilometers north of Baquba. Once the situation in Baquba stabilized, U.S. Army engineers evaluated the damaged bridge. The detonation did not collapse the bridge, but it did succeed in damaging the westbound lane to the extent that it was no longer safe for vehicles to cross.

According to the engineers, the eastbound lane could only support trucks but not heavy, tracked vehicles.

For the U.S. Army, this news was very alarming. The Diyala River bisected the 3rd Brigade area of operation, and without the bridges, supply convoys could not reach Camps Gabe or Normandy (outside of Muqdadiya). The three battalions residing in the eastern camps relied on the western Camp Warhorse for water, food, fuel, and ammunition. Only four bridges crossed the river, three in Baquba and the one on Blue Babe Highway. Additional crossing points could not be reached until traveling thirty kilometers south to Baghdad. If unable to travel around Baquba, logistical convoys would be exposed to an increased probability of being ambushed when driving their slow-moving, open-bed trucks through the heart of Baquba.

The army engineers reinforced the eastbound lane and extended a military bridge at the same location in order for the brigade to continue its essential support convoys. A company of Georgian soldiers attached to the brigade received orders to guard the bridge on Blue Babe Highway until U.S. Marine engineers could arrive to permanently reinforce both lanes of the bridge. The JCC received orders from the brigade headquarters to establish police guards on the city's three bridges crossing the Diyala River for twenty-four hours a day until further notified. Neither the U.S. nor Iraqi forces could afford for another bridge to be damaged or destroyed by the insurgents.

As the JCC worked through the afternoon with the police and traffic police to establish a schedule for guarding the bridges, Colonel Pittard arrived for an update. "So what happened in Baquba today?" he inquired as he entered the room.

I immediately walked to the situation map and began to provide a summary. No sooner had I pointed to the Mufrek police station when Colonel Pittard cut me off. "You're my liaison. I want to hear from the director."

Colonel Samir arrived in the late afternoon to assume duties as deputy director from Colonel Ali, and I was unsure about how familiar he was with the details of the morning's battle. "Sir, Colonel Samir began his shift this afternoon and was not present for the operations," I remarked from the map.

"Well, he should know what occurred based on his shift-change briefing," Colonel Pittard reminded me.

So I returned to my desk at the back of the room, apprehensive about just how much information Colonel Samir's predecessor passed along to him. However, I was pleasantly surprised by Colonel Samir's summary delivered to the brigade commander. The deputy director provided the initial time of the attacks, how many police and Iraqi Army patrols responded, and how many security personnel suffered injuries. He pointed to the icons on the map marking IED locations, and noted that the police held a suspected insurgent in custody after finding him in a sedan by the Mufrek Traffic Circle.

Pleased with the information received, Colonel Pittard encouraged the Iraqis to continue their great work. The commander's reminder to me that I was his "liaison" to the JCC echoed in my mind for some time. Politely, he was reminding a new captain (I received my promotion from first lieutenant to captain on November 1) about the necessity of empowering Iraqis to assume responsibility for handling security issues. Considering how well the Iraqi security forces did respond to the complex attacks, I realized that they had the potential, and many Iraqi leaders were committed to making their country a safer place to live.

During the next morning's security meeting, Iraqis continued to demonstrate to me that they had the ability to improve their forces and replace the U.S. Army as the first line of response for handling crises. Colonel Dehaa, the deputy director on duty for November 10, noted the importance of establishing more vehicle check points around Baquba to prevent insurgents from moving between districts or receiving support from outlying villages. His recommendation to the Iraqi Army liaison at the table was for the Iraqi Army to assume full responsibility for the city borders, and to allow the police to concentrate on handling Baquba's interior security situation. Therefore, bridges would be secure and foreign fighters isolated from supporting insurgents in the city.

Colonel Dehaa continued, "We saw yesterday that the Iraqi security forces are gaining the people's trust. Many people called the JCC to provide information about the insurgents' locations, where IEDs had been placed, and what cars the insurgents were using. The people were also glad to hear that the journalists were incorrect in reporting so many police deaths."

Around the table, colonels and majors nodded in agreement and wrote notes into their calendar books. Colonel Dehaa's comments contrasted to the discussions we had a month earlier concerning the ability of the security forces to gain the people's trust. The attacks on November 9 seemed to boost the confidence of the Iraqis as much as the Transfer of Sovereignty did at the end of June.

Such an increase in confidence would prove essential only a week later, when a more aggressive city-wide attack occurred. Around 6:00 in the morning on November 15, I once again awoke to the muffled but nevertheless distinct sounds of distant combat. The JCC staff explained to me that insurgents were attacking the Mufrek and Buhriz police stations once more.

This time however, the enemy's concept of the operation seemed more sophisticated. They stole an ambulance from Baquba General Hospital in order to disguise and execute their logistical operations. Their tactics were also sounder than in the previous week. As police and Iraqi Army patrols deployed towards Mufrek and Buhriz, they encountered heavy resistance from a variety of strongpoints established by insurgents. Highway 2 and the Mufrek Traffic Circle were seeded with IEDs. In Mufrek the same two schools as before were occupied, and insurgents established a machine gun position atop a four-story civic center on the east side of the circle.

To the south, police patrols halted at the northern edge of Buhriz after police discovered several IEDs placed on Canal Street. As police investigated one of the devices, RPGs launched from the dilapidated governor's mansion exploded around the police pickup trucks. Policemen and soldiers remained in southern Tahrir and New Baquba, where they could hear the firefight continue from both police stations. However, the insurgents succeeded in effectively blocking the security forces from reinforcing either location.

The JCC phone lines continued to ring throughout the morning. Citizens courageous enough to peek out of the gates of their homes called the police headquarters to report the location of masked riflemen throughout the city. In addition to Buhriz and Mufrek, we received reports of a half dozen fighting positions established in Old Baquba. According to several of the callers, IEDs could be spotted on Highway 2 north of the Mufrek Traffic Circle, in the direction of Camp Warhorse.

Before 8:00 in the morning, Maj. Kenneth Adgie, the brigade operations officer, radioed the JCC backroom on a brigade-wide frequency. After I provided him with a situation update, he responded, "Good report. What help do you need? Do we need to send tanks in from the north? I can have Kiowas [army helicopters] on station."

At that point, I still felt that the attack could be handled by the Iraqis with the assistance of Task Force 1-6. I told Major Adgie that armor and aviation assets would be premature at that time. The operations officer acknowledged and said that he would be waiting for my next report.

While speaking with Major Adgie, I was also cautious about asking for brigade assistance in a city that belonged to Task Force 1-6 as an area of operation. Although the JCC functioned as both a provincial and city coordination center, I was not sure that it was my place as a "liaison" to request assets from a higher headquarters to support a fight inside the artillery battalion's footprint. Maj. William Chlebowski, the Task Force 1-6 executive officer, would need to make the request.

Making such a decision was not a matter of pride — captain versus his superior, a major — in requesting support from brigade. Rather, committing forces to an area where they did not typically operate required synchronization between Task Force 1-6 and the new units. Radio frequencies needed to be shared, and internal boundaries needed to be established on maps to prevent tank and humvee units from firing into each other inadvertently. Operations officers were better suited for coordinating this than I was at the JCC.

Indeed, Task Force 1-6 was already involved in the fight. However, their priorities were concentrated in Khatoon and Old Baquba. Caleb and T. J.'s platoons supported Capt. John Bushman's B Company. In the late morning Caleb and T. J. would respond to rifle fire in Old Baquba and spend most of the day clearing pockets of resistance in that district of the city. The police and Iraqi Army would need to support themselves until U.S. forces could assist them in breaching the obstacles set between them and the besieged police stations.

As the U.S. fight moved north of Highway 5 and into Old Baquba, the governor's security convoy sped from the governor's residence in Muqdadiya to the JCC. Taking a seat in front of the situation map with General Whalid, Gov. Abdullah Rashid al Jabori intended to find out what the police plan was for resolving the crisis. When the JCC operations officer pointed to the abandoned governor's mansion in southern Tahrir to explain that insurgents using the building for cover had fixed the police on Canal Street, the governor turned to me and asked that U.S. forces destroy the dilapidated mansion with bombers.

"My police can't get to the Buhriz police station, Captain Tomlin, and the police are going to run out of ammunition soon," Governor Abdullah explained. The provincial police chief was very concerned about the situ-

Diyala Governor Abdullah Rashid al Jabori (left) and Major General Whalid (second from left), the provincial chief of police, receive status reports from Iraqi police and army leaders in the JCC on November 15, 2004. After insurgents overran police stations in Mufrek and Buhriz, Iraqi security forces coordinated their counterattack from the JCC. (Gregory Tomlin Collection)

ation in Buhriz, and he expected the station to fall into insurgent hands very soon. I did not have to speak Arabic to understand how desperate the police in the Buhriz police station were as they provided reports in high-pitched voices across the police radio frequency.

Insurgents went so far as to abduct the Buhriz police chief from his home and bring him in the front of the Buhriz station with his hands bound. As the insurgents beat the colonel, one of them screamed towards the station that the police would share a similar fate if they did not surrender the station at once. The police refused, and the insurgents subsequently shot the police colonel in the head, leaving his body on the street.

I passed the governor's request to Task Force 1-6, who forwarded the request to brigade. Shortly thereafter, Colonel Pittard called the JCC on a secure American phone line to speak to the governor directly about the issue. After a brief conversation, the governor put me on the phone to speak with Major Adgie. Two U.S. Air Force fighters would be entering Baquba air space in the next fifteen minutes to destroy the mansion-turned-strongpoint. I needed to confirm that the police on the ground were positioned at a safe distance from the impending missile launch.

However, the air strike never occurred. Minutes after the arrangement was made, the police reported that insurgents succeeded in overrunning the Mufrek police station, and two stolen police cars were heading south on Highway 2 towards Baghdad. A U.S. unmanned aerial vehicle (UAV) followed the two cars south as the brigade staff watched from a live video feed at Camp Warhorse. These two patrol cars became a priority threat that needed to be intercepted. The official government cars could be used to create vehicle borne IEDs capable of entering any number of security compounds in the national capital before causing masses of casualties. The fighters quickly altered their course and destroyed each car with its occupants, using laser-guided bombs. The brigade staff witnessed the entire process through the uninterrupted UAV coverage.

The Buhriz police station fell to the insurgents shortly thereafter. Running out of ammunition and incapable of transporting their casualties north to Baquba General Hospital because of the IEDs on Canal Street, the police withdrew from the station. Several officers removed their uniforms prior to vacating the building through the backdoor. The JCC lost radio contact with the police in Buhriz immediately after the provincial police chief learned that the Buhriz police had expended all of their ammunition.

The Iraqi security forces were not outnumbered by the insurgents, but they had clearly been outmaneuvered by the enemy. A decisive end to the day's battle would only occur if U.S. forces took the lead. Task Force 1-6 recognized that it only had the manpower to handle operations east of the Diyala River, and requested from brigade that Task Force 2-63 Armor (the brigade armor battalion positioned north of Baquba) use its tanks to clear Highway 2 and support the police in retaking the Mufrek police station.

The Task Force 2-63 response was aggressive and lethal, delivering the shock necessary to force the insurgents to displace. Once tanks cleared Highway 2 and the Mufrek Traffic Circle, the police returned to the Mufrek police station. Upon arriving at the police station, the police discovered it abandoned by the insurgents, but the rooms ravaged.

The police refused to reoccupy the station because they worried that the insurgents would return to kill them. They wanted to be at a station located directly on Highway 2 or 5, with better fields of fire and direct routes for reinforcements to use. Governor Abdullah was furious at this report, but General Whalid looked vacantly at the situation map. The police chief would not be able to convince the police to stay in Mufrek without the U.S. tanks remaining outside the front door of the station. This condition would not be met by 3rd Brigade.

By late afternoon Buhriz became everyone's focal point. Caleb and T. J. had completed their operations in Old Baquba and returned to Camp Gabe to receive orders for the mission to seize the Buhriz police station. Neither lieutenant was pleased with the new mission, especially after Spc. Michael Griffin was evacuated for his bullet wounds suffered during the day's house-to-house clearing operations.

While Task Force 1-6 planned the U.S. side of the operation, General Whalid tasked his special police unit to seize the Buhriz police station. The Iraqi Army would not support the mission, so that they could establish a greater security presence along Highway 5. By 4:00 in the afternoon, Caleb and T. J.'s platoons cleared Canal Street, and the chief's personal unit was inside the Buhriz police station. The bodies of four policemen were found on the premises, including the body of the murdered station chief. The rooms of the station were scorched black with soot; insurgents burnt office furniture and files before fleeing the building shortly before the Bradleys arrived.

Twenty minutes after the U.S. forces returned to Camp Gabe from Buhriz, the police also left the Buhriz police station to return to their provincial headquarters. Governor Abdullah and General Whalid left the JCC to meet privately in the chief's office. It could not have been a very comfortable meeting for General Whalid, based on the ill performance of his men that day. In addition to the fatalities, six police and eight civilians were seriously injured. Six police vehicles, including the two stolen cars, were damaged beyond repair. While the enemy failed to hold any new ground that day, theirs was a moral victory.

At 5:00 in the evening the provincial police headquarters came under an intense barrage of mortar and RPG fire. One stray mortar exploded in Old Baquba, killing a child. Like the climax of a 4th of July fireworks display, the fierce attack ended within minutes. It seemed as if the insurgents wanted to send a message to the security forces, reminding us that they did not suffer a total defeat that day. Without police maintaining a physical presence in the Buhriz police station, Buhriz was effectively in enemy hands. No other security patrols—U.S. or Iraqi—operated in the town that night.

At first glance, the day could be seen as a total failure for the Iraqi security forces. From the JCC, however, I observed legitimate reasons for a number of the police and Iraqi Army setbacks. IEDs plagued the streets, and the Iraqis did not have the technology that U.S. forces had to clear the 155-millimeter devices. Because the police were fixed at positions blocked by IEDs, they could not reinforce police stations until the U.S. cleared the path.

An additional concern was adequate ammunition and weaponry. With RPGs and machine guns, the insurgents often outgunned the Iraqi security forces. Police and Iraqi Army vehicle protection was conspicuously meager compared to that enjoyed by U.S. forces operating in Baquba. Even when we resorted to welding steel plates onto our humvees, U.S. soldiers always had more reliable protection from exploding IEDs and RPGs than Iraqi soldiers had by riding in the back of pickup trucks. The arguments made by the Iraqi lieutenants and sergeants sent to reoccupy the Mufrek and Buhriz police stations about refusing to stay made more sense considering these factors.

Perhaps this time the Americans were the guilty party for hoping too much, hoping that the Iraqis were fully prepared to counter the insurgency on their own. Throughout the day I witnessed Iraqi security forces attempt to reinforce their besieged comrades. In Buhriz the police held their post until they realized that death would greet them faster than reinforcements. The Buhriz police even remained in their station after watching terrorists murder their chief. If good acts were truly the essential component to achieving a safe and secure environment in Iraq, then additional training and equipment were the only solution.

While U.S. forces provided the Iraqi security forces in Diyala with uniforms, rifles, vehicles, and even RPGs, the attacks of November 15 made it apparent that the Iraqis needed more if they were to become self-sufficient. As the brigade dealt with procurement issues, Captain Edwan and I continued efforts in the JCC to build a competent staff, based on the experiences of the recent attacks. If we failed in our obligations to empower the Iraqis to make competent decisions, then we would be just as guilty of hoping that a marginal effort to prepare new Iraqi security forces was as acceptable as an Iraqi general retorting my constructive criticism with *Ensha Allah.*

chapter 16
TO BE OR NOT TO BE
Capt. Greg Tomlin, Military Advisor,
Diyala Joint Coordination Center

*W*hen Capt. Daniel Edwan and I sat down for the first time with Amer Latif, the director of the Independent Elections Commission of Iraq (IECI) for the Diyala province, we felt that we had achieved a small miracle. Amer arrived at the Joint Coordination Center (JCC) on November 21, after nearly a month of evading multiple invitations to discuss the January 2005 elections with us.

Since late October, JCC field agents drove to the IECI offices in New Baquba, and a couple IECI staffers stopped by the JCC to arrange a formal meeting. Every visit ended with both parties agreeing on a set date for a future conference. For each scheduled meeting, senior Iraqi security officials, U.S. Foreign Service officers, and planners from 3rd Brigade arrived at the JCC conference room, but the IECI director was always conspicuously absent. Fed up with his uncooperativeness, Captain Edwan took a platoon of soldiers to visit Amer at his personal office, walking straight in while Amer was giving an interview to a couple of Iraqi reporters. Realizing that we were never going to leave him alone, the IECI director assured Captain Edwan that he would come to the JCC within a week's time.

Amer arrived at the JCC with another gentleman whom he introduced as Colonel Kalifa, a police officer detailed to serve as chief of security for the IECI through the winter elections. We escorted the duo into the conference room for an uninterrupted conversation that would lay the groundwork for security operations in Diyala over the next two months. One of our interpreters and Brig. Tahsin Tawfiq Jassim, the newly appointed provincial Director of Security, also joined us in the room.

Sizing up Amer Latif, I tried to stifle a laugh. It was not that I found the man to be funny, but rather, the fact that I was finally face-to-face with the elusive individual we had nicknamed "Queen Latifa" several weeks earlier. Mr. Latif and Ms. Latifa could not have been any more dissimilar.

Election, JCC and U.S. State Department officials greet one another prior to an election security meeting in the JCC conference room. Police Colonel Kalifa (fourth from the left on the left side of the table) served as chief of security for the Diyala elections commission until his assassination on January 5, 2005. (Gregory Tomlin Collection)

With his thick mustache, carefully parted hair and wool suit, this lawyer looked very much the part of a university professor.

Following initial pleasantries, Amer quickly moved to argue that the IECI was an independent organization chartered to be an autonomous agency whose only superiors were in the IECI offices of Baghdad. Amer seemed to be concerned that involvement with members of the JCC— Iraqi or American—would cause the populace of Diyala to perceive that the police, the governor's office, and Multinational Forces were attempting to manipulate the election process.

Captain Edwan assured Amer that neither the Iraqi nor the U.S. officials intended to influence the election process. However, it was imperative that security forces be closely involved in the elections *security* process. The IECI had funds to hire a core staff, but certainly not the finances to provide for adequate protection of their offices, registration sites, polling stations, and the secure movement of election material across the province.

The voter registration period began in November and would continue through December. Despite already being three weeks into this process, the JCC did not know where the majority of the twenty-two schools were throughout the province where the IECI had set up shop for families to verify addresses and numbers of household members eligible to vote. If security officials did not know which schools were to be used, then police and Iraqi soldiers could not protect the sites from car bombs or insurgents seeking to harm Iraqi civilians.

The IECI chose to use schools as registrations sites for several practical reasons. With the schools closed for the winter holiday, children were not displaced from their classrooms. Schools constructed during the previous Iraqi regime followed a similar floor plan, thus allowing planners to standardize many of the security requirements and voting procedures from one site to the next. Most of the schools were set slightly back from the main road by a compound wall, much like traditional Arab homes. The main structure of the school stood several meters beyond the wall, with the recess yard hidden behind the building. If a large crowd gathered at one time to register, or eventually to vote, the Iraqis could mill in the playground rather than queue on the main street, where a vehicle-borne improvised explosive device (IED) might detonate.

Amer acknowledged that the IECI needed the assistance of security forces in order to assure success in the elections, but he remained concerned about the perception of his commission collaborating with U.S. soldiers. This was the exact reason why meetings at the JCC were imperative, Captain Edwan explained. The JCC was housed in an Iraqi police station; the walls of the compound prevented insurgents from observing whether visitors had appointments with Iraqi officials or the Americans. Brigadier Tahsin also shared with Amer the roles played by his staff and liaison officers.

Captain Edwan highlighted that with the ability to share information with six other JCCs in the province and having access to every government agency in both Diyala and the national government, the Baquba JCC was the logical hub for coordinating election security. The U.S. government wanted to see the Iraqi elections be an Iraqi success. In order for Multinational Forces to play a background role on election day, the U.S. was prepared to help in every step of the security planning phase. If the IECI and JCC believed that they required costly radios, unmarked cars, and barrier equipment for each polling site, then the U.S. stood ready to foot the bill.

It appeared that this dialogue was beginning to break through Amer's shell. He turned to Colonel Kalifa, instructing him to send a daily security update to the JCC. The initial report would provide the locations of the twenty-two registration sites. Could the IECI provide a permanent liaison to the JCC, we asked, just like the fire department and traffic police had established? Amer said that he would think about it. Would Amer and Colonel Kalifa be willing to attend weekly security meetings with the directors of the other JCCs in the province? Amer stated that it was a possibility. There was a reason for our urgency in pressing these issues: sixty-odd days are not a lot of time to develop a sound security plan for a general election.

Speaking English for the first time during the meeting, Amer said, "'To be or not to be, that is the question.'"

"Shakespeare," I said, with a slight grin.

Amer appeared pleased that I recognized his quote. "Yes, Shakespeare! 'To be or not to be' is what the election means for Iraq. America has been a democracy for two hundred years. Democracy is new for us in Iraq. You must be patient with us."

Captain Edwan and I looked at each other, realizing that he had a point. With our military educations and combat leadership experience, the pace of our words and actions could seem gruff to others. We could fix that perception to a degree, but had to remain relentless in pressing for support in certain matters.

Amer's choice of words also demonstrated to us that he too was dedicated to the success of his country's elections. Captain Edwan and I shared personal stakes in the mission at hand. The January 2005 elections would not only be the last significant operation during our year in Iraq, but would also serve as the litmus test as to whether our soldiers' actions and sacrifices had made a measurable improvement in the stability of Iraq. Elections marred by violence would mean failure on our part to achieve the essential tasks of our army's mission in Operation Iraqi Freedom. Amer's *Hamlet* reference reminded us that the Iraqi people were just as concerned, if not more, as the U.S. soldiers, journalists, and Foreign Service officers in seeing a free and democratic Iraq become a reality.

The following morning Colonel Kalifa returned to the JCC with his first IECI security report. He also sent copies to the governor's office and to the provincial chief of police. He handed me a large red folder that contained schematics of the twenty-two registration sites. Each blueprint was meticulously hand drawn with colored pencils. The colors represented interior and exterior walls, existing vegetation, roads, and sidewalks. When I asked who the artist was, he proudly smiled and said that he had made them. The JCC could keep the file for the day to make photocopies of the material.

With the names and locations of the schools secured, the JCC shifted from abstract planning to concrete security preparations. Using records from our daily JCC security meetings, we began to prioritize schools in the order of those that were in the most hostile areas and those which were located in areas with alarmingly low numbers of police. Turning to Brigadier Tahsin, we discussed how to involve the JCC field agents in collecting intelligence on each of the registration sites. We developed a questionnaire, which the agents would take to each school, finding out the name of the IECI site director, talking with the closest police chief about his station's involvement to protect the schools, and taking pictures of the buildings.

In many respects the registration period was our warm-up drill for the January 2005 elections. It was an opportunity for the JCC staff to become more familiar with their new duties and in handling their new equipment. During the last week of November, I spent considerable time with the field agents, teaching them how to use digital cameras and hand-held global-positioning systems (GPS). Working through a translator, it took me hours to explain that the camera will not save photos when the batteries are dead, and that the GPS will not provide a correct grid coordinate unless the display screen has three bars in the upper-right corner. Prior to their first field trips, we walked around the compound until the agents were comfortable photographing the façade of the headquarters and showing me our present grid location.

When field agents returned with inadequate information for the site questionnaire, the operations officer on duty would send the agents back to the same registration site. Because I could not personally visit the registration sites, I verified the grid location the agents reported by checking the grid on Falcon View. Falcon View is a computer system containing satellite imagery of our area of operations, and I displayed it on a large plasma screen in the JCC. There was no issue if the grid provided by the field agents matched the structure on the imagery that looked like a school. On the other hand, if the grid they returned fell in the middle of a lake or a traffic circle, then I knew something was wrong.

Many times we could correct the issue by having the field agents show me on Falcon View where a particular school was located. Initially, however, this proved difficult, because the agents did not understand the perspective of the imagery. I tried in vain with one particular agent to help him understand that he was looking at a birds-eye view of Baquba. I centered the screen on the police headquarters and showed him Highway 5, the Diyala River, and the palm groves.

Overhearing me, Colonel Kamal, the operations officer on duty, approached the screen, "You said birds-eye view. That is like flying."

"Exactly," I said, with renewed hope that we were about to have an awakening. "You were an army pilot. Can you tell Mustafa that this picture is the same as if we were flying?"

"Of course, I was a helicopter instructor for many years. I will pretend that Mustafa and I are in the cockpit," Colonel Kamal stated in English before conversing rapidly in Arabic with the field agent.

For the next ten minutes I adjusted the imagery as Colonel Kamal and Mustafa "flew" over Baquba and northeast to Muqdadiya. We zoomed in on a small building, and Colonel Kamal exclaimed with satisfaction, "There it is!"

"That can't be it," I retorted. "That's too small to be a school, and we're in the wrong city."

"No, Captain Tomlin, that is not the school; that's my family's home!" smiled Colonel Kamal. "Don't worry, we'll fly to the school next."

Ten minutes later we located the correct grid for the school Mustafa had most recently visited. By that time the entire staff had assembled around the plasma screen, and nearly everyone gained a perspective for how to use the imagery. In the months ahead, this proved invaluable when field agents and Iraqi explosive ordinance disposal (EOD) teams would return to show me exactly where IEDs were found in the province.

While my focus centered on the Baquba JCC staff, Captain Edwan concentrated on improving our communications architecture with the other JCCs in the province. Not only were the town JCC staffs learning how to use email and Yahoo! chat, but they were also introduced to reporting procedures, both laterally and higher. As Captain Edwan explained to the JCC directors during one of our new weekly provincial JCC security meetings, it was imperative to share information quickly. If an insurgent steals a police car in Muqdadiya and drives southwest, the Muqdadiya JCC needs to alert the Baquba JCC in order for the Iraqi Army or police to establish roadblocks and intercept the stolen car.

To validate that the JCC staffs were communicating, Captain Edwan designed three emergency response exercises in December and January. For each simulation he scripted an events list and left it with Brigadier

Tahsin. According to the list, the Baquba JCC would phone a particular JCC at a set time and provide the operations officer with a scenario. For instance, at 4:00 in the afternoon a call was placed to the Khalis JCC stating that insurgents raided a Khalis school used as a registration site and kidnapped the IECI employees. The Khalis JCC staff would determine how to react to the event and report their procedures to the Baquba JCC. The Baquba JCC telephone operator would record all of the exercise reports received throughout the day, and we would meet the following week to discuss everyone's performance.

On December 4, Colonel Kalifa arrived for his regular visit. Normally we would talk in the main operations room, but on this day he asked that we adjourn to the privacy of the conference room. Seated at the table with an interpreter, he handed me a letter that had been delivered the night before to the homes of nearly all registration site directors. The translator read it aloud in English.

> *Therefore, we warn all visitors to this election post or any election post, and every candidate, and those who assist them in running this election, distributing the forms, taking the signatures from the people, or who make meetings in houses, government buildings or the IECI headquarters: you are all targeted by Al Mujahedeen fighters and your names will be added to the death list, and fighters' hands will send you all to hell. Just as we did before, we will not stop kidnapping you, and we will resurrect the slaughter to separate your heads from your bodies.*

"Captain Tomlin, I have nine children. Who will support them if I am killed?" Colonel Kalifa asked.

It was a fair question, and I knew that the answer was not the Iraqi government. Pensions and insurance programs did not exist yet in the new regime. The U.S. government would provide a certain amount of money to the family, but the family would need to primarily rely on its extended family and tribe for assistance. Colonel Kalifa already knew the answer to his question. He presented me with the quandary as a way to remind me that the U.S. could not get too impatient with how the Iraqi security forces performed. If they were reluctant to act, it was not always because they were too scared for their own wellbeing. Rather, their concern often rested with the safety of their families.

Threatening letters were a significant concern for those working in the Iraqi government. From my time as a platoon leader in Baquba I was familiar with letters announcing *jihad* against the U.S. forces and the Iraqis who sympathized with the "infidels." These propaganda drops were general in nature and blanketed entire neighborhoods. Now that I was living at the JCC, the letters became more personal; they were direct threats against the people with whom I worked on a daily basis. Throughout my time at the JCC, staff members would arrive in the morning to show me a letter left at their homes and say that they would not return to the JCC again.

One of the reasons that Brigadier Tahsin became the Director of Security at the provincial JCC in late November was because Major General Ayad, the original director, quit after two grenades were detonated in front of his home in Tahrir. Brigadier Tahsin had served as an assistant director since my arrival in October. During his shifts he demonstrated the leadership qualities that both Captain Edwan and I agreed were necessary for the position of Director of Security for Diyala.

Brigadier Tahsin formerly served as a Republican Guard infantry brigade commander. His most prominent physical feature was the triangular notch missing from the bridge of his nose. As he retold the story, an Iranian bullet grazed him during the Iran-Iraq War. In fact, he had been injured five times by bullets and knives during the long conflict. As he rolled up his right pant leg to show me another bullet scar, he asked how many battle injuries I had suffered. He laughed when I told him none.

Just as I found it important for the Director of Security to lead the daily security meeting, Captain Edwan and I spent hours coaching Brigadier Tahsin to lead the weekly JCC election security meeting. I imagine that to a degree, he resented our prep time, and what general officer would not? Here were two captains, each physically unscathed by the horrors of war, telling a hardened veteran how to lead a planning session of two dozen of his countrymen.

Sometimes he rolled his eyes or quipped a terse response as I reviewed statistics or talking points with him for the umpteenth time. I think that initially he believed that I was only spending time with him prior to security meetings to impress visiting U.S. colonels and generals, or the journalists who occasionally trailed them to the JCC. By late December, when security meetings became more frequent, often without other Americans in the room barring Captain Edwan or myself, Brigadier Tahsin's attitude seemed to change. He seemed to come to realize that we cared about empowering him and the entire JCC staff to perform well and take ownership of their country.

When his outlook on our role as his advisors changed, so did his assertiveness, and the seasoned officer once again assumed command. After Captain Edwan inspected the JCC staff lounge with Brigadier Tahsin and found the room in disarray, the director assembled the staff on shift and barked orders at them to clean up their mess. He instructed his assistant directors to have their personnel wipe the dust from their desks and clean the floor of the JCC at each shift change. If the governor or provincial chief of police entered the JCC, he expected the staff to stand as a sign of respect. By lunch each day he reviewed the minutes of the daily security meeting before a field agent would carry a copy to the governor's office.

At about the same time of Brigadier Tahsin's transformation, Amer Latif became a more frequent guest in the JCC. He also dispatched a permanent liaison to the JCC who manned a work station, briefed during the daily security meetings, and even joined field agents on visits to registration sites. Most often, Amer arrived to participate in election-specific security meetings. On other occasions he arrived to meet with Maj. Teresa Wolfgang, commander of the Civil Affairs company attached to 3rd Brigade. Just as I was Brigadier Tahsin's U.S. counterpart, Major Wolfgang was Amer's. Honoring his wish for Americans to not park humvees in front of the Baqbua IECI office, the two traveled separately to the JCC. Step by step, the JCC was becoming the hub in Diyala for elections security operations.

As the sky over Baquba erupted with AK-47 tracer fire to bring in the New Year, our attention shifted from the registration period to the elections, now only thirty days away. Our progress during December was measurable, but the scope of our challenge in 2005 would be tremendously wider. In lieu of twenty-two schools, the IECI projected that they would require 254 separate polling sites on election day in order to provide Diyala's 621,000 registered voters the opportunity to cast their ballots. It appeared that the bulk of the Iraqi and American leadership remained committed to the mission, but we also knew that there was plenty of room for setbacks. We could little afford to lose a member of the team.

On January 3, Colonel Kalifa arrived at the JCC with his daily report in hand and an extra-wide smile on his face. He asked if he could have a new car, at least until the end of the month. Justifying his request, he said that shortly after he left his home that morning to drive to the provincial police headquarters, he noticed someone following him. This was not the first time that the individual had followed him. Because Colonel Kalifa drove a white Toyota Four Runner, conspicuously known as a police vehicle, he wanted to know if the JCC had a civilian car he could use. Although the JCC owned three unmarked cars, all were in use. I asked him to accompany me to the headquarters criminal investigation office, and the sergeant on duty provided me with the key to a gray Honda sedan.

Colonel Kalifa and I went outside to inspect the car. I unlocked the driver's door and sat down to ensure that the engine worked and that its gas tank was full. I turned the ignition off, satisfied that the car would be adequate. Colonel Kalifa asked me if the battery was new. I popped the hood, and together we inspected the battery. Pleased with what he saw, Colonel Kalifa shut the hood and slammed the driver's door shut.

"Colonel Kalifa," I said in exasperation, "you just locked the only key we have inside the car!"

He looked apologetic as the translator interpreted my remarks. Then he began to laugh as I withdrew my Beretta and pedantically gestured as if I were about to shatter the window with the pistol grip. Colonel Kalifa assured me that he would find a way to open the car without breaking the window, and he set off to find someone. I returned to my work in the JCC. Half an hour later, Colonel Kalifa returned to the JCC, smiling and waving the key to the Honda. He was off to visit schools that the IECI would use as polling sites so that he could make sketches, just as he made of the schools used during the registration period. It was the last time I would see him alive.

While driving to work two days later with his cousin, gunmen trailed Colonel Kalifa's car and conducted a drive-by shooting, killing both men less than three hundred meters from an Iraqi Army checkpoint. When the police brought me the news, my thoughts returned to the conversation that Colonel Kalifa and I had a month ago about who would care for his family if he were to lose his life. I prayed that his tribe would be generous in taking in the wife and nine children he left behind.

Stirring from my personal reflections, I asked the messenger where the Honda was. He reported that it was still at the checkpoint. I turned to the assistant director on duty and told him to have a tow truck haul the sedan to the provincial police headquarters immediately. It was safe to say that no one would meddle with a car within rifle range of the Iraqi Army checkpoint, but we needed to secure the car because I had a feeling that Colonel Kalifa's polling site sketches were inside. Hours later, when the tow truck pulled into our compound, the field agents found the same red folder used for the registration site schematics, only now it was thicker, with dozens more of the meticulously drawn papers.

At dusk that evening I inspected the car for myself. The driver's side window that only two days earlier I pretended to break was now shattered. Both the windshield and rear window had large holes through them. The grey cloth of the driver's headrest and the passenger's seat were crimson red. For the first time since June, when Pvt. First Class Jason Lynch was killed in Buhriz, I felt deeply saddened by the loss of life in this war.

Over the past three months I had sat through daily security meetings compiling statistics of Iraqis killed by IEDs, Iraqis killed by errant mortar rounds, and Iraqis killed by gunmen. During Ramadan, when insurgents targeted high profile government leaders, I was asked to identify bodies for my brigade headquarters, because I recognized the officials from my time at the provincial capital as a lieutenant. It did not faze me the slightest to look at photos taken by field agents at the morgue and confirm that one was an assistant governor or a provincial councilmember. These were men with whom I had curt exchanges, but Colonel Kalifa was a personable and earnest Iraqi whom I had come to know and admire.

At the beginning of that same week's election security meeting, Colonel Dana Pittard, the 3rd Brigade commander, invited those assembled in the JCC conference room to join him in a moment of silence in remembrance of Colonel Kalifa. Following the meeting, Governor Abdullah Rashid al Jabori and Colonel Pittard drove to the Kalifa household to extend their sympathies to the late colonel's family. As their motorcades departed the police headquarters, Amer introduced me to Colonel Kalifa's successor, Mohammed.

Together, Amer, Mohammed, and I faced a considerable task. During the elections security meeting Amer finally accepted the reality that the Iraqi Army and police simply did not have the required personnel to secure 254 separate polling sites. Based on the general security plan developed in Baghdad by the IECI, each polling site required ten policemen to live in the school for four days and four nights prior to election day. Some of the sites needed to be consolidated. We began our work as soon as the security meeting adjourned, and the three of us did not leave the conference room until late that night.

Irrefutably, certain polling sites could not be consolidated. If there was only one school in a remote village, then it needed to remain open to prevent voters from trekking for miles to the next closest town. However, Old Baquba did not need eleven separate schools for its one-and-a-half kilometers-square district, and we consolidated the polling sites into seven schools. Amer's greatest concern with our downscaling was that the schools would be too small to process the thousands of anticipated voters. His point was legitimate; the IECI formulated the equation used to determine the number of polling sites so that there would be about 2,500 voters per site. Acknowledging his point, we agreed to not consolidate more than three polling sites into one school, and to select the largest of the schools to hold the consolidated sites. By the end of the night we had whittled the number down to 165 schools.

We presented the final list of polling sites on January 10 to the senior Iraqi and American security leaders. While Amer's assistants planned how to organize voter booths in classrooms, JCC field agents, with a digital camera and GPS in hand, completed questionnaires about each of the schools. The U.S. task forces responsible for portions of the province dispatched platoons to conduct their own security assessments of the same sites. Everyone had ten days to complete their assessments before the province would hold an elections security rehearsal on January 20.

Diyala was divided between two U.S. brigades with six battalion-sized task forces, and JCCs shared nearly congruous boundaries with the task forces. This made the Baquba JCC the hub for updating a master database detailing everything from how many concrete barriers would be needed in front of a school to the response time of an Iraqi Army quick-reaction force to a school. I became the go-to guy for Americans and Iraqis alike who wanted to review the most current information of the province as a whole. Brigadier Tahsin continued to take a more active role in overseeing the day-by-day operations in the JCC, while I stayed cloistered in the conference room, pounding away on the keyboard of my laptop.

The day before the election rehearsal, the provincial Director of Health visited the JCC to provide a memorandum containing license plate numbers and specific locations for where he would position all hospital ambulances on election day. He also explained to Brigadier Tahsin and me that full complements of surgeons would be on duty in emergency rooms to treat victims of election day bloodshed. Finally, he asked for five tents from the U.S. Army to emplace on the grounds of the five largest hospitals in Diyala in the event of a massive casualty influx. I was astonished by the doctor's organization and forethought in requesting tents. Brigadier Tahsin handed the memorandum over to the intelligence officer to ensure that the police, traffic police, and Iraqi Army received copies, and I called the brigade planner to requisition the tents.

1st Lt. T. J. Grider, platoon leader, 4th Platoon, C Company, assists his platoon in emplacing barriers around election sites in Shifta in January 2005. (Provided with permission by Douglas Chadwick)

Early the next morning Captain Edwan and I traveled north of Baquba to the 3rd Brigade headquarters at Camp Warhorse to prepare for the day's rehearsal. Situated on an old Iraqi Army airfield, the voluminous hangar of the camp was the ideal location to house the crowd that was about to assemble. U.S. company, battalion, and brigade commanders from across Diyala sat in front of projector screens displaying satellite imagery and bilingual Microsoft PowerPoint slides. Seated next to each commander was his Iraqi Army, police, and JCC counterpart. Behind the leadership were the primary planners from the U.S. staffs and the JCCs.

If there was ever a single opportunity to do the most damage to the Multinational Forces in Diyala, January 20 was the day. A well-aimed mortar strike would have shredded the aluminum roof of the hangar to kill or maim the top brass of every security entity in the province. At least one insurgent knew about the rehearsal. About fifteen minutes before the start of the rehearsal, with most of the guests inside, I stood outside the hangar, waiting to escort the tardy deputy governor to his seat. While waiting, I received a phone call from the police headquarters reporting that his convoy finally departed Old Baquba.

Although I was content to wait outside for him to arrive, the interpreter standing next to me recommended that we advise the brigade commander of the deputy governor's expected time of arrival. Agreeing, the two of us walked into the hangar. No sooner had we approached Colonel Pittard than a piercing noise came from outside, resembling the sound of the accidental discharge of a rifle and the shattering of glass. Dozens of curious officers exited the structure to find that a single Katyusha rocket had landed less than fifty meters from the hangar. The interpreter who was accompanying me brought over a piece of shrapnel. He found it only a few meters from where we had been standing minutes earlier.

The rehearsal commenced shortly thereafter and continued without additional bombs falling from the sky. For nearly eight hours, the group studied the security plan for each individual polling site in the province and scrutinized timelines and escort rosters for ballot movement to verify and account for IECI documents. The Iraqi Army colonels and police chiefs were as responsible for briefing their portion of the plan as their U.S. colleagues. From the head table, Governor Abdullah, Lieutenant General Aziz, the 4th Iraqi Army Division commander, Maj. Gen. John Batiste, the 1st U.S. Infantry Division commander, Brigadier Tahsin, and Amer listened intently to each briefer and questioned any remark that seemed too vague.

After dark I returned to the JCC with a paper copy of the briefing slides that were covered in notes taken during the rehearsal. Although eager to begin resolving issues identified during the rehearsal, I could tell that Brigadier Tahsin and the provincial chief of police were too exhausted from the lengthy conference to concentrate further that night. We agreed to resume the following morning.

Negotiations with election, government, and security officials went well into the night on dozens of occasions. Confirming the police manning rosters for school security ran closely behind consolidating polling sites as our most arduous discussion topic. The police would require more than half of the 3,500-man force in the province to provide for the requisite ten-man teams to secure the schools. Captain Edwan facilitated nearly all meetings related to police personnel management, but I frequently attended in order to capture new agreements on the polling site spreadsheets.

Following the election rehearsal Captain Edwan, the provincial police chief, and I met with twenty-odd station chiefs from across Diyala. As I adjusted Falcon View imagery on the conference room plasma screen to locate every polling site, Captain Edwan asked each police colonel to report the name of the lieutenant or sergeant responsible for each school security team and the specific number of police who would be on station for five days and four nights. Food was brought into the conference room, and police chiefs were only excused for bathroom breaks. Finally satisfied with the list of names and numbers compiled, the provincial chief of police adjourned the meeting ten hours later.

Governor Abdullah issued a province-wide curfew effective January 23, from eight at night until five in the morning. The Iraqi Army began to establish temporary checkpoints between the towns, and the U.S. Army increased its daily patrol schedule. In addition to the increased show of force, U.S. platoons escorted supply trucks to schools to deliver concrete barriers and rolls of concertina wire from January 25 to 29. The roadblocks cordoned off the streets immediately around the schools to prevent cars from driving near the compounds, and police could use the wire to close remaining gaps. Operations appeared to be moving smoothly, and there were only a few key tasks yet to be accomplished.

When I walked into the JCC on the morning of January 29, the operations center was buzzing with an unusual amount of energy. Later that morning, Gen. George Casey, the commander of Multinational Forces–Iraq, would arrive to speak with the governor and would receive a briefing from Brigadier Tahsin and the provincial police chief. The staff was busy at work cleaning the room and excitedly conversing. I sat down next to Brigadier Tahsin to review his briefing for General Casey for the final time. The former Republican Guard commander turned to smile at me as he affixed a vine of pink plastic flowers to the front of our desk.

"They are beautiful, yes, captain?" he asked, as he cut another piece of Scotch Tape.

"Yes, sir, they are." I responded aloud, while silently telling myself that this was one of those truly bizarre moments that I would remember for the rest of my life.

Major Wolfgang arrived with two Croatian photojournalists. One worked for Reuters and the other for a French news agency. The journalists intended to cover General Casey's visit and then hoped to travel through Baquba to capture images of polling sites. They asked me if I could arrange for them to ride with a police patrol through the city, but I

The tiered provincial JCC opened only a few days prior to election day on January 30, 2005. The metallic walls behind the Diyala and Baquba maps allowed staff members to track battle emergencies and security operations with magnets designating various units. A vine of pink plastic flowers adorns the director of security's desk. (Gregory Tomlin Collection)

knew that possibility was out of the question. It had been months since Western journalists were authorized to travel without military escorts in Baquba, due to the rising threat of kidnappings and high-profile beheadings. Traveling with Colonel Pittard, Jane Arraf of CNN also arrived at the JCC, assisted by Arwa Damon and her camera crew. Jane would spend considerable time in Baquba over the next few weeks.

General Casey's visit to the JCC went smoothly. Seated next to Governor Abdullah, the U.S. commander asked the police chief if his men were ready to protect their people. The police general stated that his men would do their job. Brigadier Tahsin explained how the JCC staffs across Diyala had conducted emergency exercises to prepare their responses for a variety of crises. When General Casey said that he had no further questions and stood up to leave, Captain Edwan and I nodded to each other from across the room. Our Iraqi counterparts had done well on their own accord before their governor, the most senior U.S. military officer in Iraq, and a small pool of international journalists.

We shifted our focus to the final preparations for monitoring the elections. Task Force 1-6 sent several soldiers from their operations center at Camp Gabe to the JCC to operate as a forward command post in the heart of their area of operations. Amer had been at the JCC since the night before, and now two of his assistants joined him at a desk in the JCC, where they began telephoning IECI liaisons to the JCCs across Diyala. The Iraqi Army brigade commander sent two of his majors to the JCC from his headquarters as additional liaison support. Brigadier Tahsin ordered two shifts of his four available staffs to be on hand at the JCC for the next two days.

Late in the night on January 29, as Iraqis and Americans worked together in the operations center updating final tracking charts and maps, Major Wolfgang and I sat in the conference room with the assistant chief of police for operations. U.S. patrols were reporting that policemen were not on duty at a handful of schools. We needed the police at their polling sites before the IECI began to deliver cases of ballots to the schools after midnight. The police colonel sent for station chiefs from Baquba and phoned chiefs in Muqdadiya, where the unsecured schools were located. His dialogue with his subordinates seemed to be going in circles, and it did not appear that he was being persuasive enough. Losing my patience, I told the colonel that he broke his word, and that he had personally failed to protect the sites after we had agreed to the specific allocations of policemen days earlier.

As soon as I said this, I realized my mistake. The colonel was doing all that he could and it was to his credit that the schools had been guarded for the past four days. I could sympathize with the police colonel's challenge of keeping his men focused. If the U.S. Army were to secure a school for more than twenty-four hours, we would send at least a platoon of soldiers with 300 percent time their normal issue of ammunition and water and rations for twice the duration of the stay. Considering that we asked ten policemen to stand guard at each school with sixty rounds of ammunition apiece for four nights, it was amazing that we were having difficulty only with eighteen of the 165 schools.

The police colonels continued to discuss how to resolve the issue, when Major Wolfgang and I were interrupted by a call from the brigade headquarters at about 11:30 at night. Colonel Pittard had just received a call from Governor Abdullah, who stated that his party, the Elite of Diyala Party, did not appear on the provincial ballot! The governor wanted to have his name written onto each ballot or have a postponement for the provincial elections until other arrangements could be made.

There were many suspicious circumstances surrounding the governor's situation, and we wondered whether this was some sort of political ploy. How did Governor Abdullah know about the absence of his party, as nobody outside of the IECI knew what the ballots looked like? Why did the governor call Camp Warhorse when he knew that Diyala's IECI director sat with us in the JCC that night? He was a Sunni in a province where his sect constituted only forty percent of the populace. Did he assume, perhaps, that he could not win the governorship in a free election, and he found this to be a suitable method for saving face? Was he more afraid of disappointing the Sunni sheiks allied with his party than he was of losing to a Shi'ia? Regardless of whether there was a sinister motive or this was simply an embarrassing oversight on the part of the IECI, our job at the JCC was to find some resolution for the issue before voters arrived at the polls in less than eight hours.

Major Wolfgang asked Amer to call his Baghdad headquarters for guidance. However, the only instructions he received were from an answering machine, inviting him to call back during business hours.

"Unbelievable!" I said. "You're telling me that on the night before nation-wide elections, the Independent Elections Commission of Iraq does not have anyone available to answer the phones at their national headquarters?"

I phoned the Civil-Military Operations Center down the street from the JCC to speak with Jim Jimenez and Sherman Grandy, the two Foreign Service officers assigned to the Department of State Embed Team for Diyala. With them was a senior political specialist visiting from the embassy in Baghdad. After I recounted the situation to them, the three diplomats agreed that the U.S. government could not make any adjustments to the physical ballots or to the election timeline. A decision could only be made in Baghdad by the same people who were unable to take Amer's call. In an effort to assist, the political specialist notified the U.S. embassy in Baghdad about the Elite of Diyala Party and wrote a detailed e-mail to Carlos Venezulea, the senior United Nations observer to the IECI.

Mr. Jimenez suggested that I personally explain this to Governor Abdullah. Minutes later I called the governor at his home to explain the official position of the U.S. government. As he spoke fluent English from his years living in exile as a dentist in Manchester, England, I did not require an interpreter. With his newborn daughter, appropriately named Di-yala, crying in the background, I reported to him that Amer could not get through to the IECI in Baghdad. I also suggested, on behalf of the Foreign Service officers, that he call Prime Minister Allawi, who might be willing to raise the issue with the IECI. The governor thanked me for the informa-tion, but said he would not call Baghdad because it was the responsibility of the IECI to rectify the problem. Hanging up the phone, I agreed with Major Wolfgang that there was little else that we could do.

By one in the morning on January 30, only a handful of personnel occupied the JCC. Everyone else found corners of the police station to doze off, catching a bit of rest prior to daybreak. Finding myself unable to sleep, I occupied my time by studying the final version of the polling site spreadsheet. Every thirty minutes I also phoned the national IECI head-quarters, only to receive the same bilingual recording as Amer.

Lt. Col. Steven Bullimore, commander of Task Force 1-6, arrived at the JCC at four in the morning. He would remain at the JCC until night-fall, but before leaving Camp Gabe, he had ordered all of his platoons to pa-trol the city. On election day, U.S. patrols were not permitted to approach polling sites, but no one said that they could not patrol the highways and major roads throughout their sectors. If the insurgents chose to cause a stir, the commander intended for his task force to destroy the enemy.

Shortly after five that morning, the JCC swelled to maximum capac-ity with regular staffers, U.S. soldiers, and Iraqi security liaisons. Everyone played a specific and well-rehearsed role. Some monitored Iraqi Army and police radios to collect IED reports, dispatch Iraqi EOD teams, and update situation maps. Others tracked the opening of each polling site, estimat-ing the numbers of voters passing through and confirming the location of ballots.

One issue continued to plague us: the absence of police from eigh-teen schools in Baquba and Muqdadiya. Captain Edwan and the provincial police chief worked in the conference room to resolve this issue. Ballots could not be left unsecured at a school; therefore, polling sites without guards would not open.

By eight in the morning, few of the polling sites reported receiving more than a couple dozen voters. While still on edge, waiting for the first explosion, the lack of voters began to stress us. Perhaps the Iraqis remain-ing in their homes were also waiting for the sound of that first explosion. As Amer and Major Wolfgang stood by my desk to discuss the voter turn-out, Colonel Pittard entered the JCC. Following him in, Jane Arraf and her cameraman went about interviewing Iraqis while Gina Cavallaro, an *Army Times* reporter, began talking to soldiers from Task Force 1-6.

Colonel Pittard walked directly to Amer and asked, "How could this happen?"

He was referring to the Elite of Diylala Party debacle. Deciding that this might turn into an unpleasant conversation, I left my desk to allow them to discuss the issue through the commander's interpreter. I joined the police chief at the large provincial map covered in acetate, where he stood speaking into a handheld radio. His eyes were bloodshot, and I knew that he had shared a sleepless night with me.

Surprisingly, with the exception of several scattered small arms shootings, the polling sites were not attacked, and Diyala citizens began arriving at schools in significant numbers by nine in the morning. Leaving the JCC with Colonel Pittard after his discussion with Amer ended, Jane Arraf and her crew traveled to a polling site behind the police headquarters in Shifta. With the restriction placed on the U.S. military to not approach the polling sites, the U.S. soldiers kept their distance as the journalists entered the school under Iraqi police escort.

The small room adjacent to the JCC where we kept the U.S. Army radios had cable television. I watched live on CNN International as Jane told a London-based anchorman via video-phone about an Iraqi woman whom she observed work her way to the Baquba polling site on crutches. Her cameraman turned his focus from the reporter to film a queue of cheerful Iraqis prepared to cast their first ballots. The interview had to end prematurely because several of the men standing behind Jane began clapping spontaneously to a song that someone began bellowing off camera. This was a very good information operations message to send to the world, and reporters embedded with units throughout the country filed similar stories for their networks that morning.

A U.S. sergeant interrupted the news to tell me that Governor Abdullah's convoy had entered the police headquarters compound and that he was headed for the JCC. Meeting him by the entrance, I asked the governor if he wanted to speak with Amer. He did, but beforehand, he asked me to help him review his e-mails. I took this to mean that he wanted a computer from which to work, and I directed him to my laptop.

"No, no. Can you open my e-mail account for me? I want to see if I sent my party's application into the IECI so that we could be on the ballot," the governor inquired in his British accent.

"Sir, are you sure that somebody else in your party didn't send the

Several men stand in line while a woman moves to her own line at a school in Shifta. Voter lines were segregated between the sexes. The JCC deployed field agents to assess voter turnout and site security. (Taken by Diyala Provincial JCC field agents; Gregory Tomlin Collection)

request to the IECI?" I asked, a bit stunned that a provincial governor would not have delegated such a task to his chief of staff or political party chairman.

"No, it would have been me. I recall there being a message addressed to the IECI, but I need to see it."

I entered his username after he told me that he had a Yahoo! account. I turned the computer toward him so that he could type in his password. He turned it back toward me and told me his password aloud. The messages addressed "Hi Dad" from his older children living in England told me that this was not strictly his business account. After reviewing his in-box for messages originating from the IECI, I opened the sent messages folder to scan the subject lines of his messages.

"There are no messages sent to the IECI from this address, sir. There is a single message in your in-box from the IECI, dated from early November, inviting your party to apply for the January ballots. However, the message log says that you did not reply to this message. Are you sure that you used this account and that nobody else may have sent in the application?" I asked.

"Captain Tomlin, this is my only account, and no, nobody else would have done it. Thank you for your help," Governor Abdullah said as he stood to depart for the conference room to speak with Amer.

Governor Abdullah did not seem angry, but rather, mildly annoyed. His attitude seemed to be like that of an airplane passenger informed by a flight attendant that she had run out of his entrée choice and he would have to settle for something else. Walking over to Lieutenant Colonel Bullimore's position, I recounted my interaction with the governor to him.

"The governor let you into his email account?" my boss asked, with a mixture of amazement and amusement.

"Yes, sir, and I haven't logged out yet if you'd like to take a look," I said, laughing.

Before noon, the sound of gunfire increased in Buhriz. One of the two polling sites in the town never opened due to the absence of police, and the open site in the northern portion of the town reported that there were no voters. If there were no voters, insurgents might be inclined to raid the school, murder the IECI staffers and police, and steal the ballots. Assuming that insurgents had not attacked other polling sites because they feared retaliation by the civilian populace, there was a possibility that they might decide that burning ballots on the Al Jazeera or Arabia news networks would be the next best course of action.

We discussed closing the Buhriz polling site with Amer, who initially opposed closing any polling site. Explaining that the ballots would be transferred to a school in southern Tahrir, Amer finally relented. Colonel Pittard approved Lieutenant Colonel Bullimore's recommendation to send a platoon to Buhriz to secure the ballots and IECI workers, and transport them to Tahrir. Lt. T. J. Grider's 4th Platoon from C Company received the mission and sped to Buhriz in their Bradley Fighting Vehicles.

The timing of their deployment was fortuitous. As the Bradleys established a security perimeter around the school, one of the vehicle crews identified several men carrying rocket-propelled grenade launchers (RPG) toward the school. The insurgents were quickly killed as 4th Platoon received small arms fire from one or two AK-47s. Less than thirty minutes after their arrival, with the IECI staff and ballots inside a Bradley, T. J.'s men traveled three kilometers north to Tahrir. Despite the bloodshed, the mission occurred smoothly, and it did not appear that it would mar the success of the elections in the greater Baquba area.

Shortly after resolving the Buhriz situation, Major General Batiste, commander of the 1st Infantry Division, flew to Camp Gabe and was escorted to the JCC. It was a surprise visit, but Brigadier Tahsin and the provincial police chief were unfazed, providing an impromptu situational update to the general. Colonel Pittard recommended that the two move to the conference room for a private discussion, and the JCC personnel resumed their work.

Political party posters plaster a wall in Shifta on election day, January 30, 2005. To assist voters in recognizing different candidates, parties identified themselves with a three-digit number in addition to their official party name. (Taken by Diyala Provincial JCC field agents; Gregory Tomlin Collection)

Having returned to the JCC with Colonel Pittard, Jane Arraf wanted to know about the performance of the Iraqi security forces from a U.S. perspective. I opened a binder to show her a spreadsheet that I had maintained since my arrival. It broke down the number of IED reports received each day, whether bombs were cleared or exploded, and whether a U.S. or Iraqi EOD team cleared each device. Pointing to the monthly rollup at the end of the rows, I explained how the Iraqi EOD teams were increasingly credited for clearing IEDs. Even as we experienced a spike in the number of IEDs located in the weeks approaching the elections, the Iraqi EOD teams' missions climbed equally with the more sophisticated U.S. teams.

I also spoke with Gina Cavallaro from the *Army Times.* She and I discussed the importance of Iraqis doing things for themselves, and she asked me if security forces were gaining more confidence and independence. I assured her that they were. As an example, I singled out Brigadier Tahsin's performance, telling her that I was only successful if he and the JCC staff gained visibility and credibility. In my view the senior U.S. leader visits were a success because I did not have to say a word. The Di-

A voter dips his index finger in purple ink as an election volunteer explains the layout of a ballot at a polling site in Shifta. (Taken by Diyala Provincial JCC field agents; Gregory Tomlin Collection)

rector of Security covered the major talking points, acknowledged our principle concerns, and competently fielded questions from a four-star general, all beneath the glare of several cameras. As far as the U.S. general was concerned, I was just another officer tagging along with the brigade commander's entourage.

Her attention turned to the plasma screen behind me on the wall. Throughout the day our field agents visited polling sites in Baquba to assess the security situation and take photos. As they returned to the JCC with their reports, I downloaded their digital photos for a rolling slideshow on the television. Gina was surprised to learn that the photos were not taken by a professional photographer, and even more astonished to hear that they were taken by Iraqi JCC personnel. She handed me a thumb drive and asked if I would not mind downloading copies of the photos to it.

Although still a couple hours away from polls closing, we turned our attention to transferring ballots to a secure location. Based on the plan reviewed during the rehearsal ten days prior, election workers would count the ballots at each polling station and report their numbers to Amer's provincial staff. Once the totals were received, the ballot boxes would be consolidated in the Camp Warhorse hangar, where the IECI staffers would conduct a second count. However, by late afternoon, we realized that the threat of an attack against polling sites would proportionally increase with

A voter places her marked ballot into a ballot box in Shifta. (Taken by Diyala Provincial JCC field agents; Gregory Tomlin Collection)

the darkness that would set over the province as night approached. Major Wolfgang and Captain Edwan gained Amer's approval to have U.S. and Iraqi patrols begin transporting ballot boxes to Camp Warhorse as soon as the stations closed at five in the evening. The first count would not occur at the polling sites.

As security forces increased their movement to retrieve the ballots, a variety of IEDs, small arms attacks, and RPGs harassed the soldiers. However, the enemy attempts were weak, and only one soldier in the entire province suffered an injury. The sporadic attacks did not occur near schools that were either open or surrounded with locals. For their own reasons, the enemy made a concerted effort to not harm the civilian populace of Diyala that day.

After receiving the final closeout reports from other JCCs and polling stations, the crowd in the JCC began to thin. Task Force 1-6 soldiers collected their radio equipment and prepared to return to Camp Gabe. Lieutenant Colonel Bullimore, Captain Edwan, and I stepped into the radio room to participate in a conference call with all commanders in 3rd Brigade. Each task force commander confirmed that there were no significant security issues to report, and Colonel Pittard did not have any additional orders to provide for the night.

Returning to my desk in the operations center, I thought back to a memorandum that I wrote on November 1 and signed jointly with the Director of Security. I set out in the paper to clarify the role of the provincial JCC in the elections period. Sent in English to U.S. commanders and in Arabic to the elections commission, the governor, and security officials, we stated that, "The JCC must be seen as the centralized location for co-operative security planning and monitoring of the elections process by the Independent Elections Commission of Iraq, the Iraqi Transitional Government, Iraqi Security Forces and Coalition Forces."

On January 30, the JCC served exactly in that role. The election director shared a desk with Brigadier Tahsin. Colonel Pittard and Lieutenant Colonel Bullimore positioned their forward command posts in our operations room. The chief of police and the Iraqi Army brigade commander visited hourly for updates, and high-profile visitors toured the facility. The JCC enjoyed the capacity of communicating with the 147 opened polling sites via police radio to receive reports and provide new instructions. At each radio and telephone sat an Iraqi official, several of whom were teamed with a U.S. counterpart. With a bit of guidance and a revaluation of priorities from time to time, the Iraqis conducted business for themselves.

My head began to bob. It was only eight thirty in the evening, but I had not slept in nearly forty hours. Climbing the stairs to my room on the second floor, I fell into a deep sleep in no time at all. The following morning, with the elections visitors gone, I began to reorganize desks and clean up trash in a very quiet JCC. The operations center seemed nearly bare with only the normal shift of JCC staff officers at work. By noon Major Wolfgang and Amer arrived so that we could plan for transporting election workers to Camp Warhorse to count ballots.

As we were talking, Mr. Jimenez dropped in, beaming ear to ear. "Greg, the elections were an absolute success, and Baquba truly was a shining star. This is coming from the embassy, the State Department, and the Administration. All of Washington woke up this morning to see cheering voters at a school in downtown Baquba on CNN. It's far better than any of us expected."

Indeed, election day played out far better than anyone of us in the JCC had anticipated. We braced ourselves for suicide bombers, vehicle-borne IEDs, and complex attacks. However, our worst fears never materialized. As a whole, the Iraqi security forces demonstrated their commitment to the citizens of Diyala. The soldiers entrusted with escorting ballots through the province and the policemen responsible for securing polling sites were not the same men who shed their uniforms and disappeared from the streets of Baquba during April's Easter Offensive.

Equally as impressive were the civilians, who ignored the rumors that the elections would fail and the threats made on their lives when they left their homes to cast their votes. Although only thirty-five percent of eligible voters in Diyala went to the polls, the positive and often euphoric sentiments shared by the Iraqis at the schools promised that the turnout for the Fall 2005 constitutional reformation would be a much larger percentage.

The Iraqis did it: the elections were an Iraqi success. We could not discount the formidable role that Americans played in making the success occur, and the lives of those we lost in the war contributed to establishing the favorable security conditions to allow the elections to transpire. However, over the course of eleven months, I witnessed the Iraqi government and security forces mature and gain confidence in their abilities.

The enemy must have also witnessed this; otherwise, they would have initiated more spectacular attacks on January 30 if they believed that only U.S. forces would protect the thousands of polling sites dotting Iraq. Insurgents found themselves outnumbered by the roaming quick reaction forces, traffic control points, polling site guards, and hundreds of thousands of undaunted voters. By no means did this suggest that the enemy would lay down their weapons or end their opposition to the new Iraqi government. All of us in the JCC anticipated many more bumps on the road ahead as Iraq continued its efforts to end the insurgency, develop an equitable government, and improve its economy.

Nevertheless, the January, 2005 elections answered Amer's Shakespearean question for me: An Iraqi democracy is to be.

PART 7
up to the task

chapter 17

SECURITY
Lt. Caleb Cage, 1st Platoon Leader, C Company

On February 10, 2005, we might as well have been done with the deployment. Operation Backbreaker, the mission that had consumed so much of our recent lives, was more than a month behind us. The elections were an unmitigated success, and even those were nearly two weeks behind us. As we had been saying for months, all we had to do was make it through January, and February would not really count. Even if we were not back home with our families yet, we felt as though we had a mastery of whatever would possibly come our way in our final month in Baquba. This, of course, was a terrible mentality to have during a deployment, but that did not make it any easier to fight off.

After the elections, my platoon was sent back to Camp Gabe to rejoin the operational cycle, and February 10 marked an especially important mission for us. We had been tasked to take a convoy of six humvees down to a support base called Convoy Supply Camp Scania, several hours south of Baghdad. The purpose of the mission was to escort the entire body of equipment belonging to Task Force 1-10 Field Artillery, 3rd Infantry Division for the second half of their trip, north from Kuwait to Baquba. There was little to enjoy about this mission, minus the fact that Task Force 1-10 would replace Task Force 1-6. Even so, not much more had to be said to my soldiers to motivate them to execute this otherwise annoying, two-day logistical mission.

Of course, moving the equipment of an entire task force over enemy terrain was an infuriating and difficult process. The trip down was long, and made longer by somewhat casual enemy contact, and the return trip was fraught with mechanical breakdowns, a jackknifed wrecker (of all vehicles to jackknife), mild enemy contact, and the other standard frustrations of road-tripping in Iraq. None of that mattered in the least. Every soldier on every truck of that convoy was wearing the 3rd Infantry Division patch, a patch noticeably different from our own Big Red One. It had to mean that we were headed home soon.

I could not help but laugh when we off-loaded the vehicles back at Camp Gabe, finally, and heard the quiet grousing of the new soldiers about their new living conditions. Gabe was home to us, and the improvements over the last year seemed enormous and measurable, at least to us. These soldiers must have sounded just like we did to the 588th Engineers when we arrived a year prior. While the new soldiers were seemingly a little snobbish about their new digs, our soldiers could not fight the urge to be a little snobbish about the reputation they had honed over the course of the last year. These new guys, the thinking went, thought they knew everything and did not want to listen to anything the experts had to say. A lot had changed, the argument continued, since most of these 3rd Infantry Division solders fought in the 2003 invasion, a time before the insurgency to which we had grown accustomed.

Just like the cycle we had completed a year prior, all of the insecurity-based talk on both sides subsided when it came time to actually address the mission and the sector. It was lost on no one that, even though they had not fought the insurgency in Baquba for the last year, many of the 3rd Infantry Division soldiers had already served one tour in Iraq, *and* had been through all of the pre-deployment training that we had experienced. That is, they were more experienced than we were when we had arrived a year before. We just had more recent experience under our belts to secure the bragging rights. As the interaction between the two units increased and stabilized, so did mutual respect and relations. By February 12, the "new guys" were ready to start executing what had become the most glorious sounding phrase in the world to our wise and withered ears: the Relief in Place (RIP).

While Task Force 1-6 leadership introduced their counterparts to their new jobs and responsibilities, two companies were detailed to fall in on the footprints previously held by B and C Companies of our task force. A Company, Task Force 1-10 would replace our B Company in northern Baquba. Like my company, A Company was comprised of artillerymen serving in the role of motorized riflemen, and the organization continued to experience the growing pains that we had endured a year before. Also like my company, inexperience as riflemen was not proving to be an insurmountable obstacle for A Company when it came to addressing the mission they were assigned.

For southern Baquba and the town of Buhriz, Task Force 1-10 replaced us with their B Company, a real monster. Where the brigade leadership had decided to replace one artillery-turned-rifle company with another to secure northern Baquba, they elected to replace my company with an armor-infantry company team. C Company, Task Force 1-6 consisted of one infantry platoon with Bradley Fighting Vehicles, and three, 25-man motorized rifle platoons fighting from humvees. The new B Company had one Bradley platoon (plus another two Bradleys for the commander and executive officer), two 40-man motorized rifle platoons comprised of infantrymen, and an armor platoon with four Abrams tanks. All of which is to say that B Company, Task Force 1-10 had more manpower and firepower than Task Force 1-6 had been organized to have. For months we wondered what kind of unit would replace us, and what it would consist of. Of course, as with any proud unit, we figured that anything short of the Army's finest and fiercest would be an insult to our accomplishments, but we knew that was a little unrealistic.

Our pride aside, though, we had real reason to wonder what message the decision makers received about our sector. Before we deployed a year before, we were perplexed to hear that an artillery battalion, with a single additional infantry platoon, was being given arguably one of the toughest sectors in the brigade, while infantry and armor battalions, better trained and equipped for urban combat and maneuvers, were given less populated and more peripheral sectors of Diyala. The arguments for placing an artillery task force in Baquba, at least the ones that filtered down to our level, were generally pretty lame and so nuanced that they could hardly be taken seriously. With the sectors remaining basically the same across the board between our task force and Task Force 1-10, we were pleased to see that our company sector, southern Baquba, had been given the manpower and firepower we believed it needed to maintain what we considered to be hard-earned progress.

The RIP process was well-planned and well-delegated, thanks to the planning efforts of the C Company commander, Capt. Douglas Chadwick. We had about nine days, roughly, to bring the new platoons on board, and our time was divided between the classroom setting and real world missions. The purpose of the classroom setting was to tighten and localize the information they had no doubt received in briefings and training exercises in Kuwait before their arrival, as well as to allow for an opportunity for us, the leaders on the ground, to pass along our personal experiences to everyone as a whole. The real world training missions were designed to allow as much one-on-one time between our platoon and the new platoon as possible in order to work out as many kinks in transition as possible. The patrols and familiarizations started out consisting of seventy-five percent my platoon and twenty-five percent the new platoon and changed a little each day until the opposite was true: only my leaders were to be in the trucks, with the majority of their platoons on operations around town. We were committed to providing a better RIP than the one we remembered receiving when we arrived. Realistically, this was probably more of a motivational tool designed by our seniors to keep us focused until the very end than an actual reflection of how the RIP with the 588th Engineers had gone a year before.

Replacing me was Lt. Dan Anton, who was one of the few in his platoon without a previous deployment under his belt. Dan was an impressive leader, which was most obvious in the harmless harassment his soldiers dealt him, whether or not he was doing things correctly. He was calm, knowledgeable, eager to learn, and genuinely respected by his guys. His platoon sergeant, Sgt. First Class David Salie, was the glue that held everything together, as Lieutenant Anton told me once in private. Sergeant Salie was a massive man who had the deepest respect of his men. It was obviously the best kind of respect a leader in his position could have: part fear that he would crush you if you messed up, and part fear that you would disappoint him if you failed. This was his fourth combat deployment, an incredible number this early in the Operation Iraqi Freedom deployment cycles, and his experience was only part of the reason his men looked up to him so much. He trained his new platoon leader and showed him how to be great; he sheltered his soldiers from the common nonsense that wastes their time and puts them in harm's way; and most importantly, he cared deeply, with a remarkable brand of tough love that every one of his men admired.

The platoons did a great job of further putting their insecurities aside and gelling with each other as time went on. While my platoon sergeant and I were showing Lieutenant Anton and Sergeant Salie what we knew and what we thought would help them, their identified drivers, gunners, and squad leaders talked for hours and hours with their counterparts from my platoon. The new guys were eager to show their competence, and my guys were eager to show that it was no fluke that they had been chosen for a dangerous mission in Baquba. I was incredibly impressed with the seriousness and competence with which Lieutenant Anton's platoon approached their new mission, as well as with their eagerness to learn. After their first couple of days at Camp Gabe, I was confident that we were handing southern Baquba over to the right people.

By Valentine's Day, four days after their arrival, we were ready to move from the slideshow briefings on our sector and start conducting the mounted familiarization patrols in Baquba with our new counterparts. At around one in the afternoon, we loaded up the trucks, our convoy consisting of mostly my platoon, and the rest of our replacements. Our mission was to take them all over Baquba, show them the significant cultural and political sites, show them the routes and checkpoints, and to talk them through the firefights and improvised-explosive device (IED) attacks that we had experienced.

There was an excitement in the air when we got together for the mission briefing. My platoon was excited to finally be handing over their mission, yet weary of all things exciting at the same time. Lieutenant Anton's platoon was anxious to prove to themselves and to us that they could handle what they were about to receive. The strange overlap of emotions left a warm buzz in the air during the mission briefing and while we mounted our trucks to depart.

We executed the mission as planned. At first, we focused broadly on the big things: the Blue Dome, where they would spend much time protecting the governor and his staff; the Civil-Military Operations Center, where they would direct local Iraqis with concerns and complaints; the Provincial Police Headquarters, where, if things went as planned, they would spend more time than our platoons had, in support of Iraqi-led operations; and their brigade headquarters at Camp Warhorse, the logistical hub for the region. After traveling past the broader locations, we drove to Tahrir so they could begin to replace the maps and satellite imagery with an idea of what southern Baquba looked like in person. Despite what we told ourselves in preparing for the RIP, the entire process was all very similar to the process we had received from the engineers a year before.

As dusk approached, I was beginning to wrap up the tour of our sector in the district of Tahrir. Lieutenant Anton was sitting behind me in the lead humvee, and Sergeant Salie was sitting in the rear-right passenger seat behind my platoon sergeant, Sgt. First Class Cameron Gaines, in the trail humvee. As we headed south along Canal Street into Tahrir, I pointed towards Buhriz, a place with which we would familiarize them through a series of targeted raids at a later date. Buhriz, infamous for its capacity for violence at this point, was intriguing to look at from the outside, but the decision had been made early in the RIP to restrict travel in the town to company-sized efforts. Infantrymen or not, the RIP would not be a good time for an inexperienced platoon from Task Force 1-10 to be caught alone in a Buhriz firefight.

I was explaining to Lieutenant Anton the nature of Tahrir as I had grown to know it as our convoy slowed to turn east and into one of its neighborhoods. As we rounded the corner, an enormous detonation erupted behind us. It was the second-loudest explosion I had heard since the beginning of our deployment, the first being on November 15 when we were on the exact same piece of road, heading into Buhriz. My throat tightened as I looked back and could see our trail humvee through the rear, driver's side window. The last humvee did not make the turn, but continued south, traveling through and out of an enormous cloud of dust and smoke, seemingly losing control and driving up onto a four-foot berm that separated the shoulder of Canal Street from the canal. Fortunately, the berm slowed the humvee to a halt before the six-and-a-half ton truck full of injured and dazed personnel drove into the canal.

Sgt. Jason Brownlie was driving my vehicle and turned the vehicle around immediately, without waiting for any sort of instruction. Lieutenant Anton sat behind me, not saying a word. Without having to give the command, Staff Sgt. Ottress Thomas and Staff Sgt. Thomas Bramer, my two squad leaders in the middle two humvees, took their trucks to the north and south of the downed vehicle to provide security while we sped towards the damaged truck. During this whole time I was making a report to the task force headquarters, requesting an additional platoon for security, equipment for a medical evacuation, and a wrecker to pull home what appeared to be a destroyed vehicle.

I did not have the complete report out of my mouth before Sergeant Brownlie and one of Lieutenant Anton's squad leaders were sprinting towards the hit vehicle. The scene was already grotesque: the humvee sat awkwardly with two wheels up on the berm; the truck gunner, from the replacing platoon, was hanging out of the gunner's hatch on the top of the vehicle, screaming an eerie scream. Spc. Garrett "Doc" Larsen, my medic and the only medic on the convoy, had been blown out of the vehicle and dragged by his foot for ten yards or so until the truck stopped. He was sprawled on the ground, his foot caught between the door and the truck, and blood, streaming from his neck and ears, already pooled around his limp body.

Sergeant Brownlie and the new squad leader immediately went to work on Doc Larsen. The medic's supply bag was badly damaged, but they made do: stopping the blood flow with a compression bandage, hooking him up to an IV bag, and otherwise stabilizing and reassuring him, exactly as their training had taught them to do. He was bleeding badly from the neck and ear; he could not hear and was having trouble breathing; but, incredibly, he kept asking how everyone else was doing, while remaining perfectly calm. While they were working on Doc Larsen, others were methodically taking care of the remaining four soldiers in the vehicle. It was growing more and more obvious in the few moments that passed that not a single person in the vehicle escaped injury, and that everyone was dazed or knocked out. Sgt. Timothy Mills from my platoon, the humvee driver, was the next to be evacuated from the destroyed vehicle. He had smashed his face on the steering wheel and taken a fist-sized piece of shrapnel to his ribs, which was, thankfully, blocked mostly by his body armor. Within a moment of being revived he was pretty clearly in control of himself, if still a bit angry and groggy.

While others worked on reviving the wounded and retrieving scattered equipment, Lieutenant Anton and I began yelling inside the dust-and-smoked-out vehicle to see how everyone else was faring. It had been less than two minutes since the explosion and the methodical actions underway on the outside of the vehicle still contrasted with the confusing and cacophonous situation inside the vehicle. Through the dust, the adrenaline, and the screams, we called by name for each passenger in the vehicle. Sergeant Gaines grumbled a low, inaudible response, but we did not hear anything from Sergeant Salie.

The rooftop gunner's pain was obvious, but we could not get him out immediately. First, we knew that he was in pain, but probably otherwise all right, because the noise he was making was clear and lucid. Second, the explosion had made it nearly impossible to get to him in his broken form and drag him out. Lieutenant Anton and I both ran around to the other side and pulled Sergeant Gaines's door open. I paused for the slightest moment, gazing in disbelief at the state of the door. On an up-armored humvee, with several inches of steel armor, the IED transformed the door into something as flimsy and formless as a shattered windshield. Seeing the damage to the impacted side of the humvee, I realized why I thought it was one of the loudest explosions I had heard in Iraq.

Sergeant Gaines had gotten lucky. Yet again, he had escaped death by a matter of inches. He was dazed, angry, and peppered with shrapnel on his face and neck when we pulled open his door and pulled him out, but he was able to walk on his own once he was fully revived. The smoke began to clear a little when Lieutenant Anton and I started yelling his platoon sergeant's name again. People had been yelling his name the whole time and there had not been a response. We pulled on his door angrily, hoping that the concussion had only knocked him unconscious.

Gaining access to the passenger compartment, we immediately saw that Sergeant Salie was not so fortunate. He was dead. His door had absorbed the majority of the blast, and his body probably absorbed it further, saving everyone else in the truck, minus injuries from which they would later recover. Lieutenant Anton did not say much while we decided what to do with the gunner, who was still suspended in the rooftop gunner's hatch, yelling in terrific pain. I returned to my vehicle and radioed in a full update of all of the casualties and damage on the ground. While I was finishing my report, the recovery platoon arrived with the medical and mechanical help. It seemed like an eternity for them to arrive, of course, but we were grateful for the added help. The situation was under control, but we needed to get it all over with and behind us.

We loaded three of the wounded into the ambulance and continued to salvage the vehicle as well as we could. By the time we got it dragged free of the berm, we had emptied it, accounted for all of its weapons and radios, and figured out where everything and everyone was going to ride for the return drive. During all of the administrative functions, I had not truly realized how damaged the truck actually was. Sitting in the middle of the street hooked up to the wrecker, it was hard to miss: the passenger side doors were reduced to loosely connected shards; the quarter-inch steel roof had been peeled back as if someone had used a can-opener on it, and everything else was covered in dust and blood.

When we finally returned to the camp, we debriefed and then retired to our respective companies. Their battalion operations officer began grilling me about the operation, trying to find some negligence on my part that had caused the death of Sergeant Salie, but I quickly dispensed with his questions. Among my peers in my own task force, we were all more shocked by what had happened than interested in trying to assess blame. It was not only that we were so close to leaving, and that three members of our platoon had experienced such a close call, but also that none of us had seen an IED cause so much damage to an up-armored humvee. During patrols conducted by all of the platoons in Task Force 1-6, the humvees had always been extremely effective against the power of the menacing roadside bombs. IEDs had knocked them around some, sure, but damage like this was unprecedented.

We did not share our shock with our successors as we tried to reconsider how we would have executed the missions, patrols, and convoys throughout the previous year if we did not have the faith in the up-armored humvees that we had. How much more emotionally taxing would our year have been if we did not have faith in the protection of the up-armored humvee against an IED throughout the year before? There was no doubt that the new company's confidence was as shaken as ours was when we lost Spc. Adam Froehlich early in our deployment. Similar to what we observed in own experience, the enemy continued adapting their tactics and capabilities constantly. Everything seemed to be repeating itself.

Over the next few days, their company began to recover and grieve in their own way, while we tried to give them the necessary space to do so. Everyone knew that no matter how uncomfortable it was to do, the best thing was to continue training and continue the RIP process. The battalions held a memorial ceremony for Sergeant Salie between the missions. A few days later, the famous and fearless war journalist Joe Galloway wrote an incredibly personal and touching obituary for David Salie, whom he had met years before, during the conflict in Haiti.

As our time together wound down, I became convinced that Sergeant Salie would have been proud of his men. They were shaken, of course, but they carried on. His position as platoon sergeant was filled as well as possible, and his men never stopped doing what they had to do to get fully acclimated. Over the course of our remaining days together, I regularly heard his soldiers talking more about how great a man and leader Sergeant Salie was, and not at all talking about how uncertain the devastating attack had made them about their vulnerabilities to their enemy. As we handed over the sector to Task Force 1-10, I departed fully convinced that shaken or not, we were handing Baquba over to a group of soldiers who were up to the task.

chapter 18
DEMOCRACY
Capt. Greg Tomlin, Military Advisor,
Diyala Joint Coordination Center

*O*n February 1, 2005 I departed the Diyala Provincial Police Headquarters in an army convoy for the short journey to Camp Gabe. Although Task Force 1-6 headquarters sat less than four kilometers away from downtown Baquba, I had only returned two other times since leaving my platoon the past October. Climbing out of the humvee to clear my pistol at the front gate of the camp, I felt like a college student on a nostalgic visit to his old high school. On the whole, buildings and people appeared the same, but even the smallest renovation efforts seemed glaring to me. Like juniors rising to their own senior class, I quickly spotted new rank insignia on the collars of many of my former soldiers when we spoke. I had worked at the Joint Coordination Center (JCC) for only four months, but it seemed much longer than that. Now I was a captain, not a lieutenant, and, at least in my own mind, I was clearly a visitor to the dusty camp where I had experienced so many accomplishments and heartaches the past year.

The purpose of my visit was to participate in a briefing for the leadership of Task Force 1-10 Field Artillery, our successors in Baquba. Lt. Col. Steven Bullimore, the commander of Task Force 1-6, expected his officers to introduce their counterparts to the unique operational responsibilities of working on staff, in command, and throughout the city. As members of the 3rd Infantry Division, many soldiers in Task Force 1-10 were well acquainted with Iraq, as their division led the ground invasion in 2003. Few of the veterans, however, ventured north of Baghdad during their first tour, and even fewer had experienced the urban combat that would shape their time in Baquba.

Following the formal briefing, I met Capt. Tony Caracio, my replacement at the JCC. Tony graduated in the West Point Class of 2001, and he had already spent eighteen months in the Middle East. He served with 1-10 Field Artillery during a six-month deployment to Kuwait, prior to spending a year involved in Operation Iraqi Freedom (OIF). As a member of my year group of army officers, Tony should not have remained in his battalion for OIF III; he should have left his division to attend the Captains Career Course. However, to decrease the amount of turbulence within battalions, the army established a "stop-loss" initiative, suspending reassignment orders for many soldiers and requiring them to remain with their unit through an upcoming deployment. As the Global War on Terror progressed, it became less uncommon for soldiers to spend four or five years with the same unit, where in the past, they typically spent three years before transferring to a new assignment.

Despite whatever Tony may have personally thought about being forced to remain with his unit for a third deployment, he appeared upbeat about his new job. Confidence and a good-natured personality will go a long way when working in an advisory position, and my initial impression suggested that Tony possessed both. As we returned to the police headquarters, Tony and I discussed the potential of the Iraqi authorities to handle security efforts on their own. We agreed that the elections, which his task force missed by a few days, were a great success for the Iraqi people. The question remained, however: would the Iraqis capitalize on the momentum gained by their January achievement? It was a fair question, particularly for someone about to invest a year of his life advising Iraqi officials from a suite of offices in a small police compound. I would have three weeks to prove to Tony that, in my opinion, the Iraqis had the capacity to make measurable strides, providing that we continued to offer critical assistance while they continued to mature.

The arrival of Task Force 1-10 coincided with a visit by Colin Freeman, a reporter for the *San Francisco Chronicle,* to the police headquarters. Several days after meeting Tony, Colin and I stood before the "Diyala Most Wanted" poster in the JCC. One by one, I went down the list, explaining who had since been killed or captured, and sharing the latest speculation about those insurgent leaders who remained elusive. Most of the information was purely anecdotal for Colin. He did not travel to Baquba to learn about the capture of Abu Zuis or the most recent Al Zarqawi sighting; rather, he wanted to understand the agenda of the provincial government in the wake of peaceful elections. With so much left to be done, how would political and security officials prioritize their tasks?

For the political agenda, I directed Colin to the provincial capitol up the street, but for security forces, I felt confident in providing him with an answer. I had observed a remarkable transformation in the Iraqi security forces over the past year. In April, on the first day of the Easter Offensive, 3rd Platoon soldiers watched in disgust as Iraqi policemen tore rank insignia off of their uniforms in Tahrir and disappeared while Americans fought to counter a rising insurgency. In the months that followed, as Iraqi police and army units received better equipment, body armor to accompany their uniforms, and tactical training from multinational forces, the performance of Iraqi security forces steadily grew more reliable.

Still, recalling Caleb's challenges in securing the new Buhriz police station in December, there were plenty of reminders that Iraqi government agencies were not yet fully prepared to stand autonomously. However, there was evidence of measurable progress since the 1st Infantry Division assumed the mantle of Multinational Division-North in Iraq, one year earlier. With respect to Iraqi security forces, the most significant difference between April 2004 and February 2005 was the establishment of a core of senior leaders. It took many months of weeding through marginal and weak officers to find competent and uncorrupt generals and colonels for the Iraqi police and army, but the effort paid significant dividends. Between overseeing counterinsurgency operations and executing the Diyala election security plan, I admired many of the assertive and trustworthy senior Iraqi officers with whom I closely worked in the JCC. They shared the same resolve as many of my U.S. colleagues, and they wholly lacked the timidity of their predecessors, who were more enamored with their titles than they were with the awesome prospective of shaping a new era for their country.

With the elections complete, Iraq was also about to have its first democratically chosen political leadership assume the reigns at the provincial and national levels. Although the official results would not be announced for a few more weeks, most people in Diyala expected Mayor Ra'ad of Baquba to win the governorship. Based on his integrity and commitment to improving security and economic conditions in his city over the past tumultuous year, Governor-elect Ra'ad promised to be a superb leader for the province.

The most significant achievement of OIF II, I argued to Colin, was not the elections in itself. It was the selection of the senior leadership required to steer the government in the right direction and to charismatically charge the populace to work to improve their future. For the next year and beyond, these officials needed to mold an intermediate cohort of leaders to implement their vision, whether that would be behind the closed doors of a city council conference room or from the lead vehicle of a police patrol in Baquba.

Iraqi security forces enjoyed lengthy queues of applicants to fill junior positions as policemen and army privates whenever a hiring was announced. However, in February 2005 security forces still lacked essential midlevel leaders: the sergeants, lieutenants, and captains responsible for leading junior security forces on the harrowing missions to destroy enemy forces in the city districts and across the country. The most critical end state for OIF III would be training this middle leadership, the backbone of the Iraqi security forces. I encouraged Colin to return to the JCC in February 2006. If he found a burgeoning cadre of police sergeants leading daily patrols and army captains executing counterinsurgency operations with their companies, then Iraq was heading in the right direction.

In a major effort to train such a cohort, Multinational Forces invested heavily in police and military academies in every Iraqi province. A school also opened in Jordan, where active and retired policemen from around the world trained new Iraqi recruits for the fundamentals of enforcing the law and protecting themselves. Few such training facilities existed in early 2004, and many Iraqi policemen and soldiers received little more than an AK-47 and a uniform prior to conducting their first patrol or guard duty. Early advisors and trainers, who struggled with limited material resources and an even smaller budget, worked earnestly to produce competent security forces the year prior, but efforts were more than doubled in 2005.

Capt. Daniel Edwan designed and oversaw the construction of a small police academy on the south side of the Diyala Provincial Police Headquarters. Contractors did not finish the two-story building before we redeployed to Germany at the end of February, but Captain Edwan assisted his replacement from the 3rd Brigade Combat Team, 3rd Infantry Division in vetting police instructors and authoring a curriculum.

Being within the confines of our compound, the construction site also provided me with an opportunity to marvel at the crude but efficient construction techniques used by the Iraqis. Men layered sandstone bricks into twenty-foot walls without scaffolding and poured a concrete second floor over a questionable support structure comprised of uneven palm timbers. Although the workers did not suffer any injuries, I could only imagine what a field inspector from the Occupational Safety and Health Administration would say if he arrived onto the job site from the United States.

Over the course of his first week at the JCC, Tony shadowed me through routine meetings, and he observed how the JCC staff responded to typical emergencies, particularly in clearing improvised-explosive devices (IED). Brig. Tahsin Tawfiq Jassim, the provincial Director of Security, the JCC staff officers, and senior police leaders were all genuinely hospitable to Tony and welcomed him to the organization. Figuring out his niche in the JCC, and tailoring a few procedures to fit his personality, Tony quickly began to establish himself and assume more of my duties as military advisor.

Following our daily security meeting on February 7, Tony and I sat at a desk in the JCC, where I showed him how to make badges for new staff members. As I pointed to file directories on a laptop, a massive explosion shook the building. It was far too close to be an ordinary IED on Canal Street or Highway 5. Before I could ask the operations officer for a report, the police radio began squawking. Our translator explained that a vehicle-borne IED (VBIED) detonated fifty meters from the compound's south gate.

The gate had been opened earlier that morning to allow police applicants access to the administrative offices of the headquarters. Previously, Iraqis seeking to become policemen applied at the city police station, located between the provincial capitol and the Civil-Military Operations Center. However, after a horrific VBIED targeted a queue of aspirants and killed sixty-eight civilians on June 28, 2004, recruitment efforts moved to the provincial headquarters, away from the vulnerabilities of Highway 5.

Tony began moving towards the door. "Don't you want to see what's going on?" he asked, when he saw that I was not following his lead.

"No, our place is here," I said. "We need to coordinate for the evacuation of wounded and figure out if we should expect more attacks in the city."

While the statement was accurate, I also knew that the capable JCC staff could handle the situation without me. However, over the past year, I had also seen enough death and carnage that I had no desire to watch Iraqi policemen and ambulance drivers collect charred body parts while burqa-clad women wailed Islamic mourning prayers and beat their breasts.

Momentarily hesitating, Tony left the JCC to collect his helmet and flak vest before rushing to the south gate. Police reported that fifteen men died in the explosion, and seventeen others, including eight policemen, were injured to varying degrees. None of the dead was a policeman, but nearly all of the deceased intended to receive a blue uniform before the end of the day. As with all other massive casualty emergencies, Iraqis quickly coordinated for the evacuation of the wounded to Baquba General Hospital and the dead to the city morgue in the basement of the hospital. Perhaps it was the Islamic tradition of burying their dead before sunset that prompted the Iraqis to move so decisively at such a tragic scene.

Less than thirty minutes later, Tony returned to the JCC, his face a bit paler than when he left. "You were right," he told me, "I didn't need to be there. My place is here."

I understood. Perhaps, a year earlier I also would have jumped at the opportunity to be at the site of a VBIED. I would not have known what I was getting into, even if I thought that somehow I could help evacuate the wounded or personally kill the culprit. After a year of urban combat, however, I knew better. Tony was a veteran of the Iraq war, but he spent 2003 in the region as a conventional artilleryman, destroying enemy targets from afar with the indirect fire of his howitzers. With only a week of experience in OIF III, Tony now understood that this tour would be different. The fighting would be much more personal and in-your-face for him and his comrades in Task Force 1-10.

The violence on February 7 reminded all of us that the insurgency was not defeated just because we were congratulating each other about the success of the elections. While the VBIED detonation was the most severe attack, five other incidents marred the peace in Diyala that day alone. At 2:00 in the afternoon, errant mortar rounds missed the Diyala Provincial Police Headquarters and impacted in Tahrir, killing a five-year-old boy. Through reports to the JCC, we learned that an Iraqi soldier was knifed to death in Muqdadiya; gunmen in Khalis killed a civilian who drove Iraqi contractors to work at Camp Warhorse, the brigade headquarters; insurgents attacked a police patrol in New Baquba, but without effect; and an IED detonated in front of the home of a city councilman in Muqdadiya. No, the insurgency remained quite active within the province.

If the response of the insurgents to progress was disappointing for those of us working for stability in Iraq, the civilians who lined the street outside of the police headquarters the next day provided a promising re- tort. Dozens of men, some brothers and cousins of those killed the day prior, arrived on February 8 to apply for jobs with the police force when the administrative offices reopened. Such bravado did not go unnoticed by many of us in the JCC, who walked to the south gate to see the appli- cants for ourselves.

While daily reports continued to include a smattering of IEDs and hit-and-run attacks, Iraqi security forces did not stop their operations throughout the province. Although some missions were highly visible, other efforts remained clandestine. At 10:00 one night, the week after the VBIED explosion, Lieutenant Colonel Ishmael, commander of the 213th Iraqi Army Battalion, arrived at the JCC and asked me to meet with him in the conference room. Because he spoke passable English, presumably from his time as a special forces commando in Saddam Hussein's army, we did not require an interpreter. Closing the door behind us, I watched the battalion commander unroll a map from a mail tube that he had carried under his arm. Approaching the conference table, I immediately recognized it as a map of Baquba.

"We will capture several enemy here at midnight," he said, pointing to a block of houses in Tahrir. "You must keep the police away from Tahrir at the time of our operation."

"Sir, wouldn't you rather have the police provide the outer cordon for you?" I asked, in an effort to integrate army and police operations.

"No, Captain Tomlin, I do not want the police near us at all," he curtly replied as he returned the map to its case. "We work better alone."

It was easy for me to restrict police patrols from Tahrir, but it seemed that if Lieutenant Colonel Ishmael intended to keep his operation a secret until the last minute, the absence of normal police patrols in the city district would appear even more suspicious. However, since assuming command of the Iraqi Army battalion stationed in Baquba, the colonel preferred to handle operations independently. In his mind, he could identify spies within his own organization, but he had no control over the police, who might or might not include individuals willing to warn insurgency cells or allow enemy personnel to escape during a raid. If he was not prepared to conduct joint operations just yet, at least he was working to take action on intelligence collected about his enemy. Convincing the battalion commander to share such information and coordinate efforts with the police through the JCC would be the next step.

Lieutenant Colonel Ishmael returned to the JCC in the morning with sunken eyes but a wide grin on his face. Without asking a question, I knew that his raid proved fruitful. "We captured two people and are interrogating them now," he stated without asking to adjourn to the privacy of the conference room. "My men will bring them to the police station when we are done with them."

The army was not the only element of the Iraqi security forces conducting independent operations. A couple days later, while Tony and I stood before the huge Baquba map in the JCC with the operations officer on duty to discuss establishing a cordon around an unexploded IED, a police lieutenant rushed into the JCC. He spoke excitedly to the intelligence officer, and then approached us. Neither Tony nor I cared to speak with the lieutenant at that moment because few concerns trumped the importance of clearing an IED before it detonated.

Our translator interrupted to explain that the lieutenant and his patrol just returned from capturing the "Little Prince" in Old Baquba. Based on our unchanging expressions, the translator realized that neither of us knew who this character was, and she proceeded to explain that the "Little Prince" was al Zarqawi's lieutenant in Baquba. In addition to arresting the man, the police confiscated a copy machine and several computers from the insurgent's safe house, less than a kilometer away from the police headquarters. Many of the threatening letters that blanketed the city in the days prior to the elections were likely produced on that copier.

After ensuring that the cordon was established to allow a U.S. explosive ordinance demolition (EOD) team to destroy the IED, I ventured into the investigations offices to see the "Little Prince" for myself. Three men stood with their hands cuffed behind their backs and their faces pointed towards the wall while a policeman stood guard. Colonel Ali, the deputy police chief for operations, pointed to the man on the left, ordering him to turn around. The insurgent leader sheepishly kept his eyes oriented on the ground as I sized him up. Immediately, I understood how he earned his epithet. Not only was he relatively short, but he looked to be in his early twenties. Unlike many of the older and gruff-looking men whose mug shots appeared on the province's most wanted poster, this dangerous man should have been an undergraduate student at Baghdad University, not liaising with the most powerful Al Qaeda operative in Iraq.

Colonel Ali beamed as we walked out of the investigative offices. The police lieutenant waited for us in the corridor, evidently proud of his patrol's accomplishment. Both men had the right to be pleased. The capture of the "Little Prince" also received coverage on Iraqi and regional news networks that night. Perhaps his interrogation and the examination of his computers would also lead to the arrest of other high profile enemy figures in the province, possibly even al Zarqawi himself. It was imperative to work fast. As elusive as many of the most notorious insurgents were, we were all acutely aware that information about the whereabouts of our enemy did not remain useful for many days, sometimes becoming irrelevant after only a few hours.

Lieutenant Colonel Ishmael's midnight raid and the surprising capture of the "Little Prince" indicated to me that Iraqi security forces were becoming more assertive in policing their communities. I wanted to leave Iraq believing that we—the Americans and Iraqis with whom I served—made a difference in Iraq over the past year, but I did not want to be delusional about the security situation, either. I wanted to quantify progress as well as possible in order to shape a perception of reality grounded in truth. From the birds-eye view of the province available at the JCC, I compiled statistics about the number of IEDs, small arms attacks, and police patrols throughout Diyala. Small arms attacks against Americans dropped during my five months at the police headquarters, and the number of IEDs cleared by Iraqi EOD in lieu of the U.S. EOD increased.

However, as any statistics professor will explain, data can be manipulated to mean anything. Yes, more Iraqi civilians were contacting the six JCCs in the province to report suspicious activity, and Iraqi security forces were becoming more self-reliant. On the other hand, VBIED attacks were steadily rising, both in occurrence and devastation. A year earlier, insurgent attacks focused on U.S. forces. When the enemy realized that they could not defeat us during offenses in the spring and summer, they shifted their attacks toward Iraqi government and security officials. While assassinations continued into 2005, the resolve of the general populace to participate in the elections proved that the murder of individual leaders would not be sufficient.

In February 2005 my spreadsheet of enemy attacks throughout Diyala identified progress in areas that a year ago concerned us the most. Unfortunately, it also indicated that the insurgency was once again shifting its tactics, targeting the civilian populace at large by bombing congested intersections, army highway checkpoints, and police recruitment centers. If the enemy could not kill enough Iraqi leaders to dissuade the citizenry from supporting a democracy, then perhaps, through increasing mass chaos, they could degrade public tolerance of Multinational Forces. The enemy began to make it clear that anything, even pandemonium and suffering at large, were more desirable than seeing Iraqi domestic policy succeed. In their mind, the establishment of a freely elected parliament was too closely tied to U.S. foreign policy, and therefore, it became acceptable for Jihadists to kill innocent Iraqis by the hundreds.

By the end of February, it was time for the 1st Infantry Division to return to Germany. Tony was comfortable in his role as military advisor to the JCC, and I began to say farewell to my Iraqi colleagues. In an email to my parents in January, I asked that they send me a box of coffee table books with pictures of the United States. Over the past five months, during quiet evening hours, members of the JCC staff shared with me stories of their lives and pictures of their children, or of themselves in their old military uniforms. It seemed appropriate to share some pictures of my home with them. I presented books to Amer Latif of the Independent Election

Commission of Iraq, the three translators who worked with me the entire time, and the four deputy directors of the JCC. Brigadier Tahsin seemed very pleased with his book, and he taped to the first page a photo of the two of us sitting behind the Director of Security's desk.

Last, I requested an office call with Brig. Adel Mullan, the provincial chief of police. Originally he served as a deputy director in the JCC prior to being nominated to head the police force in late December. The former air defense artillery colonel who, as Captain Edwan irreverently pointed out, bore a striking resemblance to the Parker Brother's Monopoly man, was an unexpected selection for the important post. Although he worked competently for Brigadier Tahsin in the JCC during crises the previous fall, he had never served as a police officer. Colonel Ali, the deputy chief for operations, was a natural choice, but he had little interest in the politics or administrative responsibilities of being chief. Brigadier Adel's unassuming manner, demonstrated reliability, and understanding of the JCC structure made him a serious contender. Taking charge at the start of the election period, he proved adept at integrating his police with other Iraqi agencies, as well as holding his district chiefs accountable for their performance.

In addition to a picture book, I handed Brigadier Adel two silver eagles, the insignia of a U.S. Army colonel. Would he be willing to trade them for a set of his Iraqi Army colonel shoulder boards? I wanted to give an Iraqi set to my dad, a U.S. colonel, when I returned home. Brigadier Adel told me that he would have to return to his house in Muqdadiya first. Several hours later, a policeman entered the JCC and asked me to return to the chief's office. It was my turn to be surprised when I found out that Brigadier Adel had immediately dropped his work and ordered a police patrol to escort him home to collect the rank! Upon arriving in his office, the general handed me two sets of shoulder boards, one for winter and another for summer. Additionally, he presented me with his Iran-Iraq War Service Medal, and a photo of him as a captain, standing inside of Iran.

"Sir, I can't accept your medal," I explained through my translator. To me, it was as unthinkable as giving away my original combat patch. He placed the award back in my hand. No, he did not need it anymore, because he would not wear his army uniform again. I suggested that he should give it to a family member, but he reminded me that he did not have any children. If the rank was for my father, then he wanted me to keep the medal and photo as a token of our friendship and to mark the end of my time in his country.

In departing Brigadier Adel's office, I was reminded that there would be no transition for the Iraqis. This week marked the end of a deployment for me, but life would continue uninterruptedly the following week, with its routine of security meetings, patrols, and counterinsurgency operations. On many difficult days during the deployment, I managed to get through by reminding myself that a year is a finite period. I would return to the medieval city of Bamberg, Germany, and eventually back to the United States, but the Iraqis were already home. Their only transition would come with stability and an end to the insurgency. Until then, they would continue to endure the uncertainty of not knowing whether they would see their families each night after work.

On the evening of February 23, 2005, I bade my final goodbyes and wished Tony well as I began the journey back to Germany. As with other task forces, 1-6 Field Artillery soldiers were separated into different groups for their return flights, but I was very glad that I would travel in the same serial with Capt. Jim Gifford, the former 1st Platoon leader who received his promotion to captain the same day as me. Two days later, I became reacquainted with snow, driving on the Autobahn, and sleeping in a real bed. As with returning to the States on mid-tour leave, my friends and I wondered how smooth our transition would be. Fortunately for all of us who did make it back from Baquba, our homecoming was a welcomed and peaceful ordeal.

Two months later, while sitting behind my desk in the battalion headquarters as the assistant operations officer, a peculiar e-mail appeared in my inbox. Anyone would suspect a message sent by Mohammed Ali to be spam mail, but the subject line, "The peace," caught my attention. Upon opening it, I realized that it was sent from the Diyala Director of Security.

> *My dear friend*
>
> *I missed you alot because we remember you every day and we remember you when we see what you did for the JCC*
>
> *I respect you alot because you are very strong personality officer you didnt hestaite to take any dicesion and we will hope you will be execllant commander*
>
> *we hope all the best to you continue your job finaly*
>
> *No body con take your place here of the JCC and thanks for attentions.*
>
> *sincearly*
> *your friend*
> **BRI TAHSSIEN TAWFIQ JASSIM**

Receiving an e-mail from a former Republican Guard general made me recall the cultural class presented to us in the freezing mess tent in Hohenfels before Thanksgiving, 2003. The absurdity of the suggestion that we would be gods, by any stretch of the definition, during our deployment continued to make Caleb and me laugh. However, there was a truth that resonated in the professor's lecture. We, the young U.S. officers and soldiers sent to live in the obscure cities across Mesopotamia, had the capacity to influence Iraqi leaders in rebuilding their nation.

Lieutenants and captains in other provinces encountered similar challenges to what Captain Edwan and I faced in the Diyala JCC. We arrived with orders to advise generals and colonels, who were content to adopt the detached leadership style of Saddam Hussein. Yet with a bit of pushing and prodding, and an effort on our part to lead by example, we changed the mentality of many Iraqi officials about what it means to serve their country. Regardless of the form in which democracy evolves in Iraq, democratic leaders will be held accountable by the people they were elected or appointed to serve. If we imparted a single notion with the Iraqis to whom we said farewell, it was that in the absence of a dictator, they now have the capability to shape their own destiny.

index

Italicized page numbers refer to illustration captions.

Abrams tank, employment of, 59, 62, 64, 75, 98–99, 279
A Company, 120th Infantry Battalion, 123
Adams, John, 81–82
Adgie, Kenneth, 242–44
Afghanistan, 152, 227
Ahmed, Kamal Ibrahim, 227–28, 232–33, 235, 253
Akridge, John, 69, 84
Allawi, Ayad, 266
ammunition track. *See* Field Artillery Ammunition Supply Vehicle (FAASV)
anti-Arab, sentiment in America, 14–15
anti-Semitism, in Baquba, 149, 168
Anton, Dan, 280–84
Apache helicopter, 228
Apartheid, South African, 136
Arabia, Al, 269
artillery. *See* Field Artillery
Army Times, 83–84, 102, 165, 169, 267, 270
Arraf, Jane, 263, 266–67, 270
assassination: 183–84, 191, 244
Associated Press, 130, 134
Auf, Mayor, 29, 90, 113–14, 150
Axis of Evil, 227

Ba'ath Party, 29, 195, 221
Backbreaker, Operation, 198–207, 277

Bacon, Jason, 27, 101
Baghdad, 120–21, 134, 227–28
Baghdad Journal, 143
Balad, 74, 95, 175–76, 190
Balkans, 5, 11, 12, 152, 156, 167
Bamberg, 15, 18, 154, 175, 296
Bang-Bang Club: Images of a Hidden War, The, 128, 136
Baqi, Ayad Ibrahim, 232–33, 255
Baquba: agriculture industry, 30; city districts, 28–29; insurgent buildup, 73, 86–87; intelligence estimate of, 19–21
Baquba, New, 28, 32, 35, 248; attacks from 184, 291
Baquba, Old, 28–29, 41–42, 48, 62 293; attacks from, 54–55, 129–30, 187–92, 242
Baquba populace: anticipating insurgent attack, 53; protests, 41; response to insurgency, 58, 113, 131–33, 182, 191, 194, 273–74, 291; response to U.S. presence, 63, 148–49
Basra, 121
Batiste, John, 261, 269
Beyond Baghdad: Postmodern War and Peace, 218
Black Flag, 195–96, 211
Blue Force Tracker, 110
bomb, roadside. *See* improvised explosive device (IED)

Boggiano, Christian, 75–76. *See also* Ice
    Platoon
Boom, Camp, 27
Bosnia, 5
Bradley Fighting Vehicle: Baquba op-
    erations, 45, 82, 193; Buhriz opera-
    tions, 74, 99, 101, 109, 139–40, 166,
    204–204; capabilities of, 48–49, 64,
    169, 222; election day operations,
    269; task organization, 23, 59, 75,
    89, 98, 279
Bramer, Thomas, *71,* 204, 282
Bremmer, L. Paul, 121
Brigade Reconnaissance Troop, 89, 92,
    96, 97–98, 102, 110, 112–13, 165,
    199, 208
Brownlie, Jason, *71,* 130, 140, 190, 206,
    210, 215, 282
Buhriz: attacks from, 70, 74–75, 90–91,
    103, 139–41, 179–80, 192–94,
    204–205, 269; initial patrol of,
    33–34; origins of unrest, 29, 73,
    113; raids in, *197,* 213; routes to,
    33. *See also* Smack Down, Opera-
    tion *and* Backbreaker, Operation
Buhriz populace: response to insur-
    gency, 76–77; response to U.S.
    forces, 148
Bullimore, Steven: actions in Iraq, 39,
    95, 166, 266, 272–73; commander's
    guidance, 15–16, 53, 88, 90, 163,
    286; intelligence gathering, 129;
    personnel management, 137, 230;
    quotation, 48, 230, 269
Burduselu, Bogdan, *17,* 22, 40, 43, 50, 57,
    61–62, 81–82, 98, 101, 103–104, 112
Bush, George W., 227; election of, 9,
    11; West Point commencement
    speech, 13
Bushman, John, 52, 137–38, 187–88,
    190, 200, 243

C Battery, 1-6 Field Artillery. *See*
    C Company
C Company: assessment of enemy

threat, 34–35; incorporation of in-
    fantry platoon, 23; task organiza-
    tion for deployment, 16–18
Cable News Network (CNN), 102, 263,
    273
Caracio, Tony, 286–87, 289–91, 294, 296
Carter, Kevin, 136
Casey, George, 262–63
Carlisle Barracks, 12, 14. *See also* U.S.
    Army War College
Cavallaro, Gina, 83–84, 86, 267, 270–71
Chadwick, Douglas (Doug), 137–38,
    140–41, 160, 174, 186, 205, 279
Chechnya, 122
Chenelly, Joseph R., 169
Chicago, 161
Chlebowski, William, 41, 48, 55–60,
    112, 185, 243
Civil Affairs, 89, 96, 151, 153–56,
    164–66
Civil-Military Operations Center
    (CMOC): attack against, 42, 50; de-
    scription of, 41; rally point, 44; se-
    curity of, 126, 281; threat against,
    48, 53, 56, 63
CMOC. *See* Civil-Military Operations
    Center (CMOC)
Coalition Provisional Authority (CPA),
    41, 87, 121, 129, 157
CPA. *See* Coalition Provisional Author-
    ity (CPA)
Cochran, Jon, *71*
Cold War, 4, 10
Cold War, post-, 5, 8, 9, 119
CBS News, 98
Combat Maneuver Training Center,
    4–8, 154, 156. *See also* Hohenfels
Copp, Charles, *17,* 51, 55, 106, 110
Cortes, Frankie, *17,* 106
Cox, Travis, 127, 202
curfew, 203, 262

Dallas, 177
Damon, Arwa, 263
Danger Close, 216

democracy: development of in Iraq, 215; student roundtable on, 10

Department of Defense, 12

Department of State Embed Team, 265

Desert Storm, Operation, 119, 122, 227

DeRicco, Ryan, 178

detonation, controlled, 27, 31

Diyala Provincial Police Headquarters, 39, 107, 191, 281, 290–91; press statement, 158–59

Diyala River, 30, 253

Doha, Camp, 176, 180

Douglas, Will, *17*, 51, 55, 61–62, 103, 108

Edwan, Daniel (Dan): advising Iraqi officials, 247, 255, 261–63, 295, 297; involvement with Iraqi national elections, 248–50, 260, 266, 272; Joint Coordination Center construction, 231, 236, 253; police construction projects, 201–202, 204, 289

82nd Engineer Battalion, 26, 75, 98, 164

elections, Iraqi national: impact of, 213–14, 288; insurgent strategy for, 183, 194; polling sites, 256, 258–59, 261, 264, *268*, 271–72; security plans for, 197–99, 201, 212, 231, 235; registration sites, 250–252

elections, U.S. presidential, 180

Elite of Diyala Party, 264–65, 267

Ellis, John, 9

Ensha Allah, use of, 228, 234–35, 247

Estrada, Oscar, 164–66, 169

Eubanks, Stewart, *17*, 46, 95, 107, 109

Explosive Ordinance Demolition (EOD): Iraqi team, 80–81, 229, 294; U.S. team, 31, 45–46, 81, 83–85, 129, 239, 293–94

EOD. *See* Explosive Ordinance Demolition (EOD)

executive officer, duties of, 69

Falcon View, 252–53, 262

Fallujah, 73, 78, 181, 189, 198

Federal Emergency Management Agency (FEMA), 231

Field Artillery Officers Basic Course, 15

Field Artillery Ammunition Supply Vehicle (FAASV): limitations of, 52; urban employment of, 48–49, *54*, 55–58, 60–62

FAASV. *See* Field Artillery Ammunition Supply Vehicle (FAASV)

Field Artillery: employment in Iraq, 291; fire missions, 56, 59, 60, 64, 109–110, 207; planned target, 204

Field Manual 3-0, 151, 169

1st Armored Division, 4–5

1st Calvary Division, 145

1st Infantry Division, 4, 15, 16, 148, 161, 288, 294

588th Engineer Battalion, 20–21, 24, 27, 30, 33, 35, 39, 51, 278

force protection measures, U.S. Army garrison, 14

Forest People, The, 218

4th Infantry Division, 16, 20, 35

Freeman, Colin, 287–89

Froehlich, Adam D., 80, 285; death of, 35

Gabrielson, Dan Henry, 21, 24

Gabe, Camp: initial impressions of 24–25, 27–28; Iraqi origins of, 25–26; operations on, *25*, 39, 53, *93*, 121, 175, 210, 240, 264, 266, 278

Gaines, Cameron, 124, 127, 130–32, 134, 144, 187–91, 204, 210, 281, 283

Galloway, Joe, 285

Garcia, Jesse, *17*, 43, 46, 53, 84–85, 93–94, 100, 103

Garrant, Marcus, *71*

Georgian Army, 240

Gifford, James (Jim), 7–8, 17, 31, 39, *71*, 72, 135, 201, 296

Girasia, Eric, *71*

Gniazdowski, Sean, 175

Grandy, Sherman, 265

Green Zone, Baquba, 55–56, 58

Grider, T. J.: assisting Iraqi Security Forces, 185–87, 191–94, 202, 239, 243, 246, *260;* arrival in Baquba, 70–72; involvement on election day, 269; notoriety of, 160–63, 168; operations in Buhriz, 81, 91–96, 98, 138–41, 147, 166, 211; operations in Tahrir, 82, 84; thoughts on democratization, 213–15, 220, 224

Griffin, Michael, *71,* 189–190, 246

groves, palm: attacks from, 54–56, 77, 206–207; description of, 30; insurgent use of, 108; clearing of, 95, 139, 147, 199–200

Guellnitz, Peter, 109, 175, 207

Guttenfelder, David, 130, 134

Haiti, 285

Hamlet, 251, 274

Harmon, Jason, 190, 211, 230

Heidelberg, 151

Hernandez, Cory, *17*

Hohenfels, 4–5, 18, 297. *See also* Combat Maneuver Training Center

Hokenson, Aaron, *71*

Homer, Winslow, 143

Hope is Not a Method, 235

Hood, Fort, 35

Hoss, Michael, 154

Huber, Jesse, 125

Human Cycle, The, 218

Hunter, Wade, *17,* 21, 40, 43–44, 50, 81, 92, 94–95, 100, 103

Hussein, Qusay, 28, 32

Hussein, Saddam: 13, 229, 297; statue of, 120

Hussein, Uday, 28

Huwaydir, 28

Ice Platoon, 75–76, 98–112, 114, 125–26

imams: influence over insurgency, 62; support of Iraqi government, 130. *See also* mosque

improvised explosive device (IED): composition of, 20, 79, 82; cordon and clearing of, 31, 34–35, 81, 84, 239, 289, 292–94; employment of, 45, 48–49, 97, 99–100, 107, 150, 179, 186, 192–93, 238, 242, 282, 291; effectiveness of, 52, 239–40, 281, 283–85; reported by locals, 80; response to, 44; secondary device, 35, 85; threat of, 30, 35, 72, 79–80, 91, 96, 181, 270; triggerman, 85; vehicle-borne (VBIED), 129, *146,* 146, 209, 221, 229, 245, 250, 290, 294

IED. *See* improvised explosive device (IED)

Independent Elections Commission of Iraq (IECI): management of election, 248–50, 257, 264–65, 271; threats against, 254; election security plan, 258; exclusion of the Elite of Diyala Party, 266–68

IECI. *See* Independent Elections Commission of Iraq (IECI)

India, 217

Information Operations: definition of, 150–51; peacekeeping versus counterinsurgency value, 154–56; use in Iraq, 156–59; use in Kosovo, 152–54

Information Operations, 150–51, 169

insurgency: development of, 31, 47, 78, 85–86, 150, 198; Easter Offensive, 55–58; election day attacks, 274; illusiveness of, 53, 76–77, 88; logistical planning, 238; propaganda, 53, 159–60, 184–85, 254–55; shifting tactics, 58, 293; targeting bridges, 239–40; targeting Iraqis, 181–85; theft of ambulance, 242; theft of police car, 245; torturing Iraqis, 125 interpreter, shortage of, 54

Iran, 150, 227

Iran-Iraq War, 227, 255

Iraq: insurgency in, 8; invasion of, 3–4; household weapons law, 34; lack of electricity, 28; tribal traditions, 220

Iraqi Army: checkpoint operations, 199–200, 206; cooperation with Iraqi police, 237–38, 242–46; election day operations, 260, 264, 273; expectations of, 138, 234, 288; involvement with the Joint Coordination Center, 237, 241; operations in Buhriz, 211; operations in Tahrir, 291–92; protecting the Diyala capitol, 221–22; soldiers killed by insurgents, 183;

Iraqi Army Staff College, 227–29

Iraqi border guard, 229

Iraqi Civil Defense Corps, 113

Iraqi Freedom, Operation, 120, 142

Iraqi Interim Government, 121, 129

Iraqi National Guard, 123–125, 130, 135, 138–41, 149, 163–64, 182, 186

Iraqi police: bridge security, 240; capture of the "Little Prince," 292–93; cooperation with Iraqi Army, 186, 237–38, 242–46; election day operations, 260, 264, 273; expectations of, 138, 182, 234, 288; in media, 163–64, 221; involvement with Joint Coordination Center, 229; jurisdictional disputes, 83–84, 141; operations in Buhriz, 194, 204–207

Iraqi Republican Guard, 214, 297; 41st Armored Brigade, 25–27

Iraqi security forces (ISF): election day operations, 273; expectations of, 73, 229, 235, 254; performance of, 123, 164, 237, 241, 245–46, 293; press statement, 158–59; 2004 to 2005 comparison, 287–89

ISF. See Iraqi Security Forces (ISF)

Iraqi Transitional Government, 87, 235

Islamist Party, 130

Jabori, Abdullah Rashid al, 243–44, 246, 258, 261, 262; exclusion of name from ballot, 264–68

Jassim, Tahsin Tawfiq, 248, 250, 252–56, 259, 270, 273, 289, 295–96

Jazeera, Al, 88, 98, 142, 163, 239, 269

Jiminez, Jim, 265, 273

Joint Coordination Center, Diyala Provincial: civilian reports to, 239, 241–42; daily security meeting, 233–34, 241–42; development of, 230–31; election security operations, 248–68, 273; field agents, 229, 252, 256, 259, 271; organization of, 183, 228–29; staff training, 236, 253–54, 263

Joint Coordination Center: in Khalis, 254; in Muqdadiya, 253

JCC. See Joint Coordination Center

Joint Guardian, Operation, 155, 167

Jones, Kirby, 23, 31, 45, 57, 69–70, 122

Jordan, 150, 289

Joy, William, 17, 95, 104–105, 108

Kalifa, Colonel, 248, 249, 250–52, 254, 256; assassination of 257–58

Kerry, John F., 180

Khalis, 291

Khatoon, 28, 40, 239

Kiowa helicopter, 139, 164, 228; recovery of, 44–45

Kirkuk, 8, 121

Kosovo: air campaign, 11; peacekeeping operations, 12, 15, 151–54, 167–68, 174, 230

Kulp, Jeffrey, 167

Kuwait. See New York, Camp and Udari Ranges

Lacour, Christopher (Chris), 7, 17, 35, 64, 90, 98, 101, 110, 148

Landstuhl Army Regional Hospital, 109

Lanners, Michael, 123

Larsen, Garret (Doc), *71, 189–90,*
282–83

Lashley, Paul, 45, 56, 63–64, 126, 179

Latif, Amer, 248–49, 256, 259, 264,
266–67, 272–74, 294

LeValley, Josh, 69

Lewis, Bernard, 219

Lina, Michael, *17*

Little Prince, 293

looting: of government buildings, 26,
101; of ordnance depots, 26–27

Lloyd, Anthony, 122, 134, 136

Lynch, Jason, *17,* 42–43, 107, 112, 135,
143, 146, 210, 235, 258; death of,
110

Magill, Lance, 75

Mahdi Army, 47, 60

Marinovich, Greg, 136

Martinez, Carlos, *17*

Martinez, Winston, *17,* 50, 55, 109

Matthews, Jarrod, *17,* 106

Mayo, Clinton, 188

McDonald, Robert, 174, 177–79

media: military and, 119–121; Arab,
77–78, 79, 88, *146,* 162–64, 293;
Western, 79, 87–88, 102, 162–64,
216–18, 263. *See also* photojournalists

Merit, Trent, 193

Meyer, Dave, 175, 180

Michaud, Michael, 58

Military Advisory Council, 231–32

Miller, Gregory, 83–85

Mills, Timothy, 283

minaret speakers. *See* mosque, insurgent use of

mines, anti-personnel, 33

Miranda, Michael, 107

MK-19 grenade launcher: "big fat gun,"
49; employment of, 51, 55, 56

Mohammed, prophet, 188

mortars: effects of, 159, 291; enemy
use of, 56, 63, 108, 124, 230, 246

mosque: insurgent use of, 53–54;
Sunni, 50. *See also* imams

Mosquera, Michael, 154

Mosul, 121

Mountain People, The, 218

Mualimeen, 28, 239

Mujema, 28

Mufrek, 28, 239; attack from, 123, 159,
186

Mufrek Traffic Circle, 20, 53, 60,
237–39, 241–42, 245

Mullan, Adel, *232,* 295

Multinational Forces, 250, 294

Mumford, Steve, 142–45

Muqdadiya, 227, 231, 243, 253, 264,
266, 291, 295

Mustafa, 28

My War Gone By, I Miss it So, 122, 136

Najaf, 70, 86, 121, 181, 198

National Missile Defense Program, 12

National Public Radio, 161

National Security Strategy, 2000, 10

Naval Postgraduate School, 7

Neal, Daniel, 94–95

New Dawn, Operation, 138

New York, Camp, 19, 21

Nichols, Justin, 104–105

night-vision device: use of, 94, 114;
street light effects on, 50

Nordquist, Joseph C., 21

Normandy, Camp 240

North Atlantic Treaty Organization
(NATO), 11, 167

North Korea, 227

Nutter, Fred, 167, 230

Olympics, Iraqi soccer team, 144

1-6 Field Artillery, Task Force: area
of operations, 26, 29, 123, 243,
245; authors' assignment to, 15;
election operations, 264, 266–67,

272; initial impression of enemy, 30–31; redeployment, 296; task organization for deployment, 16–17

1-10 Field Artillery, Task Force, 277, 285, 286, 291

Oosterbroek, Ken, 136

Paladin, 59, 64, 109. *See also* Field Artillery

peacekeeping, 5. *See also* Kosovo, peacekeeping operations *and* 2-63 Armor, Task Force, in Kosovo

Pentagon, 227

Peters, Ralph, 218

Phantom Fury, Operation, 180, 198

Phillips, Gary, 31–34

photojournalists: impact of reporting, 145; in Baquba, 121–123, 127–130, 132–133, 134–137; moral detachment, 122; moral questioning, 133, 142

Pineda, Jorge (Paco), *71*, 223–24

Pittard, Dana: commander's guidance, 113, 166, 196, 272; involvement with Iraqi national elections, 258, 261, 263–64, 266–67, 169–70, 273; involvement with Joint Coordination Center, 231, 240–41, 244; involvement with Military Advisory Council, 232; quotation, 157, 165

Pojman, Louis, 218

police academy, 289

police station: attacks in Buhriz, 236–39, 242–46; construction of in Buhriz, 199–207, 288; attacks in Mufrek, 236–39, 242–46

Poynter, Barry, *17*, 42–43, 46, 101, 104–105

Prakash, Neil, 175, 180

Psychological Operations, 151–56

Punisher Platoon: Al Sadr Party raid, 60; Baquba operations, 125–26, 191–94, 202, 211, 222, 243; Buhriz

operations, 59–60, 70, 92–96, 98, 138–41, 147; composition of, 23; Najaf operations, 70; notoriety of, 161

Putnam, James, 15

Qaeda, Al, 9, 15, 72, 78, 196–97, 211, 293

Quiroz, Ismael, *71,* 139, 193

Ra'ad, Mayor, 113, 288

Ramadan, 173–74, 183–85, 188, 194, 198, 258

Reagan, Ronald, 12

Reason, 149

Reformation, 235

relativism, cultural, 217–19

Relief in Place: Task Force 1-6 to Task Force 1-10, 278–85; 588th Engineers to Task Force 1-6, 30, 35, 280

Reno, 175

Rest and Relaxation (R and R), 174–80

Reuters, 262

Rocket Propelled Grenade (RPG): effectiveness of, 43–46, 59–60, 98, 126, 229; enemy employment of, 42, 50–51, 60, 74, 90, 100–101, 123, 140–41, 179, 187, 204–205, 211, 246; enemy source of, 27

RPG. *See* Rocket Propelled Grenade (RPG)

Rolling Stone, 216

Roman, Richard, *17,* 49, 106, 108–109

Ramos, Phillip, *17*

Rosen, Nir, 149, 169

Rumsfeld, Donald, 11–12

Sadr City, 47

Sadr Party, al, 48, 60

Sadr, Muqtada al, 47, 70

Samarra, 73, 198

San Francisco Chronicle, 287

Salie, David, 280–81, 283, 285; death of, 284

Saudi Arabia, 150

Scania, Convoy Supply Camp, 277

Septi, Hussein Ali, 89, 91–92, 94–96, 196

Sheiks' Council, 232

Shi'ia: demographics in Baquba, 29; holiday, 53

Shifta, 28, 31–32, 56, *63, 260, 267, 268, 270, 271, 272*

shoot houses. *See* tactics, room clearing procedures

Sill, Fort, 15

Silva, Joao, 127–28, 130, 132–33, 136–37

Smack Down, Operation, 89–96, 97–113, 121

sniper operations: counter-enemy, 104–105; counter-IED, 77, 80; enemy 98

Southern Justice, Operation, 138–41

Soviets, 4, 11

Star Wars Program, 12

stop-loss, 287

Student Conference on U.S. Affairs (SCUSA), 9–11

Sullivan, Gordon, 235

Sunni: attacks on Shi'ias, 184; demographics in Baquba and Buhriz, 29; Shi'ia resentment of, 29

Sunni Triangle, 16, 121, 175, 198

sustainment operations, 6

Sunni Triangle, 29

Syria, 150, 200, 211–12

Szczurowsky, Richard, 107, 111

tactics: attrition warfare, 89, 114; counterinsurgency, 64–65; high ground, 99, 114–15; movement to contact definition, 61; room clearing procedures, 22–23; vehicle search operations, 31–33

Tahrir, 28–29, 255, 269, 282, 292; attacks from, 42, 44, 50–52, 54–55, 60, 63–64, 111; improvements to, 157; description of, 52, 54, *57*; suspicious activity in, 62–63

Taliban, 13, 227

Task Force 1–6. *See* 1–6 Field Artillery, Task Force

terrorists: pre-2001 attacks, 11; September 11th attacks, 12

3rd Brigade Combat Team, 4, 5, 7, 26, 155, 196, 240, 246, 258, 272

3rd Infantry Division, 16, 35, 277–78, 286, 289

Tikrit, 28

Thomas, Ottress, 189, 204, 282

Tigris River, *74*

transfer of authority. *See* Relief in Place

Transfer of Sovereignty: impact of, 137–38, 242; insurgent efforts to derail, 73, 85–86, 87, 121; Iraqi preparation for, 113–14, 123–24, 182; media coverage of, 122, 163

Trebuchet, Operation, 208

Turnbull, Colin, 218–19

Twin Bridges, 32

Twin Towers, 227

2-63 Armor, Task Force: in Kosovo, 150, 152–53, 167; in Baquba, 59–60, 142, 245

2-2 Infantry, Task Force, 23, 231

Udari Ranges, 21–22

United Nations (UN), 154, 167, 265

U.S. Air Force, air strikes in Baquba, 124–125, *126,* 245–46

U.S. Army, Iraqi perception of, 7–8

U.S. Army War College, 12–15, 151. *See also* Carlisle Barracks

U.S. Military Academy, 9–13, 119, 218

USA Today, 218

unmanned aerial vehicle (UAV), 92, 97–98, 108, 245

UAV. *See* unmanned aerial vehicle (UAV)

Vandayburg, Allan, 210; death of, 59–60

Vargas, Manuel, *17*

Vega, Javier, *17*

VBIED. *See* improvised explosive device (IED), vehicle-borne (VBIED)
Venezulea, Carlos, 265
Vietnam, 229
Villanueva, Ray, *17*
Vitina, 151, 154, 167

Waddell, Rick, 9
Waggoner, Wesley, *17,* 108
Walter Reed Army Hospital, 190
Walters, Marvin, 101
Warhorse, Camp: detainment facility, 210, 238; election security operations, 260, 271, 273; medical center, 60, 109; operations on, 45, 129, 240, 291; 3rd Brigade Combat Team headquarters, 41, 83, 123, 245, 265, 281
Washington Post, The, 127–28, 134, 145, 164, 166, 169
Weapons of Mass Destruction (WMD), 11
WMD. *See* Weapons of Mass Destruction

Weeks, Arthur, 58, 71–72, 98, 185
Wenzel, Dustin, 206
West Point. *See* U.S. Military Academy
Whalid, Major General, 84, 237–38, 243–44, 246
What Went Wrong?, 219
White, Dwayne, 23
Whitney, Peter, 228
Williams, Clayton, *17*
Wilson, Scott, 127
Wolf, Middleton, *17*
Wolfgang, Teresa, 256, 262, 264–66, 272–73
Woodall, Andrea Bruce, 127, 130, 134–35, 137, 145–46

Yahoo!, 236, 253, 268
Yon, Michael, 216–18, 220
Yugoslavia, 122

Zaragoza, Thomas, *71,* 188, 224
Zarqawi, Abu Musab al, 287, 293
Zuis, Abu, 195–99, 208–212, 287

ISBN-13: 978-1-60344-038-7
ISBN-10: 1-60344-038-0